DevOps

The SEI Series in Software Engineering

Software Engineering Institute of Carnegie Mellon University and Addison-Wesley

 Software Engineering Institute | **Carnegie Mellon University**

Visit **informit.com/sei** for a complete list of available publications.

The **SEI Series in Software Engineering** is a collaborative undertaking of the Carnegie Mellon Software Engineering Institute (SEI) and Addison-Wesley to develop and publish books on software engineering and related topics. The common goal of the SEI and Addison-Wesley is to provide the most current information on these topics in a form that is easily usable by practitioners and students.

Titles in the series describe frameworks, tools, methods, and technologies designed to help organizations, teams, and individuals improve their technical or management capabilities. Some books describe processes and practices for developing higher-quality software, acquiring programs for complex systems, or delivering services more effectively. Other books focus on software and system architecture and product-line development. Still others, from the SEI's CERT Program, describe technologies and practices needed to manage software and network security risk. These and all titles in the series address critical problems in software engineering for which practical solutions are available.

Make sure to connect with us!
informit.com/socialconnect

 Addison Wesley | **informIT** the trusted technology learning source | Safari

DevOps

A Software Architect's Perspective

Len Bass
Ingo Weber
Liming Zhu

✦✦Addison-Wesley

New York • Boston • Indianapolis • San Francisco
Toronto • Montreal • London • Munich • Paris • Madrid
Capetown • Sydney • Tokyo • Singapore • Mexico City

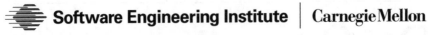

The SEI Series in Software Engineering

For information about buying this title in bulk quantities, or for special sales opportunities (which may include electronic versions; custom cover designs; and content particular to your business, training goals, marketing focus, or branding interests), please contact our corporate sales department at corpsales@pearsoned.com or (800) 382-3419.

For government sales inquiries, please contact governmentsales@pearsoned.com.

For questions about sales outside the U.S., please contact international@pearsoned.com.

Visit us on the Web: informit.com/aw

Library of Congress Cataloging-in-Publication Data

Bass, Len.
  DevOps : a software architect's perspective / Len Bass, Ingo Weber, Liming Zhu.—First [edition].
    pages   cm.—(The SEI series in software engineering)
  Includes bibliographical references and index.
  ISBN 978-0-13-404984-7 (hardcover : alk. paper)
  1. Software architecture. 2. Computer software—Development.
3. Operating systems (Computers) I. Weber, Ingo M. II. Zhu, Liming, 1975- III. Title.
  QA76.76.D47B377 2015
  005.1′2—dc23

                                                                              2015007093

ISBN-13: 978-0-13-404984-7
ISBN-10: 0-13-404984-5

Text printed in the United States on recycled paper at Courier in Westford, Massachusetts.
2   16

Contents

Preface

We have been investigating problems in operations for several years and have, naturally, been tracking the DevOps movement. It is moving up the Gartner Hype Curve and has a solid business reason for existing. We were able to find treatments from the IT manager's perspective (e.g., the novel *The Phoenix Project: A Novel about IT, DevOps, and Helping Your Business Win*) and from the project manager's perspective (e.g., *Continuous Delivery: Reliable Software Releases Through Build, Test, and Deployment Automation*). In addition, there is a raft of material about cultural change and what it means to tear down barriers between organizational units.

What frustrated us is that there is very little material from the software architect's perspective. Treating operations personnel as first-class stakeholders and listening to their requirements is certainly important. Using tools to support operations and project management is also important. Yet, we had the strong feeling that there was more to it than stakeholder management and the use of tools.

Indeed there is, and that is the gap that this book intends to fill. DevOps presents a fascinating interplay between design, process, tooling, and organizational structure. We try to answer two primary questions: What technical decisions do I, as a software architect, have to make to achieve the DevOps goals? What impact do the other actors in the DevOps space have on me?

The answers are that achieving DevOps goals can involve fundamental changes in the architecture of your systems and in the roles and responsibilities required to get your systems into production and support them once they are there.

Just as software architects must understand the business context and goals for the systems they design and construct, understanding DevOps requires understanding organizational and business contexts, as well as technical and operational contexts. We explore all of these.

The primary audience for this book is practicing software architects who have been or expect to be asked, "Should this project or organization adopt DevOps practices?" Instead of being asked, the architect may be told. As with all books, we expect additional categories of readers. Students who are interested in learning more about the practice of software architecture should find interesting material here. Researchers who wish to investigate DevOps topics can find important background material. Our primary focus, however, is on practicing architects.

Previewing the Book

We begin the book by discussing the background for DevOps. Part One begins by delving into the goals of DevOps and the problems it is intended to solve. We touch on organizational and cultural issues, as well as the relationship of DevOps practices to agile methodologies.

In Chapter 2, we explore the cloud. DevOps practices have grown in tandem with the growth of the cloud as a platform. The two, in theory, are separable, but in practice virtualization and the cloud are important enablers for DevOps practices.

In our final background chapter, Chapter 3, we explore operations through the prism of the Information Technology Infrastructure Library (ITIL). ITIL is a system of organization of the most important functions of an operations group. Not all of operations are included in DevOps practices but understanding something of the responsibilities of an operations group provides important context, especially when it comes to understanding roles and responsibilities.

Part Two describes the deployment pipeline. We begin this part by exploring the microservice architectural style in Chapter 4. It is not mandatory that systems be architected in this style in order to apply DevOps practices but the microservice architectural style is designed to solve many of the problems that motivated DevOps.

In Chapter 5, we hurry through the building and testing processes and tool chains. It is important to understand these but they are not our focus. We touch on the different environments used to get a system into production and the different sorts of tests run on these environments. Since many of the tools used in DevOps are used in the building and testing processes, we provide context for understanding these tools and how to control them.

We conclude Part Two by discussing deployment. One of the goals of DevOps is to speed up deployments. A technique used to achieve this goal is to allow each development team to independently deploy their code when it is ready. Independent deployment introduces many issues of consistency. We discuss different deployment models, managing distinct versions of a system that are simultaneously in production, rolling back in the case of errors, and other topics having to do with actually placing your system in production.

Part Two presents a functional perspective on deployment practices. Yet, just as with any other system, it is frequently the quality perspectives that control the design and the acceptance of the system. In Part Three, we focus on crosscutting concerns. This begins with our discussion of monitoring and live testing in Chapter 7. Modern software testing practices do not end when a system is placed into production. First, systems are monitored extensively to detect problems, and secondly, testing continues in a variety of forms after a system has been placed into production.

Another crosscutting concern is security, which we cover in Chapter 8. We present the different types of security controls that exist in an environment, spanning those that are organization wide and those that are specific system wide. We discuss the different roles associated with achieving security and how these roles are evaluated in the case of a security audit.

Security is not the only quality of interest, and in Chapter 9 we discuss other qualities that are relevant to the practices associated with DevOps. We cover topics such as performance, reliability, and modifiability of the deployment pipeline.

Finally, in Part Three we discuss business considerations in Chapter 10. Practices as broad as DevOps cannot be adopted without buy-in from management. A business plan is a typical means of acquiring this buy-in; thus, we present the elements of a business plan for DevOps adoption and discuss how the argument, rollout, and measurement should proceed.

In Part Four we present three case studies. Organizations that have implemented DevOps practices tell us some of their tricks. Chapter 11 discusses how to maintain two datacenters for the purpose of business continuity; Chapter 12 presents the specifics of a continuous deployment pipeline; and Chapter 13 describes how one organization is migrating to a microservice architecture.

We close by speculating about the future in Part Five. Chapter 14 describes our research and how it is based on viewing operations as a series of processes, and Chapter 15 gives our prediction for how the next three to five years are going to evolve in terms of DevOps.

Acknowledgments

Books like this require a lot of assistance. We would like to thank Chris Williams, John Painter, Daniel Hand, and Sidney Shek for their contributions to the case studies, as well as Adnene Guabtni, Kanchana Wickremasinghe, Min Fu, and Xiwei Xu for helping us with some of the chapters.

Manuel Pais helped us arrange case studies. Philippe Kruchten, Eoin Woods, Gregory Hartman, Sidney Shek, Michael Lorant, Wouter Geurts, and Eltjo Poort commented on or contributed to various aspects of the book.

We would like to thank Jean-Michel Lemieux, Greg Warden, Robin Fernandes, Jerome Touffe-Blin, Felipe Cuozzo, Pramod Korathota, Nick Wright, Vitaly Osipov, Brad Baker, and Jim Watts for their comments on Chapter 13.

Addison-Wesley did their usual professional and efficient job in the production process, and this book has benefited from their expertise.

Finally, we would like to thank NICTA and NICTA management. NICTA is funded by the Australian government through the Department of Communications and the Australian Research Council through the ICT Centre of Excellence Program. Without their generous support, this book would not have been written.

Legend

We use four distinct legends for the figures. We have an architectural notation that identifies the key architectural concepts that we use; we use Business Process Model and Notation (BPMN) to describe some processes, Porter's Value Notation to describe a few others, and UML sequence diagrams for interleaving sequences of activities. We do not show the UML sequence diagram notation here but the notation that we use from these other sources is:

Architecture

Person   Group

FIGURE P.1   People, both individual and groups

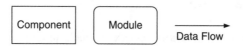

Component   Module   Data Flow

FIGURE P.2   Components (runtime entities), modules (code-time collections of entities), and data flow

Database   Data Object   VM   VM Image   DNS Entry or IP Address

FIGURE P.3   Specialized entities

FIGURE P.4 Collections of entities

BPMN

We use Business Process Model and Notation (BPMN) for describing events and activities [OMG 11].

Event (start)   Event (end)   Exclusive Gateway   Repetition

FIGURE P.5 Event indications

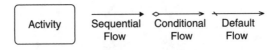

Activity   Sequential   Conditional   Default
            Flow   Flow   Flow

FIGURE P.6 Activities and sequences of activities

Porter's Value Chain

This notation is used to describe processes (which, in turn, have activities modelled in BPMN).

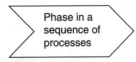

Phase in a
sequence of
processes

FIGURE P.7 Entry in a value chain

PART ONE

BACKGROUND

This part provides the necessary background for the remainder of the book. DevOps is a movement that envisions no friction between the development groups and the operations groups. In addition, the emergence of DevOps coincides with the growth of the cloud as a basic platform for organizations, large and small. Part One has three chapters.

In Chapter 1, we define DevOps and discuss its various motivations. DevOps is a catchall term that can cover several meanings, including: having development and operations speak to each other; allowing development teams to deploy to production automatically; and having development teams be the first responders when an error is discovered in production. In this chapter, we sort out these various considerations and develop a coherent description of what DevOps is, what its motivations and goals are, and how it is going about achieving those goals.

In order to understand how certain DevOps practices work, it is necessary to know how the cloud works, which we discuss in Chapter 2. In particular, you should know how virtual machines work, how IP addresses are used, the role of and how to manipulate Domain Name System (DNS) servers, and how load balancers and monitors interact to provide on-demand scaling.

DevOps involves the modifications of both Dev and Ops practices. In Chapter 3, we discuss Ops in its totality. It describes the services that Ops provides to the organization and introduces Ops responsibilities, from supporting deployed applications to enforcing organization-wide security rules.

1

What Is DevOps?

1.1 Introduction

The question this book attempts to answer is "Why should I care about DevOps, and what impact does it have on me?" The long answer will be found by reading the book, but the short answer is that if you are involved in building software systems and your organization is interested in reducing the time to market for new features, then you should care. This is the motivation for DevOps, and DevOps practices will influence the way that you organize teams, build systems, and even the structure of the systems that you build. If you are a software engineering student or researcher then you should care how the adoption of DevOps practices could influence the problems that you choose to work on. If you are an educator you should care because incorporating DevOps material into your curriculum will help educate your students about modern development practices.

We begin by defining DevOps and providing a short example. Then we present the motivation for the movement, the DevOps perspective, and barriers to the success of DevOps. Much of the writing on DevOps discusses various organizational and cultural issues. In this first chapter, we summarize these topics, which frame the remainder of the book.

Defining DevOps

DevOps has been classified as "on the rise" with respect to the Gartner Hype Cycle for Application Development in 2013. This classification means that the

term is becoming a buzz word and, as such, is ill defined and subject to over-
blown claims. Our definition of DevOps focuses on the goals, rather than the
means.

> *DevOps is a set of practices intended to reduce the time between
> committing a change to a system and the change being placed into
> normal production, while ensuring high quality.*

Before we delve more deeply into what set of practices is included, let's
look at some of the implications of our definition.

- The quality of the deployed change to a system (usually in the form of
  code) is important. Quality means suitability for use by various stakeholders
  including end users, developers, or system administrators. It also includes
  availability, security, reliability, and other "ilities." One method for ensuring
  quality is to have a variety of automated test cases that must be passed
  prior to placing changed code into production. Another method is to test the
  change in production with a limited set of users prior to opening it up to the
  world. Still another method is to closely monitor newly deployed code for
  a period of time. We do not specify in the definition how quality is ensured
  but we do require that production code be of high quality.
- The definition also requires the delivery mechanism to be of high quality.
  This implies that reliability and the repeatability of the delivery mechanism
  should be high. If the delivery mechanism fails regularly, the time required
  increases. If there are errors in how the change is delivered, the quality of
  the deployed system suffers, for example, through reduced availability or
  reliability.
- We identify two time periods as being important. One is the time when a
  developer commits newly developed code. This marks the end of basic
  development and the beginning of the deployment path. The second time
  is the deploying of that code into production. As we will see in Chapter 6,
  there is a period after code has been deployed into production when
  the code is being tested through live testing and is closely monitored
  for potential problems. Once the code has passed live testing and close
  monitoring, then it is considered as a portion of the normal production
  system. We make a distinction between deploying code into production for
  live testing and close monitoring and then, after passing the tests, promoting
  the newly developed code to be equivalent to previously developed code.
- Our definition is goal oriented. We do not specify the form of the practices
  or whether tools are used to implement them. If a practice is intended to
  reduce the time between a commit from a developer and deploying into
  production, it is a DevOps practice whether it involves agile methods, tools,
  or forms of coordination. This is in contrast to several other definitions.
  Wikipedia, for example, stresses communication, collaboration, and
  integration between various stakeholders without stating the goal of such

communication, collaboration, or integration. Timing goals are implicit. Other definitions stress the connection between DevOps and agile methods. Again, there is no mention of the benefits of utilizing agile methods on either the time to develop or the quality of the production system. Still other definitions stress the tools being used, without mentioning the goal of DevOps practices, the time involved, or the quality.

- Finally, the goals specified in the definition do not restrict the scope of DevOps practices to testing and deployment. In order to achieve these goals, it is important to include an Ops perspective in the collection of requirements—that is, significantly earlier than committing changes. Analogously, the definition does not mean DevOps practices end with deployment into production; the goal is to ensure high quality of the deployed system throughout its life cycle. Thus, monitoring practices that help achieve the goals are to be included as well.

DevOps Practices

We have identified five different categories of DevOps practices below. These are mentioned in writings about DevOps and satisfy our definition.

- Treat Ops as first-class citizens from the point of view of requirements. These practices fit in the high-quality aspect of the definition. Operations have a set of requirements that pertain to logging and monitoring. For example, logging messages should be understandable and usable by an operator. Involving operations in the development of requirements will ensure that these types of requirements are considered.
- Make Dev more responsible for relevant incident handling. These practices are intended to shorten the time between the observation of an error and the repair of that error. Organizations that utilize these practices typically have a period of time in which Dev has primary responsibility for a new deployment; later on, Ops has primary responsibility.
- Enforce the deployment process used by all, including Dev and Ops personnel. These practices are intended to ensure a higher quality of deployments. This avoids errors caused by ad hoc deployments and the resulting misconfiguration. The practices also refer to the time that it takes to diagnose and repair an error. The normal deployment process should make it easy to trace the history of a particular deployment artifact and understand the components that were included in that artifact.
- Use continuous deployment. Practices associated with continuous deployment are intended to shorten the time between a developer committing code to a repository and the code being deployed. Continuous deployment also emphasizes automated tests to increase the quality of code making its way into production.

- Develop infrastructure code, such as deployment scripts, with the same set of practices as application code. Practices that apply to the development of infrastructure code are intended to ensure both high quality in the deployed applications and that deployments proceed as planned. Errors in deployment scripts such as misconfigurations can cause errors in the application, the environment, or the deployment process. Applying quality control practices used in normal software development when developing operations scripts and processes will help control the quality of these specifications.

Figure 1.1 gives an overview of DevOps processes. At its most basic, DevOps advocates treating Operations personnel as first-class stakeholders. Preparing a release can be a very serious and onerous process. (We describe that in the section "Release Process.") As such, operations personnel may need to be trained in the types of runtime errors that can occur in a system under development; they may have suggestions as to the type and structure of log files, and they may provide other types of input into the requirements process. At its most extreme, DevOps practices make developers responsible for monitoring the progress and errors that occur during deployment and execution, so theirs would be the voices suggesting requirements. In between are practices that cover team practices, build processes, testing processes, and deployment processes. We discuss the continuous deployment pipeline in Chapters 5 and 6. We also cover monitoring, security, and audits in subsequent chapters.

You may have some questions about terminology with the terms *IT professional*, *operator*, and *operations personnel*. Another related term is *system administrator*. The IT professional subsumes the mentioned roles and others, such as help desk support. The distinction in terminology between operators and system administrators has historical roots but is much less true today. Historically, operators had hands-on access to the hardware—installing and configuring hardware, managing backups, and maintaining printers—while system administrators were responsible for uptime, performance, resources, and security of computer systems. Today it is the rare operator who does not take on some duties formerly assigned to a system administrator. We will use the term *operator* to refer to anyone who performs computer operator or system administration tasks (or both).

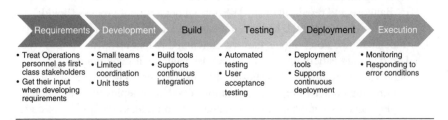

FIGURE 1.1   DevOps life cycle processes [Notation: Porter's Value Chain]

Example of Continuous Deployment: IMVU

IMVU, Inc. is a social entertainment company whose product allows users to connect through 3D avatar-based experiences. This section is adapted from a blog written by an IMVU engineer.

> IMVU does continuous integration. The developers commit early and often. A commit triggers an execution of a test suite. IMVU has a thousand test files, distributed across 30–40 machines, and the test suite takes about nine minutes to run. Once a commit has passed all of its tests, it is automatically sent to deployment. This takes about six minutes. The code is moved to the hundreds of machines in the cluster, but at first the code is only made live on a small number of machines (canaries). A sampling program examines the results of the canaries and if there has been a statistically significant regression, then the revision is automatically rolled back. Otherwise the remainder of the cluster is made active. IMVU deploys new code 50 times a day, on average.

The essence of the process is in the test suite. Every time a commit gets through the test suite and is rolled back, a new test is generated that would have caught the erroneous deployment, and it is added to the test suite.

Note that a full test suite (with the confidence of production deployment) that only takes nine minutes to run is uncommon for large-scale systems. In many organizations, the full test suite that provides production deployment confidence can take hours to run, which is often done overnight. A common challenge is to reduce the size of the test suite judiciously and remove "flaky" tests.

1.2   Why DevOps?

DevOps, in many ways, is a response to the problem of slow releases. The longer it takes a release to get to market, the less advantage will accrue from whatever features or quality improvements led to the release. Ideally, we want to release in a continuous manner. This is often termed *continuous delivery* or *continuous deployment*. We discuss the subtle difference between the two terms in Chapters 5 and 6. In this book, we use the term *continuous deployment* or just *deployment*. We begin by describing a formal release process, and then we delve more deeply into some of the reasons for slow releases.

Release Process

Releasing a new system or version of an existing system to customers is one of the most sensitive steps in the software development cycle. This is true whether the system or version is for external distribution, is used directly by consumers, or is strictly for internal use. As long as the system is used by more than one person, releasing a new version opens the possibility of incompatibilities or failures, with subsequent unhappiness on the part of the customers.

Consequently, organizations pay a great deal of attention to the process of defining a release plan. The following release planning steps are adapted from Wikipedia. Traditionally, most of the steps are done manually.

1. Define and agree on release and deployment plans with customers/ stakeholders. This could be done at the team or organizational level. The release and deployment plans will include those features to be included in the new release as well as ensure that operations personnel (including help desk and support personnel) are aware of schedules, resource requirements are met, and any additional training that might be required is scheduled.

2. Ensure that each release package consists of a set of related assets and service components that are compatible with each other. Everything changes over time, including libraries, platforms, and dependent services. Changes may introduce incompatibilities. This step is intended to prevent incompatibilities from becoming apparent only after deployment. In Chapter 5, we discuss the ways of ensuring all of these compatibilities. Managing dependencies is a theme that will surface repeatedly throughout this book.

3. Ensure that the integrity of a release package and its constituent components is maintained throughout the transition activities and recorded accurately in the configuration management system. There are two parts to this step: The first is to make sure that old versions of a component are not inadvertently included in the release, and the second is to make sure that a record is kept of the components of this deployment. Knowing the elements of the deployment is important when tracking down errors found after deployment. We discuss the details of deployment in Chapter 6.

4. Ensure that all release and deployment packages can be tracked, installed, tested, verified, and/or uninstalled or rolled back, if appropriate. Deployments may need to be *rolled back* (new version uninstalled, old version redeployed) under a variety of circumstances, such as errors in the code, inadequate resources, or expired licenses or certificates.

The activities enumerated in this list can be accomplished with differing levels of automation. If all of these activities are accomplished primarily through human coordination then these steps are labor-intensive, time-consuming, and error-prone. Any automation reflects an agreement on the release process whether at the team or organization level. Since tools are typically used more than once, an agreement on the release process encoded into a tool has persistence beyond a single release.

In case you are tempted to downplay the seriousness of getting the deployment correct, you may want to consider recent media reports with substantial financial costs.

- On August 1, 2012, Knight Capital had an upgrade failure that ended up costing (US) $440 million.
- On August 20, 2013, Goldman Sachs had an upgrade failure that, potentially, could cost millions of dollars.

These are just two of the many examples that have resulted in downtime or errors because of upgrade failure. Deploying an upgrade correctly is a significant and important activity for an organization and, yet, one that should be done in a timely fashion with minimal opportunity for error. Several organizations have done surveys to document the extent of deployment problems. We report on two of them.

- XebiaLabs is an organization that markets a deployment tool and a continuous integration tool. They did a survey in 2013 with over 130 responses. 34% of the respondents were from IT services companies with approximately 10% each from health care, financial services, and telecommunications companies. 7.5% of the respondents reported their deployment process was "not reliable," and 57.5% reported their deployment process "needs improvement." 49% reported their biggest challenge in the deployment process was "too much inconsistency across environments and applications." 32.5% reported "too many errors." 29.2% reported their deployments relied on custom scripting, and 35.8% reported their deployments were partially scripted and partially manual.
- CA Technologies provides IT management solutions to their customers. They commissioned a survey in 2013 that had 1,300 respondents from companies with more than (US) $100 million revenue. Of those who reported seeing benefits from the adoption of DevOps, 53% said they were already seeing an increased frequency of deployment of their software or services and 41% said they were anticipating seeing an increased frequency of deployment. 42% responded that they had seen improved quality of deployed applications, and 49% responded they anticipated seeing improved quality.

Although both surveys are sponsored by organizations with a vested interest in promoting deployment automation, they also clearly indicate that the speed and quality of deployments are a concern to many companies in a variety of different markets.

Reasons for Poor Coordination

Consider what happens after a developer group has completed all of the coding and testing for a system. The system needs to be placed into an environment where:

- Only the appropriate people have access to it.

- It is compatible with all of the other systems with which it interacts in the environment.
- It has sufficient resources on which to operate.
- The data that it uses to operate is up to date.
- The data that it generates is usable by other systems in the environment.

Furthermore, help desk personnel need to be trained in features of the new system and operations personnel need to be trained in troubleshooting any problems that might occur while the system is operating. The timing of the release may also be of significance because it should not coincide with the absence of any key member of the operations staff or with a new sales promotion that will stress the existing resources.

None of this happens by accident but each of these items requires coordination between the developers and the operations personnel. It is easy to imagine a scenario where one or more of these items are not communicated by the development personnel to the operations personnel. A common attitude among developers is "I finished the development, now go and run it." We explore the reasons for this attitude when we discuss the cultural barrier to adoption of DevOps.

One reason that organizations have processes to ensure smooth releases is that coordination does not always happen in an appropriate manner. This is one of the complaints that motivated the DevOps movement.

Limited Capacity of Operations Staff

Operations staff perform a variety of functions but there are limits as to what they can accomplish or who on the staff is knowledgeable in what system. Consider the responsibilities of a modern operations person as detailed in Wikipedia.

- Analyzing system logs and identifying potential issues with computer systems
- Introducing and integrating new technologies into existing datacenter environments
- Performing routine audits of systems and software
- Performing backups
- Applying operating system updates, patches, and configuration changes
- Installing and configuring new hardware and software
- Adding, removing, or updating user account information; resetting passwords, etc.
- Answering technical queries and assisting users
- Ensuring security
- Documenting the configuration of the system
- Troubleshooting any reported problems
- Optimizing system performance
- Ensuring that the network infrastructure is up and running

- Configuring, adding, and deleting file systems
- Maintaining knowledge of volume management tools like Veritas (now Symantec), Solaris ZFS, LVM

Each of these items requires a deep level of understanding. Is it any wonder that when we asked the IT director of an Internet-based company what his largest problem was, he replied "finding and keeping qualified personnel."

The DevOps movement is taking a different approach. Their approach is to reduce the need for dedicated operations personnel through automating many of the tasks formerly done by operations and having developers assume a portion of the remainder.

1.3 DevOps Perspective

Given the problems we have discussed and their long-standing nature, it is no surprise that there is a significant appeal for a movement that promises to reduce the time to market for new features and reduce errors occurring in deployment. DevOps comes in multiple flavors and with different degrees of variation from current practice, but two themes run consistently through the different flavors: automation and the responsibilities of the development team.

Automation

Figure 1.1 shows the various life cycle processes. The steps from build and testing through execution can all be automated to some degree. We will discuss the tools used in each one of these steps in the appropriate chapters, but here we highlight the virtues of automation. Some of the problems with relying on automation are discussed in Section 1.7.

Tools can perform the actions required in each step of the process, check the validity of actions against the production environment or against some external specification, inform appropriate personnel of errors occurring in the process, and maintain a history of actions for quality control, reporting, and auditing purposes.

Tools and scripts also can enforce organization-wide policies. Suppose the organization has a policy that every change has to have a rationale associated with the change. Then prior to committing a change, a tool or script can require a rationale to be provided by the individual making the change. Certainly, this requirement can be circumvented, but having the tool ask for a rationale will increase the compliance level for this policy.

Once tools become central to a set of processes, then the use of these tools must also be managed. Tools are invoked, for example, from scripts, configuration changes, or the operator's console. Where console commands are complicated, it is advisable to script their usage, even if there is only a handful of commands being used. Tools may be controlled through specification files, such as Chef cookbooks or Amazon CloudFormation—more on these later. The scripts, configuration files, and specification files must be subject to the same quality control as the application code itself. The scripts and files should also be under version control and subject to examination for corrections. This is often termed "infrastructure-as-code."

Development Team Responsibilities

Automation will reduce the incidence of errors and will shorten the time to deployment. To further shorten the time to deployment, consider the responsibilities of operations personnel as detailed earlier. If the development team accepts DevOps responsibilities, that is, it delivers, supports, and maintains the service, then there is less need to transfer knowledge to the operations and support staff since all of the necessary knowledge is resident in the development team. Not having to transfer knowledge removes a significant coordination step from the deployment process.

1.4   DevOps and Agile

One of the characterizations of DevOps emphasizes the relationship of DevOps practices to agile practices. In this section, we overlay the DevOps practices on IBM's Disciplined Agile Delivery. Our focus is on what is added by DevOps, not an explanation of Disciplined Agile Delivery. For that, see *Disciplined Agile Delivery: A Practitioner's Approach*. As shown in Figure 1.2, Disciplined Agile Delivery has three phases—inception, construction, and transition. In the DevOps context, we interpret transition as deployment.

DevOps practices impact all three phases.

1. *Inception phase*. During the inception phase, release planning and initial requirements specification are done.

    a. Considerations of Ops will add some requirements for the developers. We will see these in more detail later in this book, but maintaining backward compatibility between releases and having features be software switchable are two of these requirements. The form and content of operational log messages impacts the ability of Ops to troubleshoot a problem.

    b. Release planning includes feature prioritization but it also includes coordination with operations personnel about the scheduling of the release and determining what training the operations personnel require to support the new release. Release planning also includes ensuring

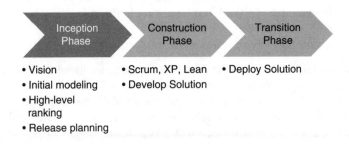

FIGURE 1.2   Disciplined Agile Delivery phases for each release. (Adapted from *Disciplined Agile Delivery: A Practitioner's Guide* by Ambler and Lines) [Notation: Porter's Value Chain]

compatibility with other packages in the environment and a recovery plan if the release fails. DevOps practices make incorporation of many of the coordination-related topics in release planning unnecessary, whereas other aspects become highly automated.

2. *Construction phase.* During the construction phase, key elements of the DevOps practices are the management of the code branches, the use of continuous integration and continuous deployment, and incorporation of test cases for automated testing. These are also agile practices but form an important portion of the ability to automate the deployment pipeline. A new element is the integrated and automated connection between construction and transition activities.

3. *Transition phase.* In the transition phase, the solution is deployed and the development team is responsible for the deployment, monitoring the process of the deployment, deciding whether to roll back and when, and monitoring the execution after deployment. The development team has a role of "reliability engineer," who is responsible for monitoring and troubleshooting problems during deployment and subsequent execution.

1.5   Team Structure

In this section, the usual size of and roles within a development team with DevOps responsibilities are discussed.

Team Size

Although the exact team size recommendation differs from one methodology to another, all agree that the size of the team should be relatively small. Amazon has a "two pizza rule." That is, no team should be larger than can be fed from two pizzas. Although there is a fair bit of ambiguity in this rule—how big the pizzas are, how hungry the members of the team are—the intent is clear.

The advantages of small teams are:

- They can make decisions quickly. In every meeting, attendees wish to express their opinions. The smaller the number of attendees at the meeting, the fewer the number of opinions expressed and the less time spent hearing differing opinions. Consequently, the opinions can be expressed and a consensus arrived at faster than with a large team.
- It is easier to fashion a small number of people into a coherent unit than a large number. A coherent unit is one in which everyone understands and subscribes to a common set of goals for the team.
- It is easier for individuals to express an opinion or idea in front of a small group than in front of a large one.

The disadvantage of a small team is that some tasks are larger than can be accomplished by a small number of individuals. In this case the task has to be broken up into smaller pieces, each given to a different team, and the different pieces need to work together sufficiently well to accomplish the larger task. To achieve this, the teams need to coordinate.

The team size becomes a major driver of the overall architecture. A small team, by necessity, works on a small amount of code. We will see that an architecture constructed around a collection of microservices is a good means to package these small tasks and reduce the need for explicit coordination—so we will call the output of a development team a "service." We discuss the ways and challenges of migrating to a microservice architecture driven by small teams in Chapter 4 and the case study in Chapter 13 from Atlassian.

Team Roles

We lift two of the roles in the team from Scott Ambler's description of roles in an agile team.

Team lead. This role, called "Scrum Master" in Scrum or team coach or project lead in other methods, is responsible for facilitating the team, obtaining resources for it, and protecting it from problems. This role encompasses the soft skills of project management but not the technical ones such as planning and scheduling, activities which are better left to the team as a whole.

Team member. This role, sometimes referred to as developer or programmer, is responsible for the creation and delivery of a system. This includes modeling, programming, testing, and release activities, as well as others.

Additional roles in a team executing a DevOps process consist of service owner, reliability engineer, gatekeeper, and DevOps engineer. An individual can perform multiple roles, and roles can be split among individuals. The assignment of roles to individuals depends on that individual's skills and workload as well as the skills and amount of work required to satisfy the role. We discuss some examples of team roles for adopting DevOps and continuous deployment in the case study in Chapter 12.

Service Owner

The service owner is the role on the team responsible for outside coordination. The service owner participates in system-wide requirements activities, prioritizes work items for the team, and provides the team with information both from the clients of the team's service and about services provided to the team. The requirements gathering and release planning activities for the next iteration can occur in parallel with the conception phase of the current iteration. Thus, although these activities require coordination and time, they will not slow down the time to delivery.

The service owner maintains and communicates the vision for the service. Since each service is relatively small, the vision involves knowledge of the clients of the team's service and the services on which the team's service depends. That is, the vision involves the architecture of the overall system and the team's role in that architecture.

The ability to communicate both with other stakeholders and with other members of the team is a key requirement for the service owner.

Reliability Engineer

The reliability engineer has several responsibilities. First, the reliability engineer monitors the service in the time period immediately subsequent to the deployment. This may involve the use of canaries (live testing of a small number of nodes) and a wide variety of metrics taken from the service. We will discuss both of those concepts in more detail later in this book. Second, the reliability engineer is the point of contact for problems with the service during its execution. This means being on call for services that require high availability. Google calls this role "Site Reliability Engineer."

Once a problem occurs, the reliability engineer performs short-term analysis to diagnose, mitigate, and repair the problem, usually with the assistance of automated tools. This can occur under very stressful conditions (e.g., in the middle of the night or a romantic dinner). The problem may involve reliability engineers from other teams. In any case, the reliability engineer has to be excellent at troubleshooting and diagnosis. The reliability engineer also has to have a comprehensive grasp of the internals of the service so that a fix or workaround can be applied.

In addition to the short-term analysis, the reliability engineer should discover or work with the team to discover the root cause of a problem. The "5 Whys" is a technique to determine a root cause. Keep asking "Why?" until a process reason is discovered. For example, the deployed service is too slow and the immediate cause may be an unexpected spike in workload. The second "why" is what caused the unexpected spike, and so on. Ultimately, the response is that stress testing for the service did not include appropriate workload characterization. This process reason can be fixed by improving the workload characterization for the stress testing. Increasingly, reliability engineers need to be competent developers, as they need to write high-quality programs to automate the repetitive part of the diagnosis, mitigation, and repair.

Gatekeeper

Netflix uses the steps given in Figure 1.3 from local development to deployment.

Each arrow in this figure represents a decision to move to the next step. This decision may be done automatically (in Netflix's case) or manually. The manual role that decides to move a service to the next step in a deployment pipeline is a gatekeeper role. The gatekeeper decides whether to allow a version of a service or a portion of a service through "the gate" to the next step. The gatekeeper may rely on comprehensive testing results and have a checklist to use to make this decision and may consult with others but, fundamentally, the responsibility for allowing code or a service to move on through the deployment pipeline belongs to the gatekeeper. In some cases, the original developer is the gatekeeper before deployment to production, making a decision informed by test results but carrying the full responsibility. Human gatekeepers (*not* the original developer) may be required by regulators in some industries such as the financial industry.

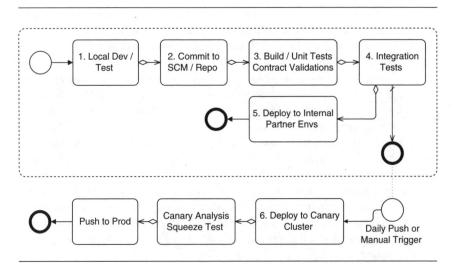

FIGURE 1.3   Netflix path to production. (Adapted from http://techblog.netflix .com/2013/11/preparing-netflix-api-for-deployment.html) [Notation: BPMN]

Mozilla has a role called a *release coordinator* (sometimes called release manager). This individual is designated to assume responsibility for coordinating the entire release. The release coordinator attends triage meetings where it is decided what is in and what is omitted from a release, understands the background context on all work included in a release, referees bug severity disputes, may approve late-breaking additions, and can make the back-out decision. In addition, on the actual release day, the release coordinator is the point for all communications between developers, QA, release engineering, website developers, PR, and marketing. The release coordinator is a gatekeeper.

DevOps Engineer

Examine Figure 1.2 again with an eye toward the use of tools in this process. Some of the tools used are code testing tools, configuration management tools, continuous integration tools, deployment tools, or post-deployment testing tools.

Configuration management applies not only to the source code for the service but also to all of the input for the various tools. This allows you to answer questions such as "What changed between the last deployment and this one?" and "What new tests were added since the last build?"

Tools evolve, tools require specialized knowledge, and tools require specialized input. The DevOps engineer role is responsible for the care and feeding of the various tools used in the DevOps tool chain. This role can be filled at the individual level, the team level, or the organizational level. For example, the organization may decide on a particular configuration management tool that all should use. The team will still need to decide on its branching strategies, and individual developers may further create branches. Policies for naming and access will exist and possibly be automatically enforced. The choice of which release of the configuration management tool the development teams will use is a portion of the DevOps engineer's role, as are the tailoring of the tool for the development team and monitoring its correct use by the developers. The DevOps engineering role is inherent in automating the development and deployment pipeline. How this role is manifested in an organizational or team structure is a decision separate from the recognition that the role exists and must be filled.

1.6 Coordination

One goal of DevOps is to minimize coordination in order to reduce the time to market. Two of the reasons to coordinate are, first, so that the pieces developed by the various teams will work together and, second, to avoid duplication of effort. The *Oxford English Dictionary* defines coordination as "the organization of the different elements of a complex body or activity so as to enable them to work together effectively." We go more deeply into the concept of coordination and its mechanisms in this section.

Forms of Coordination

Coordination mechanisms have different attributes.

- *Direct*—the individuals coordinating know each other (e.g., team members).
- *Indirect*—the coordination mechanism is aimed at an audience known only by its characterization (e.g., system administrators).
- *Persistent*—the coordination artifacts are available after the moment of the coordination (e.g., documents, e-mail, bulletin boards).
- *Ephemeral*—the coordination, per se, produces no artifacts (e.g., face to face meetings, conversations, telephone/video conferencing). Ephemeral coordination can be made persistent through the use of human or mechanical recorders.
- *Synchronous*—individuals are coordinating in real time, (e.g., face to face).
- *Asynchronous*—individuals are not coordinating in real time (e.g., documents, e-mail).

Coordination mechanisms are built into many of the tools used in DevOps. For example, a version control system is a form of automated coordination that keeps various developers from overwriting each other's code. A continuous integration tool is a form of coordinating the testing of the correctness of a build.

Every form of coordination has a cost and a benefit. Synchronous coordination requires scheduling and, potentially, travel. The time spent in synchronous coordination is a cost for all involved. The benefits of synchronous coordination include allowing the people involved to have an immediate opportunity to contribute to the resolution of any problem. Other costs and benefits for synchronous coordination depend on the bandwidth of communication, time zone differences, and persistence of the coordination. Each form of coordination can be analyzed in terms of costs and benefits.

The ideal characteristics of a coordination mechanism are that it is low cost in terms of delay, preparation required, and people's time, and of high benefit in terms of visibility of the coordination to all relevant stakeholders, fast resolution of any problems, and effectiveness in communicating the desired information.

The Wikipedia definition of DevOps that we mentioned earlier stated that "communication, collaboration, and integration" are hallmarks of a DevOps process. In light of our current discussion of coordination, we can see that too much manual communication and collaboration, especially synchronous, defeats the DevOps goal of shorter time to market.

Team Coordination

Team coordination mechanisms are of two types—human processes and automated processes. The DevOps human processes are adopted from agile processes and are designed for high-bandwidth coordination with limited persistence.

Stand-up meetings and information radiators are examples of human process coordination mechanisms.

Automated team coordination mechanisms are designed to protect team members from interference of their and others' activities (version control and configuration management systems), to automate repetitive tasks (continuous integration and deployment), and to speed up error detection and reporting (automated unit, integration, acceptance, and live production tests). One goal is to provide feedback to the developers as quickly as possible.

Cross-team Coordination

Examining the release process activities again makes it clear that cross-team coordination is the most time-consuming factor. Coordination must occur with customers, stakeholders, other development teams, and operations. Therefore, DevOps processes attempt to minimize this coordination as much as possible. From the development team's perspective, there are three types of cross-team coordination: upstream coordination with stakeholders and customers, downstream coordination with operations, and cross-stream coordination with other development teams.

The role of the service owner is to perform upstream coordination. Downstream coordination is accomplished by moving many operations responsibilities to the development team. It is cross-team coordination that we focus on now. There are two reasons for a development team to coordinate with other development teams—to ensure that the code developed by one team works well with the code developed by another and to avoid duplication of effort.

1. *Making the code pieces work together.* One method for supporting the independent work of different development teams while simplifying the integration of this work is to have a software architecture. An architecture for the system being developed will help make the pieces work together. Some further coordination is still necessary, but the architecture serves as a coordinating mechanism. An architecture specifies a number of the design decisions to create an overall system. Six of these design decisions are:

   a. *Allocation of responsibilities.* In DevOps processes, general responsibilities are specified in the architecture but specific responsibilities are determined at the initiation of each iteration.
   b. *Coordination model.* The coordination model describes how the components of an architecture coordinate at runtime. Having a single coordination model for all elements removes the necessity of coordination about the coordination model.
   c. *Data model.* As with responsibilities, the data model objects and their life cycle are specified in the architecture but refinements may occur at iteration initiation.

    d. *Management of resources.* The resources to be managed are determined by the architecture. The limits on these resources (e.g., buffer size or thread pool size) may be determined during iteration initiation or through system-wide policies specified in the architecture.

    e. *Mapping among architectural elements.* The least coordination is required among teams if these mappings are specified in the architecture and in the work assignments for the teams. We return to this topic when we discuss the architectural style we propose for systems developed with DevOps processes, in Chapter 4.

    f. *Binding time decisions.* These are specified in the overall architecture. Many runtime binding values will be specified through configuration parameters, and we will discuss the management of the configuration parameters in Chapter 5.

2. *Avoiding duplication of effort.* Avoiding duplication of effort and encouraging reuse is another argument for coordination among development teams. DevOps practices essentially argue that duplication of effort is a necessary cost for shorter time to market. There are two portions to this argument. First, since the task each team has to accomplish is small, any duplication is small. Large potential areas of duplication, such as each team creating their own datastore, are handled by the architecture. Second, since each team is responsible for its own service, troubleshooting problems after deployment is faster with code written by the team, and it avoids escalating a problem to a different team.

1.7   Barriers

If DevOps solves long-standing problems with development and has such clear benefits, why haven't all organizations adopted DevOps practices? In this section we explore the barriers to their adoption.

Culture and Type of Organization

Culture is important when discussing DevOps. Both across organizations and among different groups within the same organization, cultural issues associated with DevOps affect its form and its adoption. Culture depends not only on your role but also on the type of organization to which you belong.

    One of the goals of DevOps is to reduce time to market of new features or products. One of the tradeoffs that organizations consider when adopting DevOps practices is the benefits of reduced time to market versus the risks of something going awry. Almost all organizations worry about risk. The risks that a particular organization worries about, however, depend on their domain of activity. For some organizations the risks of problems occurring outweigh a time-to-market advantage.

- Organizations that operate in regulated domains—financial, health care, or utility services—have regulations to which they must adhere and face penalties, potentially severe, if they violate the regulations under which they operate. Even organizations in regulated domains may have products that are unregulated. So a financial organization may use DevOps processes for some products. For products that require more oversight, the practices may be adaptable, for example, by introducing additional gatekeepers. We discuss security and audit issues in Chapter 8.
- Organizations that operate in mature and slow-moving domains— automotive or building construction—have long lead times, and, although their deadlines are real, they are also foreseeable far in advance.
- Organizations whose customers have a high cost of switching to another supplier, such as Enterprise Resource Planning systems, are reluctant to risk the stability of their operations. The cost of downtime for some systems will far outweigh the competitive advantage of introducing a new feature somewhat more quickly.

For other organizations, nimbleness and fast response are more important than the occasional error caused by moving too fast.

- Organizations that rely on business analytics to shape their products want to have shorter and shorter times between the gathering of the data and actions inspired by the data. Any errors that result can be quickly corrected since the next cycle will happen quickly.
- Organizations that face severe competitive pressure want to have their products and new features in the marketplace before their competitors.

Note that these examples do not depend on the size of the organization but rather the type of business they are in. It is difficult to be nimble if you have regulators who have oversight and can dictate your operating principles, or if your lead time for a product feature is measured in years, or if your capital equipment has a 40-year estimated lifetime.

The point of this discussion is that businesses operate in an environment and inherit much of the culture of that environment. See Chapter 10 for more details. Some DevOps practices are disruptive, such as allowing developers to deploy to production directly; other DevOps practices are incremental in that they do not affect the overall flow of products or oversight. Treating operations personnel as first-class citizens should fall into this nondisruptive category.

It is possible for a slow-moving organization to become more nimble or a nimble organization to have oversight. If you are considering adopting a DevOps practice then you need to be aware of three things.

1. *What other practices are implicit in the practice you are considering?*
    You cannot do continuous deployment without first doing continuous
    integration. Independent practices need to be adopted prior to adopting
    dependent practices.
2. *What is the particular practice you are considering?* What are its
    assumption, its costs, and its benefits?
3. *What is the culture of your business, and what are the ramifications of
    your adopting this particular DevOps practice?* If the practice just affects
    operations and development, that is one thing. If it requires modification
    to the entire organizational structure and oversight practices, that is quite
    another. The difficulty of adopting a practice is related to its impact on
    other portions of the organization. But even if the adoption focuses on
    a single development team and a few operators, it is important that the
    DevOps culture is adopted by all people involved. A commonly reported
    way of failing in the adoption of DevOps is to hire a DevOps engineer and
    think you are done.

Type of Department

One method for determining the culture of an organization is to look at what
kinds of results are incentivized. Salespeople who work on commission work
very hard to get sales. CEOs who are rewarded based on quarterly profits are
focused on the results of the next quarter. This is human nature. Developers are
incentivized to produce and release code. Ideally, they are incentivized to produce error-free code but there is a Dilbert cartoon that shows the difficulty of
this: The pointy-headed boss offers $10 for every bug found and fixed, and Wally
responds, "Hooray, I am going to write me a new minivan this afternoon." In any
case, developers are incentivized to get their code into production.

Operations personnel, on the other hand, are incentivized to minimize downtime. Minimizing downtime means examining and removing causes of downtime. Examining anything in detail takes time. Furthermore, avoiding change
removes one of the causes of downtime. "If it ain't broke, don't fix it" is a well-
known phrase dating back over decades.

Basically, developers are incentivized to change something (release new
code), and operations personnel are incentivized to resist change. These two different sets of incentives breed different attitudes and can be the cause of culture
clashes.

Silo Mentality

It is easy to say that two departments in an organization have a common goal—
ensuring the organization's success. It is much more difficult to make this happen
in practice. An individual's loyalty tends to be first to her or his team and sec-
ondarily to the overall organization. If the development team is responsible for

defining the release plan that will include what features get implemented in what priority, other portions of the organization will see some of their power being usurped and, potentially, their customers become unhappy. If activities formerly performed by operations personnel are now going to be performed by developers, what happens to the operations personnel who now have less to do?

These are the normal ebbs and flows of organizational politics but that does not make them less meaningful and less real.

Tool Support

We described the advantages of automating processes previously, and these advantages are real. They do not come without a cost, however.

- There must be expertise in the installation, configuration, and use of each tool. Tools have new releases, inputs, and idiosyncrasies. Tool expertise has to be integrated into the organization.
- If the organization uses common processes across a wide variety of development teams, then there must be a means of defining these common processes and ensuring that all of the development teams obey them. Use of a tool means subscribing to the process implicit in that tool. See the case study in Chapter 12 for an example of the definition of common processes.

Personnel Issues

According to the Datamation 2012 IT salary guide, a software engineer earns about 50% more than a systems administrator. So by moving a task from a system administrator (Ops) to a software engineer (Dev), the personnel performing the task cost 50% more. Thus, the time spent performing the task must be cut by a third just to make the performance of the task cost the same amount. A bigger cut is necessary to actually gain time, with automation being the prevalent method to achieve these time savings. This is the type of cost/benefit analysis that an organization must go through in order to determine which DevOps processes to adopt and how to adopt them.

Developers with a modern skill set are in high demand and short supply, and they also have a heavy workload. Adding more tasks to their workload may exacerbate the shortage of developers.

1.8 Summary

The main takeaway from this chapter is that people have defined DevOps from different perspectives, such as operators adopting agile practices or developers taking operations responsibilities, among others. But one common objective is to reduce the time between the conception of a feature or improvement as a business idea to its eventual deployment to users.

DevOps faces barriers due to both cultural and technical challenges. It can have a huge impact on team structure, software architecture, and traditional ways of conducting operations. We have given you a taste of this impact by listing some common practices. We will cover all of these topics in detail throughout the rest of the book.

Some of the tradeoffs involved in DevOps are as follows:

- *Creation of a need to support DevOps tools.* This tool support is traded off against the shortening of the time to market of new functions.
- *Moving responsibilities from IT professionals to developers.* This tradeoff is multifaceted. The following are some of the facets to be considered:

  - The cost to complete a task from the two groups.
  - The time to complete a task from the two groups.
  - The availability of personnel within the two groups.
  - The repair time when an error is detected during execution. If the error is detected quickly after deployment, then the developer may still have the context information necessary to diagnose it quickly, whereas if the error is initially diagnosed by IT personnel, it may take time before the error gets back to the developer.

- *Removing oversight of new features and deployment.* This tradeoff is between autonomy for the development teams and overall coordination. The efficiencies of having autonomous development teams must outweigh the duplications of effort that will occur because of no overall oversight.

All in all, we believe that DevOps has the potential to lead IT onto exciting new ground, with high frequency of innovation and fast cycles to improve the user experience. We hope you enjoy reading the book as much as we enjoyed writing it.

1.9 For Further Reading

You can read about different takes on the DevOps definition from the following sources:

- Gartner's Hype Cycle [Gartner] categorizes DevOps as on the rise: http://www.gartner.com/DisplayDocument?doc_cd=249070.
- AgileAdmins explains DevOps from an agile perspective: http://theagileadmin.com/what-is-devops/.

You can find many more responses from the following recent surveys and industry reports:

- XebiaLabs has a wide range of surveys and state of industry reports on DevOps-related topics that can be found at http://xebialabs.com/xl-resources/whitepapers/
- CA Technologies' report gives some insights into business' different understanding of DevOps and can be found at http://www.ca.com/us/collateral/white-papers/na/techinsights-report-what-smart-businesses-know-about-devops.aspx

While some vendors or communities extended continuous integration tools toward continuous deployment, many vendors also released completely new tools for continuous delivery and deployment.

- The popular continuous integration tool Jenkins has many third-party plug-ins including some workflows extending into continuous deployment. You can find some plug-ins from Cloudbees at http://www.slideshare.net/cloudbees
- IBM acquired UrbanCode recently. UrbanCode is one of the new vendors providing a continuous delivery tool suite [InfoQ 13].
- ThoughtWorks also released its own continuous deployment pipeline suite called Go, which can be found at http://www.go.cd/

Some of the basic conceptual information in this chapter comes from the following Wikipedia links:

- One definition of DevOps we refer to is found at http://en.wikipedia.org/wiki/System_administrator
- The steps in a release or deployment plan are adapted from http://en.wikipedia.org/wiki/Deployment_Plan
- The duties of an operator are listed in http://en.wikipedia.org/wiki/DevOps.
- The 5 Whys originated at Toyota Motors and are discussed in http://en.wikipedia.org/wiki/5_Whys

There are also discussions around whether or not continuous deployment is just a dream [BostInno 11]. Scott Ambler has not only coauthored (with Mark Lines) a book on disciplined agile delivery [Ambler 12], he also maintains a blog from which we adapted the description of the roles in a team [Ambler 15].

Netflix maintains a technical blog where they discuss a variety of issues associated with their platform. Their deployment steps are discussed in [Netflix 13].

Mozilla's Release Coordinator role is discussed in [Mozilla].

Len Bass, Paul Clements, and Rick Kazman discuss architectural decisions on page 73 and subsequently in *Software Architecture in Practice* [Bass 13].

The discussion of IMVU is adapted from a blog written by Timothy Fitz [Fitz 09].

2

The Cloud as a Platform

We've redefined cloud computing to include everything that we already do.
... The computer industry is the only industry that is more fashion-driven than women's fashion.
... We'll make cloud computing announcements because if orange is the new pink, we'll make
orange blouses. I'm not going to fight this thing.
—Larry Ellison

2.1 Introduction

The standard analogy used to describe the cloud is that of the electric grid. When you want to use electricity, you plug a device into a standard connection and turn it on. You are charged for the electricity you use. In most cases, you can remain ignorant of the mechanisms the various electric companies use to generate and distribute electricity. The exception to this ignorance is if there is a power outage. At that point you become aware that there are complicated mechanisms underlying your use of electricity even if you remain unaware of the particular mechanisms that failed.

The National Institute of Standards and Technology (NIST) has provided a characterization of the cloud with the following elements:

- *On-demand self-service.* A consumer can unilaterally provision computing capabilities, such as server time and network storage, as needed automatically without requiring human interaction with each service provider.
- *Broad network access.* Capabilities are available over the network and accessed through standard mechanisms that promote use by heterogeneous thin or thick client platforms (e.g., mobile phones, tablets, laptops, and workstations).
- *Resource pooling.* The provider's computing resources are pooled to serve multiple consumers using a multi-tenant model, with different

physical and virtual resources dynamically assigned and reassigned according to consumer demand. There is a sense of location independence in that the customer generally has no control over or knowledge of the exact location of the provided resources but may be able to specify location at a higher level of abstraction (e.g., country, state, or datacenter). Examples of resources include storage, processing, memory, and network bandwidth.

- *Rapid elasticity.* Capabilities can be elastically provisioned and released, in some cases automatically, to scale rapidly outward and inward commensurate with demand. To the consumer, the capabilities available for provisioning often appear to be unlimited and can be appropriated in any quantity at any time.
- *Measured service.* Cloud systems automatically control and optimize resource use by leveraging a metering capability at some level of abstraction appropriate to the type of service (e.g., storage, processing, bandwidth, and active user accounts). Resource usage can be monitored, controlled, and reported, thereby providing transparency for both the provider and consumer of the utilized service.

From the perspective of operations and DevOps, the most important of these characteristics are on-demand self-service and measured (or metered) service. Even though the cloud provides what appear to be unlimited resources that you can acquire at will, you must still pay for their use. As we will discuss, the other characteristics are also important but not as dominant as on-demand self-service and paying for what you use.

Implicit in the NIST characterization is the distinction between the provider and the consumer of cloud services. Our perspective in this book is primarily that of the consumer. If your organization runs its own datacenters then there may be some blurring of this distinction, but even in such organizations, the management of the datacenters is not usually considered as falling within the purview of DevOps.

NIST also characterizes the various types of services available from cloud providers, as shown in Table 2.1. NIST defines three types of services, any one of which can be used in a DevOps context.

- *Software as a Service (SaaS).* The consumer is provided the capability to use the provider's applications running on a cloud infrastructure. The applications are accessible from various client devices through either a thin client interface, such as a web browser (e.g., web-based e-mail) or an application interface. The consumer does not manage or control the underlying cloud infrastructure including networks, servers, operating systems, storage, or even individual application capabilities, with the possible exception of limited user-specific application configuration settings.

TABLE 2.1   Cloud Service Models

Service Model	Examples
SaaS: Software as a Service	E-mail, online games, Customer Relationship Management, virtual desktops, etc.
PaaS: Platform as a Service	Web servers, database, execution runtime, development tools, etc.
IaaS: Infrastructure as a Service	Virtual machines, storage, load balancers, networks, etc.

- *Platform as a Service (PaaS).* The consumer is provided the capability to deploy onto the cloud infrastructure consumer-created or acquired applications created using programming languages, libraries, services, and tools supported by the provider. The consumer does not manage or control the underlying cloud infrastructure including networks, servers, operating systems, or storage, but has control over the deployed applications and possibly configuration settings for the application-hosting environment.
- *Infrastructure as a Service (IaaS).* The consumer is provided the capability to provision processing, storage, networks, and other fundamental computing resources where the consumer is able to deploy and run arbitrary software, which can include operating systems and applications. The consumer does not manage or control the underlying cloud infrastructure but has control over operating systems, storage, and deployed applications; and possibly limited control of select networking components (e.g., host firewalls).

We first discuss the mechanisms involved in the cloud, and then we discuss the consequences of these mechanisms on DevOps.

2.2   Features of the Cloud

The fundamental enabler of the cloud is virtualization over hundreds of thousands of hosts accessible over the Internet. We begin by discussing IaaS-centric features, namely, virtualization and IP management, followed by some specifics of PaaS offerings. Then we discuss general issues, such as the consequences of having hundreds of thousands of hosts and how elasticity is supported in the cloud.

Virtualization

In cloud computing, a virtual machine (VM) is an emulation of a physical machine. A VM image is a file that contains a bootable operating system and some software installed on it. A VM image provides the information required to launch a VM (or more precisely, a VM instance). In this book, we use "VM" and "VM instance" interchangeably to refer to an instance. And we use "VM image" to refer to the file used to launch a VM or a VM instance. For example, an Amazon Machine Image (AMI) is a VM image that can be used to launch Elastic Compute Cloud (EC2) VM instances.

When using IaaS, a consumer acquires a VM from a VM image by using an application programming interface (API) provided by the cloud provider for that purpose. The API may be embedded in a command-line interpreter, a web interface, or another tool of some sort. In any case, the request is for a VM with some set of resources—CPU, memory, and network. The resources granted may be hosted on a computer that is also hosting other VMs (multi-tenancy) but from the perspective of the consumer, the provider produces the equivalent of a stand-alone computer.

Creating a Virtual Machine

In order to create a VM, two distinct activities are performed.

- The user issues a command to create a VM. Typically, the cloud provider has a utility that enables the creation of the VM. This utility is told the resources required by the VM, the account to which the charges accrued by the VM should be charged, the software to be loaded (see below), and a set of configuration parameters specifying security and the external connections for the VM.
- The cloud infrastructure decides on which physical machine to create the VM instance. The operating system for this physical machine is called a *hypervisor*, and it allocates resources for the new VM and "wires" the new machine so that it can send and receive messages. The new VM is assigned an IP address that is used for sending and receiving messages. We have described the situation where the hypervisor is running on bare metal. It is also possible that there are additional layers of operating system–type software involved but each layer introduces overhead and so the most common situation is the one we described.

Loading a Virtual Machine

Each VM needs to be loaded with a set of software in order to do meaningful work. The software can be loaded partially as a VM and partially as a result of the activated VM loading software after launching. A VM image can be created by loading and configuring a machine with the desired software and data, and then copying the memory contents (typically in the form of the virtual hard disk) of the machine to a persistent file. New VM instances from that VM image (software and data) can then be created at will.

The process of creating a VM image is called *baking* the image. A *heavily* baked image contains all of the software required to run an application and a *lightly* baked image contains only a portion of the software required, such as an operating system and a middleware container. We discuss these options and the related tradeoffs in Chapter 5.

Virtualization introduces several types of uncertainty that you should be aware of.

- Because a VM shares resources with other VMs on a single physical machine, there may be some performance interference among the VMs. This situation may be particularly difficult for cloud consumers as they usually have no visibility into the co-located VMs owned by other consumers.
- There are also time and dependability uncertainties when loading a VM, depending on the underlying physical infrastructure and the additional software that needs to be dynamically loaded. DevOps operations often create and destroy VMs frequently for setting up different environments or deploying new versions of software. It is important that you are aware of these uncertainties.

IP and Domain Name System Management

When a VM is created, it is assigned an IP address. IP addresses are the means by which messages are routed to any computer on the Internet. IP addresses, their routing, and their management are all complicated subjects. A discussion of the Domain Name System (DNS), and the persistence of IP addresses with respect to VMs follows.

DNS

Underlying the World Wide Web is a system that translates part of URLs into IP addresses. This function concerns the domain name part of the URL (e.g., ssrg.nicta.com.au), which can be resolved to an IP address through the DNS. As a portion of normal initiation, a browser, for example, is provided with the address of a DNS server. As shown in Figure 2.1, when you enter a URL into your browser, it sends that URL to its known DNS server which, in association with a larger network of DNS servers, resolves that URL into an IP address.

The domain name indicates a routing path for the resolution. The domain name ssrg.nicta.com.au, for example, will go first to a root DNS server to look up how to resolve .au names. The root server will provide an IP address for the Australian DNS server where .com names for Australia are stored. The .com.au server will provide the IP address of the nicta DNS server, which in turn provides an IP address for ssrg.

The importance of this hierarchy is that the lower levels of the hierarchy— .nicta and .ssrg—are under local control. Thus, the IP address of ssrg within the .nicta server can be changed relatively easily and locally.

Furthermore, each DNS entry has an attribute named time to live (TTL). TTL acts as an expiration time for the entry (i.e., the mapping of the domain

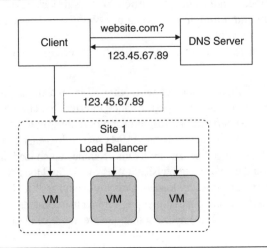

FIGURE 2.1   DNS returning an IP address [Notation: Architecture]

name and the IP address). The client or the local DNS server will cache the entry, and that cached entry will be valid for a duration specified by the TTL. When a query arrives prior to the expiration time, the client/local DNS server can retrieve the IP address from its cache. When a query arrives after the expiration time, the IP address has to be resolved by an authoritative DNS server. Normally the TTL is set to a large value; it may be as large as 24 hours. It is possible to set the TTL to as low as 1 minute. We will see in our case studies, Chapters 11–13, how the combination of local control and short TTL can be used within a DevOps context.

One further point deserves mention. In Figure 2.1, we showed the DNS returning a single IP address for a domain name. In fact, it can return multiple addresses. Figure 2.2 shows the DNS server returning two addresses.

The client will attempt the first IP address and, in the event of no response, will try the second, and so forth. The DNS server may rotate the order of the servers in order to provide some measure of load balancing.

Multiple sites can exist for several reasons:

- *Performance.* There are too many users to be served by a single site; consequently, multiple sites exist.
- *Reliability.* If one site fails to respond for some reason, the client can attempt the second site.
- *Testing.* The second site may provide some features or a new version that you want to test within a limited production environment. In this case, access to the second site is restricted to the population you want to perform the tests on. More details on this method are given in Chapters 5 and 6.

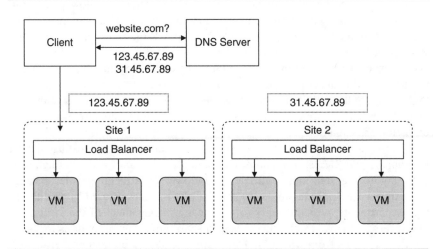

FIGURE 2.2   DNS returning two addresses for a single URL [Notation: Architecture]

Persistence of IP Addresses with Respect to VMs

The IP address assigned to a virtual machine on its creation persists as long as that VM is active. A VM becomes inactive when it is terminated, paused, or stopped. In these cases, the IP address is returned to the cloud provider's pool for reassignment.

One consequence of IP reassignment is: If one VM within your application sends a message to another VM within your application it must verify that the IP address of the recipient VM is still current. Consider the following sequence where your application contains at least VM_A and VM_B.

1. VM_B receives a message from VM_A.
2. VM_A fails.
3.   The cloud provider reassigns the IP address of VM_A.
4. VM_B responds to the originating IP address.
5.   The message is delivered to a VM that is not a portion of your application.

In order to avoid this sequence either you must ask the cloud provider for persistent IP addresses (often available at a premium) or your application VMs must verify, prior to sending a message, that the recipient is still alive and has the same IP address. We discuss a mechanism for verifying the aliveness of a VM in Chapter 4.

Platform as a Service

Many of the aspects we discussed so far are IaaS-specific. When using PaaS offerings, you can abstract from many of these details, since PaaS services reside at a higher level of the stack and hide underlying details to a degree.

As stated in the NIST definition earlier, PaaS offerings allow you to run applications in predefined environments. For instance, you can compile a Java web application into a web application archive (WAR) file and deploy it on hosted web application containers. You can then configure the service to your specific needs, for example, in terms of the number of underlying (often standardized) resources, and connect the application to hosted database management systems (SQL or NoSQL). While most PaaS platforms offer hosted solutions, either on their own infrastructure or on an IaaS base, some platforms are also available for on-premise installation.

Most PaaS platforms provide a set of core services (e.g., hosting of Java web apps, Ruby Gems, Scala apps, etc.) and a catalogue of add-ons (e.g., specific monitoring solutions, autoscaling options, log streaming, and alerting, etc.). In a way, PaaS are similar to some of the services offered by traditional Ops departments, which usually took over the management of the infrastructure layers and gave development teams a set of environment options for hosting their systems from which the Dev teams could pick and choose. However, using a provider PaaS with worldwide availability usually means that you have more add-ons and newer options more quickly than in traditional Ops departments.

Similarly to IaaS, if you are inexperienced with a particular PaaS offering, you first have to learn how to use it. This includes platform-specific tools, structures, configuration options, and logic. While getting started is relatively easy in most PaaS platforms, there are intricate, complex details in commands and configurations that take time to master.

The additional abstraction of PaaS over IaaS means that you can focus on the important bits of your system—the application. You do not have to deal with the network configuration, load balancers, operating systems, security patches on the lower layers, and so on. But it also means you give up visibility into and control over the underlying layers. Where this is acceptable, it might be well worthwhile to use a PaaS solution. However, when you end up needing the additional control at a later stage, the migration might be increasingly hard.

Distributed Environment

In this section, we explore some of the implications of having hundreds of thousands of servers within a cloud provider's environment. These implications concern the time involved for various operations, the probability of failure, and the consequences of these two aspects on the consistency of data.

Time

Within a stand-alone computer system, there are large variations in the time required to read an item from main memory and the time required to read a data item from a disk. The actual numbers change over time because of the improvements in hardware speed, but just to give some idea of the difference, accessing 1MB (roughly one million bytes) sequentially from main memory takes on the order of 12μs (microseconds). Accessing an item from a spinning disk requires on the order of 4ms (milliseconds) to move the disk head to the correct location. Then, reading 1MB takes approximately 2ms.

In a distributed environment where messages are the means of communication between the various processes involved in an application, a round trip within the same datacenter takes approximately 500μs and a round trip between California and the Netherlands takes around 150ms.

One consequence of these numbers is that determining what data to maintain in memory or on the disk is a critical performance decision. Caching allows for maintaining some data in both places but introduces the problem of keeping the data consistent. A second consequence is that where persistent data is physically located will also have a large impact on performance. Combining these two consequences with the possibility of failure, discussed in the next section, leads to a discussion of keeping data consistent using different styles of database management systems.

Failure

Although any particular cloud provider may guarantee high availability, these guarantees are typically for large segments of their cloud as a whole and do not refer to the components. Individual component failure can thus still impact your application. The list below presents some data from Google about the kinds of failures that one can expect within a datacenter. As you can see, the possibilities for individual element failure are significant. Amazon released some data stating that in a datacenter with ~64,000 servers with 2 disks each, on average more than 5 servers and 17 disks fail each day.

Below is a list of problems arising in a datacenter in its first year of operation (from a presentation by Jeff Dean, Google):

- ~0.5 overheating (power down most machines in <5 minutes, ~1–2 days to recover)
- ~1 PDU failure (~500–1,000 machines suddenly disappear, ~6 hours to come back)
- ~1 rack-move (plenty of warning, ~500–1,000 machines powered down, ~6 hours)
- ~1 network rewiring (rolling ~5% of machines down over 2-day span)
- ~20 rack failures (40–80 machines instantly disappear, 1–6 hours to get back)
- ~5 racks go wonky (40–80 machines see 50% packet loss)
- ~8 network maintenances (4 might cause ~30-minute random connectivity losses)
- ~12 router reloads (takes out DNS for a couple minutes)
- ~3 router failures (have to immediately pull traffic for an hour)
- ~dozens of minor 30-second blips for DNS

- ~1,000 individual machine failures
- ~thousands of hard drive failures
- slow disks, bad memory, misconfigured machines, flaky machines, etc.
- long-distance links: wild dogs, sharks, dead horses, drunken hunters, etc.

What do these failure statistics mean from an application or operations perspective? First, any particular VM or portion of a network may fail. This VM or network may be performing application or operation functionality. Second, since the probability of failure of serial use of components is related to the product of the failure rate of the individual components, the more components involved in a request, the higher the probability of failure. We discuss these two possibilities separately.

Failure of a VM

One of the major decisions the architect of a distributed system makes is how to divide state among the various pieces of an application. If a stateless component fails, it can be replaced without concern for state. On the other hand, state must be maintained somewhere accessible to the application, and getting state and computation together in the same VM will involve some level of overhead. We distinguish three main cases.

1. *A stateless component.* If a VM is stateless, then failure of a VM is recovered by creating another instance of the same VM image and ensuring that messages are correctly routed to it. This is the most desirable situation from the perspective of recovering from failure.

2. *Client state.* A session is a dialogue between two or more components or devices. Typically, each session is given an ID to provide continuity within the dialogue. For example, you may log in to a website through one interaction between your browser and a server. Session state allows your browser to inform the server in successive messages that you have been successfully logged in and that you are who you purport to be. Sometimes the client will add additional state for security or application purposes. Since client state must be sent with a message to inform the server of the context or a set of parameters, it should be kept to a minimum.

3. *Application state* contains the information specific to an application or a particular user of an application. It may be extensive, such as a knowledge base or the results of a web crawler, or it may be small, such as the current position of a user when watching a streaming video. We identify three categories of application state.

    a. *Small amounts of persistent state.* The persistent state must be maintained across multiple sessions or across failure of either servers or clients. Small amounts of persistent state could be maintained in a flat file or other structure on a file system. The application can maintain this state either per user or for the whole application. Small amounts of state could also be cached using a tool that maintains a persistent state across VM instances such as ZooKeeper or Memcached.

b. *Moderate amounts of persistent or semi-persistent state.* The timing numbers we saw earlier suggest that it is advantageous to cache those portions of persistent state that are used frequently in computations. It is also advantageous to maintain state across different instances of a VM that allows the sharing of this state. In some sense, this is equivalent to shared memory at the hardware level except that it is done across different VMs across a network. Tools such as Memcached are intended to manage moderate amounts of shared state that represent cached database entries or generated pages. Memcached automatically presents a consistent view of the data to its clients, and by sharing the data across servers, it provides resilience in the case of failure of a VM.

c. *Large amounts of persistent state.* Large amounts of persistent state can be kept in a database managed by a database management system or in a distributed file system such as Hadoop Distributed File System (HDFS). HDFS acts as a network- (or at least a cluster-) wide file system and automatically maintains replicas of data items to protect against failure. It provides high performance through mechanisms such as writing data as 64MB blocks. Large block sizes lead to inefficient writing of small amounts of data. Hence, HDFS should be used for large amounts of data. Since an HDFS file is available throughout a cluster, any client that fails will not lose any data that has been committed by HDFS.

The Long Tail

Many natural phenomena exhibit a normal distribution as shown in Figure 2.3a. Values are mostly spread around the mean with a progressively smaller likelihood of values toward the edges. In the cloud, many phenomena such as response time to requests show a long-tail distribution, like the one depicted in Figure 2.3b. This result is often due to the increased probability of failure with more entities involved, and the failure of one component causes response time to be an order slower than usual (e.g., until a network packet is routed through a different link, after the main network link broke and the error has been detected).

A long tail has been observed in map-reduce completion times, in response to search queries and in launching instances in Amazon cloud. In the latter case, the median time to satisfy a launch instance request was 23 seconds, but 4.5% of the requests took more than 36 seconds.

Although this has not been proven, our intuition is that the skewness of a distribution (the length of the long tail) is a function of the number of different elements of the cloud that are activated in order to satisfy a request. In other words, simple requests such as computation, reading a file, or receiving a local message will have a distribution closer to normal. Complicated requests such as extensive map-reduce jobs, searches across a large database, or launching virtual instances will have a skewed distribution such as a long tail.

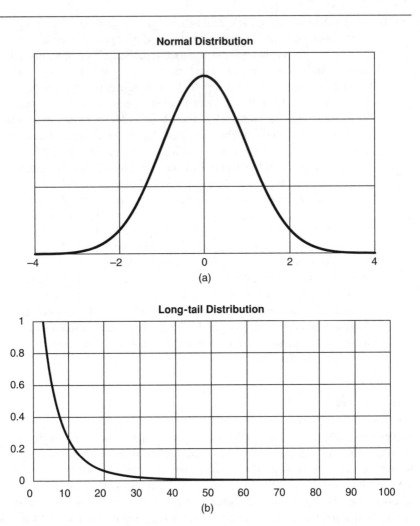

FIGURE 2.3   (a) A normal distribution where values cluster around the mean, and the median and the mean are equal. (b) A long-tail distribution where some values are exceedingly far from the median.

A request that takes an exceedingly long time to respond should be treated as a failure. However, one problem with such a request is that there is no way of knowing whether the request has failed altogether or is going to eventually complete. One mechanism to combat the long tail is to cancel a request that takes too long, for example, more than the 95th percentile of historical requests, and to reissue that request.

Consistency

Given the possibility of failure, it is prudent to replicate persistent data. Given two copies of a data item, it is desirable that when a client reads a data item, the client would get the same value regardless of which copy it read. If all copies of a data item have the same value at a particular instant they are said to be *consistent* at that instant. Recall that it takes time to write a data value to persistent storage.

Consistency is maintained in a distributed system by introducing locks that control the sequence of access to individual data items. Locking data items introduces delays in accessing those data items; consequently, there are a variety of different schemes for maintaining consistency and reducing the delay caused by locks. Regardless of the scheme used, the availability of data items will be impacted by the delays caused by the introduction of locks.

In addition, in the cloud persistent data may be partitioned among different locales to reduce access time, especially if there is a large amount of data. Per a theoretical result called the CAP (Consistency, Availability, Partition Tolerance) theorem, it is not possible to simultaneously have fully available, consistent, and partitioned data. *Eventual consistency* means that distributed, partitioned, and replicated data will be consistent after a period of time even if not immediately upon a change to a data item—the replicas will become consistent eventually.

NoSQL Databases

For a variety of reasons, including the CAP theorem and the overhead involved in setting up a relational database system, a collection of database systems have been introduced that go under the name NoSQL. Originally the name literally meant *No* SQL, but since some of the systems now support SQL, it now stands for *Not Only* SQL.

NoSQL systems use a different data model than relational systems. Relational systems are based on presenting data as tables. NoSQL systems use data models ranging from key-value pairs to graphs. The rise of NoSQL systems has had several consequences.

- NoSQL systems are not as mature as relational systems, and many features of relational systems such as transactions, schemas, and triggers are not supported by these systems. The application programmer must implement these features if they are needed in the application.
- The application programmer must decide which data model(s) are most appropriate for their use. Different applications have different needs with respect to their persistent data, and these needs must be understood prior to choosing a database system.
- Applications may use multiple database systems for different needs. Key-value stores can deal with large amounts of semistructured data efficiently. Graph database systems can maintain connections among data items efficiently. The virtue of using multiple different database systems

is that you can better match a system with your needs. The case study in Chapter 11 gives an example of the use of multiple database systems for different purposes. Licensing costs and increased maintenance costs are the drawbacks of using multiple different database systems.

Elasticity

Rapid elasticity and provisioning is one of the characteristics of the cloud identified by NIST. Elasticity means that the number of resources such as VMs used to service an application can grow and shrink according to the load. Monitoring the utilization of the existing resources is one method for measuring the load.

Figure 2.4 shows clients accessing VMs through a load balancer and a monitor determining CPU and I/O utilization of the various VMs, grouped together in a scaling group. The monitor sends its information to the scaling controller, which has a collection of rules that determine when to add or remove the server in the scaling group. These rules can be reactive (e.g., "when utilization has reached a certain stage, add an additional server") or proactive (e.g., "add additional servers at 7:00 am and remove them at 6:00 pm"). When a rule to add a new server is triggered, the scaling controller will create a new virtual machine and ensure that it is loaded with the correct software. The new VM is then registered with the load balancer, and the load balancer will now have an additional VM to distribute messages to. It is also possible to control scaling through various APIs. We see an example of this in Chapter 12.

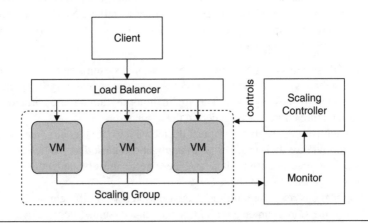

FIGURE 2.4   Monitoring used as input to scaling [Notation: Architecture]

2.3 DevOps Consequences of the Unique Cloud Features

Three of the unique aspects of the cloud that impact DevOps are: the ability to create and switch environments simply, the ability to create VMs easily, and the management of databases. We begin by discussing environments.

Environments

An environment in our context is a set of computing resources sufficient to execute a software system, including all of the supporting software, data sets, network communications, and defined external entities necessary to execute the software system.

The essence of this definition is that an environment is self-contained except for explicitly defined external entities. An environment is typically isolated from other environments. In Chapter 5, we see a number of environments such as the Dev, integration, user testing, and production environments. In the case study in Chapter 12, the life cycle of an environment is explicitly a portion of their deployment pipeline. Having multiple environments during the development, testing, and deployment processes is not a unique feature of the cloud, but having the ability to simply create and migrate environments is—as is the ease of cloning new instances. The isolation of one environment from another is enforced by having no modifiable shared resources. Resources that are read-only, such as feeds of one type or another, can be shared without a problem. Since an environment communicates with the outside world only through defined external entities, these entities can be accessed by URLs and, hence, managed separately. Writing to or altering the state of these external entities should only be done by the production environment, and separate external entities must be created (e.g., as dummies or test clones) for all other environments.

One method of visualizing an environment is as a silo. Figure 2.5 shows two variants of two different environments—a testing environment and a production environment. Each contains slightly different versions of the same system. The two load balancers, responsible for their respective environments, have different IP addresses. Testing can be done by forking the input stream to the production environment and sending a copy to the testing environment as shown in Figure 2.5a. In this case, it is important that the test database be isolated from the production database. Figure 2.5b shows an alternative situation. In this case, some subset of actual production messages is sent to the test environment that performs live testing. We discuss canary testing and other methods of live testing in Chapter 6. Moving between environments can be accomplished in a single script that can be tested for correctness prior to utilizing it. In Chapter 6, we will see other techniques for moving between testing and production environments.

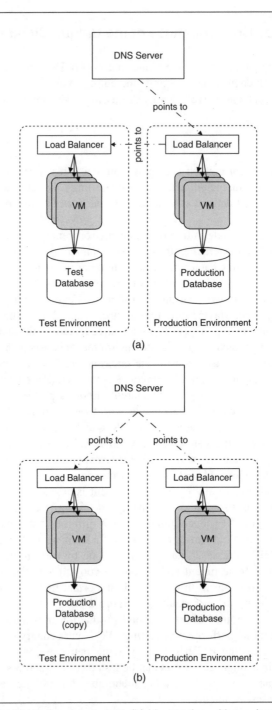

FIGURE 2.5 (a) Using live data to test. (b) Live testing with a subset of users. [Notation: Architecture]

A consequence of easily switching production from one environment to another is that achieving business continuity becomes easier. Business continuity means that businesses can continue to operate in the event of a disaster occurring either in or to their main datacenter. In Chapter 11, we see a case study about managing multiple datacenters, but for now observe that there is no requirement that the two environments be co-located in the same datacenter. There is a requirement that the two databases be synchronized if the goal is quickly moving from one environment to a backup environment.

Creating Virtual Machines Easily

One of the problems that occurs in administering the cloud from a consumer's perspective arises *because* it is so easy to allocate new VMs. Virtual machines need to have the latest patches applied, just as physical machines, and need to be accounted for. Unpatched machines constitute a security risk. In addition, in a public cloud, the consumer pays for the use of VMs. We know of an incident in a major U.S. university where a student went away for the summer without cleaning up her or his allocation and returned to find a bill of $80,000.

The term *VM sprawl* is used to describe the complexity in managing too many VMs. Similarly, the challenges of having too many VM images is called *image sprawl*. Tools exist, such as Janitor Monkey, to scan an account and determine which machines are allocated and how recently they have been used. Developing and enforcing a policy on the allocation of machines and archiving of VM images is one of the activities necessary when utilizing the cloud as a platform.

Data Considerations

The economic viability of the cloud coincided with the advent of NoSQL database systems. Many systems utilize multiple different database systems, both relational and NoSQL. Furthermore, large amounts of data are being gathered from a variety of sources for various business intelligence or operational purposes. Just as computational resources can be added in the cloud by scaling, storage resources can also be added. We begin by discussing the HDFS that provides storage for applications in a cluster. HDFS provides the file system for many NoSQL database systems. We then discuss the operational considerations associated with distributed file systems.

HDFS

HDFS provides a pool of shared storage resources. An application accesses HDFS through a normal file system interface in Java, C, or other popular languages. The commands available include open, create, read, write, close, and append. Since the storage provided by HDFS is shared by multiple applications, a manager controls the name space of file names and allocates space when an application wishes to write a new block. This manager also provides information so that applications can perform direct access to particular blocks. There also is a pool of storage nodes.

In HDFS the manager is called the NameNode, and each element of the storage pool is called a DataNode. There is one NameNode with provision for a hot backup. Each DataNode is a separate physical computer or VM. Applications are restricted to write a fixed-size block—typically 64MB. When an application wishes to write a new block to a file it contacts the NameNode and asks for the DataNodes where this block will be stored. Each block is replicated some number of times, typically three. The NameNode responds to a request for a write with a list of the DataNodes where the block to be written will be stored, and the application then writes its block to each of these DataNodes.

Many features of HDFS are designed to guard against failure of the individual DataNodes and to improve the performance of HDFS. For our purposes, the essential element is that HDFS provides a pool of storage sites that are shared across applications.

Operational Considerations

The operational considerations associated with a shared file system such as HDFS are twofold.

1. Who manages the HDFS installation? HDFS can be either a shared system
    among multiple applications, or it can be instantiated for a single application.
    In case of a single application, its management will be the responsibility of the
    development team for that application. In the shared case, the management of
    the system must be assigned somewhere within the organization.
2. How is the data stored within HDFS protected in the case of a disaster?
    HDFS itself replicates data across multiple DataNodes, but a general failure
    of a datacenter may cause HDFS to become unavailable or the data being
    managed by HDFS to become corrupted or lost. Consequently, business
    continuity for those portions of the business dependent on the continued
    execution of HDFS and access to the data stored within HDFS is an issue
    that must be addressed.

2.4   Summary

The cloud has emerged as a major trend in IT during recent years. Its characteristics include metered usage (pay-per-use) and rapid elasticity, allowing the scaling out of an application to virtually infinite numbers of VMs. If architected properly, applications can indeed scale quickly, and thus you can avoid disappointing users when your new app goes "viral" and your user numbers double every couple of hours. Additionally, when the demand decreases you are not stuck with major hardware investments, but can simply release resources that are no longer needed.

Using the cloud opens up many interesting opportunities, but also means you have to deal with many of the concerns of distributed computing:

- The cloud rests on a platform that is inherently distributed and exploits virtualization to allow rapid expansion and contraction of the resources available to a given user.
- IP addresses are the key to accessing the virtualized resources and are associated with URLs through the DNS entries and can be manipulated to allow for the various forms of testing through the isolation of environments.
- Within large distributed environments, failure of the individual components is to be expected. Failure must be accommodated. The accommodations involve management of state and recognizing and recovering from requests that take an exceedingly long time.
- From an operational perspective, controlling the proliferation of VMs, managing different database management systems, and ensuring the environments meet the needs of the development and operations tasks are new considerations associated with the cloud.

2.5 For Further Reading

NIST's definition of the cloud is part of the special publication SP 800-145 [NIST 11].

The latency numbers for different types of memory and network connections are derived from http://www.eecs.berkeley.edu/~rcs/research/interactive_latency.html

Jeff Dean's keynote address lists problems in a new datacenter [Dean].

James Hamilton from Amazon Web Services gives insights into failures that occur at scale in the presentation at http://www.slideshare.net/AmazonWebServices/cpn208-failuresatscale-aws-reinvent-2012

Memcached system's website can be found at http://memcached.org/

More information about HDFS and its architecture is available:

- http://hadoop.apache.org/docs/r1.2.1/hdfs_design.html
- http://itm-vm.shidler.hawaii.edu/HDFS/ArchDocOverview.html

The long-tail distribution and some of its occurrences are described in [Dean 13].

Outliers in MapReduce are discussed in this PowerPoint presentation [Kandula].

The paper "Mechanisms and Architectures for Tail-Tolerant System Operations in Cloud" proposes methods and architecture tactics to tolerate long-tail behavior [Lu 15].

Netflix's Janitor Monkey helps to keep VM and image sprawl under control; see the following website: https://github.com/Netflix/SimianArmy/wiki/Janitor-Home

The CAP theorem was first proposed by Erick Brewer and proven by Gilbert and Lynch [Gilbert 02].

3

Operations

*There is a core of thinkers within the DevOps community
who understand what IT management is about
and are sensible about the use of ITIL within a DevOps context;
and there are others with a looser grasp on reality...*
—Rob England, http://www.itskeptic.org/devops-and-itil

3.1 Introduction

Just as DevOps does not subsume Dev, it does not subsume Ops. To understand DevOps, however, it is important to be aware of the context that people in Ops or Dev come from. In this chapter, we present the activities that an IT operations group carries out. How many of these activities are suitable for a DevOps approach is a matter for debate, and we will comment on that debate.

One characterization of Ops is given in the Information Technology Infrastructure Library (ITIL). ITIL acts as a kind of coarse-grained job description for the operations staff. ITIL is based on the concept of "services," and the job of Ops is to support the design, implementation, operation, and improvement of these services within the context of an overall strategy. Figure 3.1 shows how ITIL views these activities interacting.

We first describe the services for which Ops historically has had responsibility. Then we return to Figure 3.1 to discuss the service life cycle. Finally, we discuss how DevOps fits into this overall picture.

3.2 Operations Services

An operations service can be the provisioning of hardware, the provisioning of software, or supporting various IT functions. Services provided by operations also include the specification and monitoring of service level agreements (SLAs), capacity planning, business continuity, and information security.

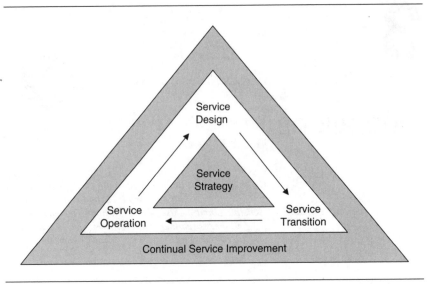

FIGURE 3.1   Service life cycle (Adapted from ITIL)

Provisioning of Hardware

Hardware can be physical hardware owned by the organization, or it can be virtual hardware managed by a third party or a cloud provider. It can also be used by individuals, projects, or a large portion of an organization. Table 3.1 shows these possibilities.

- *Physical hardware.*
  - *Individual hardware.* Individual hardware includes laptops, desktops, tablets, and phones used by and assigned to individuals. Typically, Ops will have standard configurations that they support. Whether the actual ordering and configuring of the hardware is done by operations or by the individuals will vary from organization to organization. The degree of enforcement of the standardized configurations will also vary from organization to organization. At one extreme, Ops provides each employee with some set of devices that have been locked so that only approved software and configuration settings can be loaded. Compatibility among the configurations is provided by the standardization. At the other extreme, Ops provides guidelines but individuals can order whatever hardware they wish and provision it however they wish. Compatibility among the configurations is the responsibility of the individuals.

TABLE 3.1 Types of Hardware Used by Individuals, Projects, and Organizations

Used by	Physical Hardware	Virtual Hardware
Individuals	Laptops, desktops, tablets, smartphones	Virtual machines for development and unit tests
Projects	Integration servers, version control servers	Virtual machines used for integration and version control
Organization	Servers for services such as printers, network infrastructure	Virtual machines used for organization-wide services

- *Project hardware.* Project hardware typically includes integration servers and version control servers, although these could be managed in an organization context. The requirements for project hardware are set by the project, and Ops can be involved in ordering, configuring, and supporting project hardware to the extent dictated by the organization or by negotiation between the project and Ops.
- *Organization-wide hardware.* This hardware is the responsibility of Ops. Any datacenters or generally available servers such as mail servers are managed and operated by Ops.

- *Virtual hardware.* Virtualized hardware can also be personal, project-specific, or organization-wide. It follows the pattern of physical hardware. Projects are generally responsible for the specification and management of virtualized project hardware, and Ops is generally responsible for the specification and management of virtualized organization-wide hardware. Ops typically has responsibility for the overall usage of virtualized hardware, and they may have budgetary input when a project considers their VM requirements. Note that much of the physical hardware on a project or organization level could actually be virtualized on private or public cloud resources. Exceptions include network infrastructure for devices, printers, and datacenters.

Provisioning of Software

Software is either being developed internally (possibly through contractors) or acquired from a third party. The third-party software is either project-specific, in which case it follows the pattern we laid out for hardware (the management and support of the software is the responsibility of the project); or it is organization-specific, in which case the management and support of the software is the responsibility of Ops. Delays in fielding internally developed software is one motivation for DevOps, and we will return to the relation between traditional operations and DevOps at the end of this chapter.

Table 3.2 shows the responsibilities for the different types of software.

TABLE 3.2   Responsibilities for Different Types of Software

Developed by	Supported by
Project	Project
Third party	Operations or projects, depending on breadth of use
Operations	Operations
DevOps group	DevOps group

IT Functions

Ops supports a variety of functions. These include:

- *Service desk operations.* The service desk staff is responsible for handling all incidents and service requests and acts as first-level support for all problems.
- *Technology experts.* Ops typically has experts for networks, information security, storage, databases, internal servers, web servers and applications, and telephony.
- *Day-to-day provisioning of IT services.* These include periodic and repetitive maintenance operations, monitoring, backup, and facilities management.

The people involved in the Ops side of DevOps typically come from the last two categories. Day-to-day IT services include the provisioning of new software systems or new versions of current systems, and improving this process is a main goal of DevOps. As we will see in the case study in Chapter 12, information security and network experts are also involved in DevOps, at least in the design of a continuous deployment pipeline, which is ideally shared across the organization to promote standardization and avoid drifting over time.

Service Level Agreements

An organization has a variety of SLAs with external providers of services. For example, a cloud provider will guarantee a certain level of availability. Ops traditionally is responsible for monitoring and ensuring that the SLAs are adhered to. An organization also has a variety of SLAs with its customers. Ops has traditionally been responsible for ensuring that an organization meets its external SLAs. Similarly to external SLAs, Ops is usually responsible for meeting internal SLAs, for example, for an organization's own website or e-mail service. Dev and DevOps are becoming more responsible for application SLAs and external SLAs in the DevOps movement.

All of these functions involve monitoring and analyzing various types of performance data from servers, networks, and applications. See Chapter 7 for an extensive discussion of monitoring technology. See also Chapter 10 for a discussion of what to monitor from the perspective of business.

Capacity Planning

Ops is responsible for ensuring that adequate computational resources are available for the organization. For physical hardware, this involves ordering and configuring machines. The lead time involved in ordering and configuring the hardware needs to be accounted for in the planning.

More importantly, Ops is responsible for providing sufficient resources so that consumers of an organization's products can, for instance, browse offerings, make orders, and check on the status of orders. This involves predicting workload and the characteristics of that workload. Some of this prediction can be done based on historical data but Ops also needs to coordinate with the business in case there are new products or promotions being announced. DevOps emphasizes coordination between Ops and Development but there are other stakeholders involved in coordination activities. In the case of capacity planning, these other stakeholders are business and marketing. With cloud elasticity, the pay-as-you-go model, and the ease of provisioning new virtual hardware, capacity planning is becoming more about runtime monitoring and autoscaling rather than planning for purchasing hardware.

Business Continuity and Security

In the event a disaster occurs, an organization needs to keep vital services operational so that both internal and external customers can continue to do their business. Two key parameters enable an organization to perform a cost/benefit analysis of various alternatives to maintain business continuity:

- *Recovery point objective (RPO)*. When a disaster occurs, what is the maximum period for which data loss is tolerable? If backups are taken every hour then the RPO would be 1 hour, since the data that would be lost is that which accumulated since the last backup.
- *Recovery time objective (RTO)*. When a disaster occurs, what is the maximum tolerable period for service to be unavailable? For instance, if a recovery solution takes 10 minutes to access the backup in a separate datacenter and another 5 minutes to instantiate new servers using the backed-up data, the RTO is 15 minutes.

The two values are independent since some loss of data may be tolerable, but being without service is not. It is also possible that being without service is tolerable but losing data is not.

Figure 3.2 shows three alternative backup strategies with different RPOs. In the case study in Chapter 11, we describe the alternative used by one organization. Another alternative is discussed in the case study in Chapter 13, which uses the services of the cloud provider to do replication.

1. Figure 3.2a shows an external agent—the backup process—copying the database periodically. No application support is required but the backup process should copy a consistent version of the database. That is, no updates are currently being applied. If the backup process is external to the database management system, then transactions may be in process and so the activation of the backup should be carefully performed. In this case, the RPO is the period between two backups. That is, if a disaster occurs just prior to the backup process being activated, all changes in the period from the last backup will be lost.

2. Figure 3.2b shows an alternative without an external agent. In this case, the database management system creates a copy periodically. The difference between 3.2a and 3.2b is that in 3.2b, guaranteeing consistency is done by the database management system, whereas in 3.2a, consistency is guaranteed by some mechanism that governs the activation of the backup process. As with 3.2a, the RPO is the period between taking copies. If the database is a relational database management system (RDBMS) offering some level of replication (i.e., a transaction only completes a commit when the replica database has executed the transaction as well), then transactions lost in the event of a disaster will be those not yet committed to the replicating database. The cost, however, is increased overhead per transaction.

3. Figure 3.2c modifies Figure 3.2b by having the database management system log every write. Then the data can be re-created by beginning with the backup database and replaying the entries in the log. If both the log and the backup database are available during recovery, the RPO is 0 since all data is either in the backup database or in the log. The protocol for committing a transaction to the production database is that no transaction is committed until the respective log entry has been written. It is possible in this scheme that some transactions have not been completed, but no data from a completed transaction will be lost. This scheme is used by high-reliability relational database management systems. It is also used by distributed file systems such as Hadoop Distributed File System (HDFS).

When considering RTO (i.e., how quickly you can get your application up and running after an outage or disaster), alternatives include: using multiple datacenters as discussed in the case study in Chapter 11 or using distinct availability zones or regions offered by a cloud provider, or even using several cloud providers.

By considering RTO and RPO, the business can perform a cost/benefit analysis of a variety of different disaster recovery techniques. Some of these

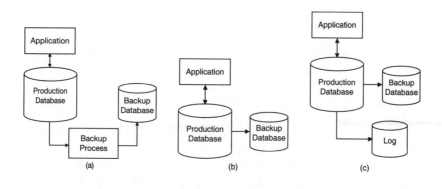

FIGURE 3.2 Database backup strategies. (a) An independent agent performing the backup. (b) The database management system performing the backup. (c) The database management system performing the backup and logging all transactions. [Notation: Architecture]

techniques will involve application systems architecture such as replication and maintaining state consistency in the different replicas. Other techniques such as periodic backups can be performed with any application architecture. Using stateless servers on the application tier and different regions within a cloud provider results in a short RTO but does not address RPO.

Traditionally, Ops is responsible for the overall security of computer systems. Securing the network, detecting intruders, and patching operating systems are all activities performed by Ops. Chapter 8 discusses security and its maintenance in some depth.

Service Strategy

We now return to the ITIL life cycle shown in Figure 3.1. At the center of the figure are strategies for each of the services that we have enumerated: hardware provisioning, software provisioning, IT functions, capacity planning, business continuity, and information security.

Developing a strategy is a matter of deciding where you would like your organization to be in a particular area within a particular time frame, determining where you currently are, and deciding on a path from the current state to the desired state. The desired state is affected by both internal and external events. Internal events such as personnel attrition, hardware failure, new software releases, marketing, and business activities will all affect the desired state. External events such as acquisitions, government policies, or consumer reaction will also affect the desired state. The events that might occur all have some probability of occurrence, thus, strategic planning shares some elements with for-tune telling.

Understanding future demands in terms of resources and capabilities will help in strengthening the areas that are not covered at present. If, for example, you want to move some of your organization's applications to the cloud within the next year, then it is important to know if you have people with the right skill set in your organization. If not, you need to decide whether to hire new talent or develop the skills of some existing employees, or a mix of both. Future demands may lead to continual service improvement initiatives.

Strategic planning takes time and coordination among stakeholders. Its virtues are not so much the actual plan that emerges but the consideration of multiple viewpoints and constraints that exist within an organization. As such, defining a service strategy should be done infrequently and should result in loose guidelines that can be approached in shorter time frames. We discuss the strategy planning of migrating to microservices and its implementation in the case study in Chapter 13.

Service Design

Before a new or changed service is implemented, it must be designed. As with any design, you need to consider not only the functions that the service aims to achieve but also a variety of other qualities. Some of the considerations when designing a service are:

- What automation is going to be involved as a portion of the service? Any automation should be designed according to the principles of software design. In general, these include the eight principles that Thomas Erl articulated for service design:

  - Standardized contract
  - Loose coupling
  - Abstraction
  - Reusability
  - Autonomy
  - Statelessness
  - Discoverability
  - Composability

- What are the governance and management structures for the service? Services need to be managed and evolved. People responsible for the performance of the service and changes to the service should be identified by title if not by name.
- What are the SLAs for the service? How is the service to be measured, and what monitoring structure is necessary to support the measurement?

- What are the personnel requirements for the service? Can the service be provided with current personnel, or do personnel with specific skills need to be hired or contracted? Alternatively, will the service be outsourced altogether?
- What are the compliance implications of the service? What compliance requirements are satisfied by the service, and which are introduced?
- What are the implications for capacity? Do additional resources need to be acquired and what is the time frame for this acquisition?
- What are the business continuity implications of the service? Must the service be continued in the event of a disaster and how will this be accomplished?
- What are the information security implications of the service? What data is sensitive and must be protected, and who has responsibility for that data?

The ITIL volume on service design discusses all of these issues in detail.

Service Transition

Service transition subsumes all activities between service design and operation, namely, all that is required to successfully get a new or changed service into operation. As such, much of the content of this book is related to service transition insofar as it affects the introduction of new versions of software.

Transition and planning support includes aspects of: resources, capacity, and change planning; scoping and goals of the transition; documentation requirements; consideration of applicable rules and regulations; financial planning; and milestones. In essence, service transition covers the implementation and delivery phases of a service. DevOps and continuous deployment require the delivery part of service transition to be highly automated so it can deal with high-frequency transition and provide better quality control. Many of these considerations are discussed in Chapters 5 and 6.

In addition to implementing the considerations enumerated in the section on service design, service transition involves extending the knowledge of the new or revised service to the users and the immediate supporters of that service within operations.

Suppose, for example, a new version of a deployment tool is to be implemented. Questions such as the following three need to be answered:

- Are all features of the old version supported in the new version? If not, what is the transition plan for supporting users of the old version?
- Which new features are introduced? How will the scripts for the deployment tool be modified, and who is responsible for that modification?
- Will the new version require or support a different configuration of servers, which includes both testing/staging and production servers?

Tools involved in a deployment pipeline change just as other software does. One of the implications of "infrastructure-as-code" is that these changes need to be managed in the same fashion as changes to software developed by customer use. Some aspects of this management may be implicit in the deployment pipeline, and other aspects may need attention. ITIL distinguishes three change models:

- Standard changes (e.g., often-occurring and low-risk)
- Normal changes
- Emergency changes

Each of these types of change should be managed differently and will require different levels of management attention and oversight. Many more details are discussed in the ITIL volume on service transition.

Service Operation

While software developers and architects are most concerned with development, operation is where the customer benefits from good design, implementation, and transition—or not. Support plays a major role here, in particular for incident and failure management. Monitoring and adaptation are other major concerns. We discuss more concerns in Chapter 9.

Service Operation Concepts

During operation, *events* are defined by ITIL as "any detectable or discernible occurrence that has significance for the management of the IT infrastructure or the delivery of IT service and evaluation of the impact a deviation might cause to the services." Events are created by configuration items, IT services, or monitoring tools. More concretely, monitoring tools can actively pull event information from configuration items or services, or they can (passively) receive them. Events of interest during operation include

- Status information from systems and infrastructure
- Environmental conditions, such as smoke detectors
- Software license usage
- Security information (e.g., from intrusion detection)
- Normal activity, such as performance metrics from servers and applications

An *incident*, according to ITIL, is "any event which disrupts, or which could disrupt, a service." They are raised by users (e.g., over the phone or by e-mail), technical personnel, support desk staff, or monitoring tools. Incident management is one area where DevOps will have an impact.

Core activities of incident management are

- Logging the incident
- Categorization and prioritization

- Initial diagnosis
- Escalation to appropriately skilled or authorized staff, if needed
- Investigation and diagnosis, including an analysis of the impact and scope of the incident
- Resolution and recovery, either through the user under guidance from support staff, through the support staff directly, or through internal or external specialists
- Incident closure, including recategorization if appropriate, user satisfaction survey, documentation, and determination if the incident is likely to recur

Incident management is one of the areas where DevOps is changing the traditional operations activities. Incidents that are related to the operation of a particular software system are routed to the development team. Regardless of who is on call for a problem, incidents must still be logged and their resolution tracked. In Part Five, we discuss how we can automate such failure detection, diagnosis, and recovery with the help of DevOps and a process view.

3.3 Service Operation Functions

Monitoring is of central importance during operations, as it allows collecting events, detecting incidents, and measuring to determine if SLAs are being fulfilled; it provides the basis for service improvement. SLAs can also be defined and monitored for operations activities, for example, for the time to react to incidents.

Monitoring can be combined with some *control*, for example, as done in autoscaling for cloud resources, where an average CPU load among the pool of web servers of, say, 70% triggers a rule to start another web server. Control can be *open-loop* or *closed-loop*. Open-loop control (i.e., monitoring feedback is not taken into account) can be used for regular backups at predefined times. In closed-loop control, monitoring information is taken into account when deciding on an action, such as in the autoscaling example. Closed-loop feedback cycles can be nested into more complex control loops, where lower-level control reacts to individual metrics and higher-level control considers a wider range of information and trends developing over longer time spans. At the highest level, control loops can link the different life-cycle activities. Depending on the measured deviations from the desired metrics, continual service improvement can lead to alterations in service strategy, design, or transition—all of which eventually comes back to changes in service operation.

The results of the monitoring are analyzed and acted upon by either the Dev or Ops group. One decision that must be made when instituting DevOps processes is: Which group is responsible for handling incidents? See Chapter 10 for a discussion of incident handling. One DevOps practice is to have the development group analyze the monitoring of the single system that they developed. Monitoring of multiple systems including the infrastructure will be the responsibility of the Ops group, which is also responsible for the escalation procedure for any incidents that require handling through one or more development teams.

3.4 Continual Service Improvement

Every process undertaken by an organization should be considered from the perspective of: How well is the process working? How can the process be improved? How does this process fit in the organization's overall set of processes?

All of the Ops services we discussed—the provisioning of hardware and software, IT support functions, specification and monitoring of SLAs, capacity planning, business continuity, and information security—are organizational processes. They should be monitored and evaluated from the perspective of the questions we have identified.

Organizationally, each of these services should have an owner, and the owner of a service is the individual responsible for overseeing its monitoring, evaluation, and improvement.

Continual service improvement's main focus is to achieve better alignment between IT services and business needs—whether the needs have changed or are the same. If the needs have changed, desired changes to the IT services can concern scope, functionality, or SLAs. If the business needs are the same, IT services can be extended to better support them, but their improvement can also focus on increasing the efficiency. DevOps is concerned with bringing those changes into practice more quickly and reliably.

Figure 3.3 depicts the seven-step process for improvement, as suggested by ITIL. This data-driven process starts off with an identification of the vision, strategy, and goals that are driving the current improvement cycle. Based on that, Step 1 defines what should be measured so as to gain an understanding of what should be improved, and after the improvement is completed, if the desired goals were achieved. Metrics can roughly be divided into the three categories: technology, process, and service.

The actual data gathering is performed in Step 3. Here it is important to establish baselines—if they do not exist already—for later comparison. Furthermore, the collection of the data (who collects it and how, when, and how frequently it is collected) needs to be specified clearly. In Step 4, the data is processed (e.g., by aggregating data from different sources or over specified time intervals). Analyzing the data is done in Step 5. In Step 6, the information derived from the analysis is presented and corrective actions are determined. The chosen corrective actions are then implemented in Step 7. These actions can impact all phases of the service life cycle—that is, strategy, design, transition, or operation.

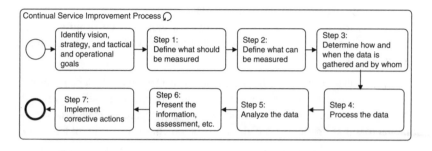

FIGURE 3.3 Continual service improvement process (Adapted from ITIL)
[Notation: BPMN]

3.5 Operations and DevOps

After discussing the core concepts and phases of ITIL, we now highlight how
interactions between traditional IT Ops and DevOps can be shaped in the future.
Our basic message is that ignoring ITIL because it looks heavyweight and not
suited for the processes of DevOps is shortsighted and will require relearning the
lessons incorporated into the ITIL framework.

Ops is responsible for provisioning of hardware and software; personnel with
specialized skills; specification and monitoring of SLAs; capacity planning; business
continuity; and information security. Most of these responsibilities have aspects that
are included both inside and outside of DevOps processes. Any discussion of which
aspects of Ops are to be included in DevOps must take into consideration all of the
activities that Ops currently performs and involves both functional activities, personnel skills, and availability. The aspects of these activities that impact DevOps are:

- *Hardware provisioning*. Virtualized hardware may be allocated by a
  development team or application with more automation.
- *Software provisioning*. Internally developed software will be deployed by
  Dev. Other software is provisioned by Ops.
- *IT function provision*. To the extent that a Dev team is responsible for
  incident management and deployment tools, it must have people with the
  expertise to perform these tasks.
- *Specification and monitoring of SLAs*. For those SLAs that are specific to a
  particular application, Dev will be responsible for monitoring, evaluating,
  and responding to incidents.
- *Capacity planning*. Dev is responsible for capacity planning for individual
  applications, and Ops is responsible for overall capacity planning.
- *Business continuity*. Dev is responsible for those aspects of business
  continuity that involve the application architecture, and Ops is responsible

for the remainder. Ops can provide services and policies for business continuity, which in turn are used by Dev.

- *Information security*. Dev is responsible for those aspects of information security that involve a particular application, and Ops is responsible for the remainder.

The number of people who are involved in DevOps will depend on which processes are adopted by the organization. One organization estimates that 20% of the Ops team and 20% of the Dev team are involved in DevOps processes. Some factors that impact the breadth of involvement of the different teams are:

- The extent to which Dev becomes the first responder in the event of an incident
- Whether there is a separate DevOps group responsible for the tools used in the continuous deployment pipeline
- The skill set and availability of personnel from the two groups

One difference between ITIL's service transition and the DevOps approach is that ITIL assumes fairly large release packages where careful planning, change management, and so on are feasible—in contrast to the high-frequency small releases encountered in typical DevOps scenarios. Rob Spencer suggests in a blog post to view DevOps releases as "concurrent streams of smaller deliverables" and gives the following example in Table 3.3.

Most rows in Table 3.3 now contain criteria that can be seen as invariants in the cycles of the development process. In DevOps, the typical frequency of these invariants is significantly higher than in ITIL. Yet, the processes and roles in the right-hand column are taken from ITIL, thus making use of proven methods

TABLE 3.3   Release Package Examples (Adapted from R. Spencer's blog post)

Stream	Frequency	ITIL Roles/Processes
1 Code objects checked in, tested, and deployed	Daily	Research & Development Management (R&DM), Service Asset and Configuration Management (SACM)
2 Knowledge updates created and tested for the new functional requirements	Every other day	SACM, Service Validation and Testing (SV&T), Knowledge Management
3 Formal Operational acceptance tests	2 times/week	SV&T, Service Level Management (SLM), Business Relationship Manager (BRM), App/Tech Function Managers
4 Hardware deliveries	As required	R&DM, Tech Management
5 Early Life Support and Continual Service Improvement	Daily	Continual Service Improvement (CSI), SLM, BRM, Service Owner

and processes. Notably, the last row contains the now-joint stream of "Early Life Support and Continual Service Improvement." Given that releases are daily, the early life support phase is effectively never-ending.

While many startups would consider such an approach overkill, larger and more mature organizations will find defining the relation between DevOps and ITIL useful, and this approach could increase the acceptance of and buy-in to DevOps.

3.6 Summary

ITIL provides general guidance for the activities of Ops. These activities include provisioning of hardware and software; providing functions such as service desk operations and specialized technology experts; and day-to-day provisioning of IT services. As with many such process specification standards, ITIL provides general guidance on how activities are to be carried out rather than specific guidance. For example, instead of saying "measure A with a goal of X," ITIL says something like "for goal X, choose the measurements that will allow you to determine X."

Organizational activities should satisfy some strategic purpose for the organization and need to be designed, implemented, monitored, and improved. DevOps practices with the goals of reducing the time from developer commit to production and rapid repair of discovered errors will impact some of the types of services provided by Ops and will provide mechanisms for monitoring and improving those services. The specifics of the impact of DevOps on Ops will depend on the type of organization and the particular DevOps practices that are adopted.

One method of viewing the relationship between DevOps and ITIL is that DevOps provides continuous delivery of the various ITIL services rather than requiring those services to be packaged into a major release.

3.7 For Further Reading

ITIL is a standardization effort begun by the government of the United Kingdom in the 1980s. It has gone through a series of revisions, consolidations, amendments, and so forth. The latest version of ITIL is from 2011. It is published in five volumes [Cannon 11; Hunnebeck 11; Lloyd 11; Rance 11; Steinberg 11].

Thomas Erl has written extensively about design issues of services in a service-oriented architecture sense, but his requirements are more generally applicable than just for software. We applied them to the services provided by operations. See his book *Service-Oriented Architecture: Principles of Service Design*, which describes designing services [Erl 07].

Some blogs that discuss ITIL and its relation to DevOps are

- "DevOps and ITIL: Continuous Delivery Doesn't Stop at Software" [Spencer 14]
- "What is IT Service?" [Agrasala 11]
- FireScope is a company involved in enterprise monitoring: See the blog "What is an IT Service?" [FireScope 13]

Recovery point objective (RPO) is defined and contrasted with recovery time objective (RTO) in a Wikipedia article at http://en.wikipedia.org/wiki/Recovery_point_objective

PART TWO

THE DEPLOYMENT PIPELINE

In this part, we focus on the methods for placing code into production as quickly as possible, while maintaining high quality. These methods are manifested as a pipeline, where the code has to pass quality gates one by one before reaching production. The deployment pipeline is the place where the architectural aspects and the process aspects of DevOps intersect. The goals of minimizing the coordination requirements between different development teams, minimizing the time required to integrate different development branches, having a high-quality set of tests, and placing the code into production with high speed and quality are covered in the three chapters in this part.

In Chapter 4, we explain the microservice architecture and argue why it satisfies many of the coordination requirements and, hence, removes the requirement for explicit coordination prior to deployment.

Requirements for a continuous deployment pipeline mandate that testing be efficient and only a limited amount of merging needs to be done. We discuss these issues in Chapter 5.

Once code is "production ready" there are a number of options for actually deploying the code. Several different all-or-nothing deployment strategies exist, as well as several different partial deployment strategies. One common deployment strategy results in multiple versions of a service being simultaneously active and this, in turn, raises questions of consistency. Furthermore, allowing any team to deploy at any time results in potential inconsistency between clients and the services they are using. We discuss these and other issues in Chapter 6.

4

Overall Architecture

> *A distributed system is one in which the failure of a computer*
> *you didn't even know existed can render you own computer unusable.*
> —Leslie Lamport

In this chapter we begin to see the structural implications of the DevOps practices. These practices have implications with respect to both the overall structure of the system and techniques that should be used in the system's elements. DevOps achieves its goals partially by replacing explicit coordination with implicit and often less coordination, and we will see how the architecture of the system being developed acts as the implicit coordination mechanism. We begin by discussing whether DevOps practices necessarily imply architectural change.

4.1 Do DevOps Practices Require Architectural Change?

You may have a large investment in your current systems and your current architecture. If you must re-architect your systems in order to take advantage of DevOps, a legitimate question is "Is it worth it?" In this section we see that some DevOps practices are independent of architecture, whereas in order to get the full benefit of others, architectural refactoring may be necessary.

Recall from Chapter 1 that there are five categories of DevOps practices.

1. Treat Ops as first-class citizens from the point of view of requirements. Adding requirements to a system from Ops may require some architectural modification. In particular, the Ops requirements are likely to be in the area of logging, monitoring, and information to support incident handling. These requirements will be like other requirements for modifications to a

system: possibly requiring some minor modifications to the architecture but, typically, not drastic modifications.

2. Make Dev more responsible for relevant incident handling. By itself, this change is just a process change and should require no architectural modifications. However, just as with the previous category, once Dev becomes aware of the requirements for incident handling, some architectural modifications may result.

3. Enforce deployment process used by all, including Dev and Ops personnel. In general, when a process becomes enforced, some individuals may be required to change their normal operating procedures and, possibly, the structure of the systems on which they work. One point where a deployment process could be enforced is in the initiation phase of each system. Each system, when it is initialized, verifies its pedigree. That is, it arrived at execution through a series of steps, each of which can be checked to have occurred. Furthermore, the systems on which it depends (e.g., operating systems or middleware) also have verifiable pedigrees.

4. Use continuous deployment. Continuous deployment is the practice that leads to the most far-reaching architectural modifications. On the one hand, an organization can introduce continuous deployment practices with no major architectural changes. See, for example, our case study in Chapter 12. On the other hand, organizations that have adopted continuous deployment practices frequently begin moving to a microservice-based architecture. See, for example, our case study in Chapter 13. We explore the reasons for the adoption of a microservice architecture in the remainder of this chapter

5. Develop infrastructure code with the same set of practices as application code. These practices will not affect the application code but may affect the architecture of the infrastructure code.

4.2 Overall Architecture Structure

Before delving into the details of the overall structure, let us clarify how we use certain terminology. The terms *module* and *component* are frequently overloaded and used in different fashions in different writings. For us, a module is a code unit with coherent functionality. A component is an executable unit. A compiler or interpreter turns modules into binaries, and a builder turns the binaries into components. The development team thus directly develops modules. Components are results of the modules developed by development teams, and so it is possible to speak of a team developing a component, but it should be clear that the development of a component is an indirect activity of a development team.

As we described in Chapter 1, development teams using DevOps processes are usually small and should have limited inter-team coordination. Small teams imply that each team has a limited scope in terms of the components they develop. When a team deploys a component, it cannot go into production unless the component is compatible with other components with which it interacts. This compatibility can be ensured explicitly through multi-team coordination, or it can be ensured implicitly through the definition of the architecture.

An organization can introduce continuous deployment without major architectural modifications. For example, the case study in Chapter 12 is fundamentally architecture-agnostic. Dramatically reducing the time required to place a component into production, however, requires architectural support:

- Deploying without the necessity of explicit coordination with other teams reduces the time required to place a component into production.
- Allowing for different versions of the same service to be simultaneously in production leads to different team members deploying without coordination with other members of their team.
- Rolling back a deployment in the event of errors allows for various forms of live testing.

Microservice architecture is an architectural style that satisfies these requirements. This style is used in practice by organizations that have adopted or inspired many DevOps practices. Although project requirements may cause deviations to this style, it remains a good general basis for projects that are adopting DevOps practices.

A microservice architecture consists of a collection of services where each service provides a small amount of functionality and the total functionality of the system is derived from composing multiple services. In Chapter 6, we also see that a microservice architecture, with some modifications, gives each team the ability to deploy their service independently from other teams, to have multiple versions of a service in production simultaneously, and to roll back to a prior version relatively easily.

Figure 4.1 describes the situation that results from using a microservice architecture. A user interacts with a single consumer-facing service. This service, in turn, utilizes a collection of other services. We use the terminology *service* to refer to a component that provides a service and *client* to refer to a component that requests a service. A single component can be a client in one interaction and a service in another. In a system such as LinkedIn, the service depth may reach as much as 70 for a single user request.

Having an architecture composed of small services is a response to having small teams. Now we look at the aspects of an architecture that can be specified globally as a response to the requirement that inter-team coordination be minimized. We discuss three categories of design decisions that can be made globally as a portion of the architecture design, thus removing the need for inter-team

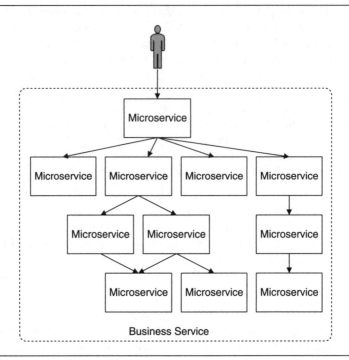

FIGURE 4.1   User interacting with a single service that, in turn, utilizes multiple other services [Notation: Architecture]

coordination with respect to these decisions. The three categories are: the coordination model, management of resources, and mapping among architectural elements.

Coordination Model

If two services interact, the two development teams responsible for those services must coordinate in some fashion. Two details of the coordination model that can be included in the overall architecture are: how a client discovers a service that it wishes to use, and how the individual services communicate.

   Figure 4.2 gives an overview of the interaction between a service and its client. The service registers with a registry. The registration includes a name for the service as well as information on how to invoke it, for example, an endpoint location as a URL or an IP address. A client can retrieve the information about the service from the registry and invoke the service using this information. If the registry provides IP addresses, it acts as a local DNS server—local, because typically, the registry is not open to the general Internet but is within the environment of the application. Netflix Eureka is an example of a cloud service registry that acts as a DNS server. The registry serves as a catalogue of available services, and

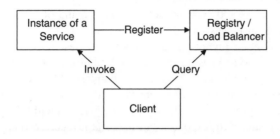

FIGURE 4.2   An instance of a service registers itself with the registry, the client queries the registry for the address of the service and invokes the service. [Notation: Architecture]

can further be used to track aspects such as versioning, ownership, service level agreements (SLAs), etc., for the set of services in an organization. We discuss extensions to the registry further in Chapter 6.

There will typically be multiple instances of a service, both to support a load too heavy for a single instance and to guard against failure. The registry can rotate among the instances registered to balance the load. That is, the registry acts as a load balancer as well as a registry. Finally, consider the possibility that an instance of a service may fail. In this case, the registry should not direct the client to the failed instance. By requiring the service to periodically renew its registration or proactively checking the health of the service, a guard against failure is put in place. If the service fails to renew its registration within the specified period, it is removed from the registry. Multiple instances of the service typically exist, and so the failure of one instance does not remove the service. The above-mentioned Netflix Eureka is an example for a registry offering load balancing. Eureka supports the requirement that services periodically renew their registration.

The protocol used for communication between the client and the service can be any remote communication protocol, for example, HTTP, RPC, SOAP, etc. The service can provide a RESTful interface or not. The remote communication protocol should be the only means for communication among the services. The details of the interface provided by the service still require cross-team coordination. When we discuss the example of Amazon later, we will see one method of providing this coordination. We will also see an explicit requirement for restricting communication among services to the remote communication protocol.

Management of Resources

Two types of resource management decisions can be made globally and incorporated in the architecture—provisioning/deprovisioning VMs and managing variation in demand.

Provisioning and Deprovisioning VMs

New VMs can be created in response to client demand or to failure. When the demand subsides, instances should be deprovisioned. If the instances are stateless (i.e., they do not retain any information between requests), a new instance can be placed into service as soon as it is provisioned. Similarly, if no state is kept in an instance, deprovisioning becomes relatively painless: After a cool-down period where the instance receives no new requests and responds to existing ones, the instance can be deprovisioned. The cool-down period should therefore be long enough for an instance to respond to all requests it received (i.e., the backlog). If you deprovision an instance due to reduced demand, the backlog should be fairly small—in any other case this action needs to be considered carefully. An additional advantage of a stateless service is that messages can be routed to any instance of that service, which facilitates load sharing among the instances.

This leads to a global decision to maintain state external to a service instance. As discussed in Chapter 2, large amounts of application state can be maintained in persistent storage, small amounts of application state can be maintained by tools such as ZooKeeper, and client state should not be maintained on the provider's side anyway.

Determining which component controls the provisioning and deprovisioning of a new instance for a service is another important aspect. Three possibilities exist for the controlling component.

1. A service itself can be responsible for (de)provisioning additional instances. A service can know its own queue lengths and its own performance in response to requests. It can compare these metrics to thresholds and (de) provision an instance itself if the threshold is crossed. Assuming that the distribution of requests is fair, in some sense, across all instances of the service, one particular instance (e.g., the oldest one) of the service can make the decision when to provision or deprovision instances. Thus, the service is allowed to expand or shrink capacity to meet demand.

2. A client or a component in the client chain can be responsible for (de) provisioning instances of a service. For instance, the client, based on the demands on it, may be aware that it will shortly be making demands on the service that exceed a given threshold and provisions new instances of the service.

3. An external component monitors the performance of service instances (e.g., their CPU load) and (de)provisions an instance when the load reaches a given threshold. Amazon's autoscaling groups provide this capability, in collaboration with the CloudWatch monitoring system.

Managing Demand

The number of instances of an individual service that exist should reflect the demand on the service from client requests. We just discussed several different methods for provisioning and deprovisioning instances, and these methods make different assumptions about how demand is managed.

- One method for managing demand is to monitor performance. Other decisions to be made include determining how to implement monitoring (e.g., whether done internally by running a monitoring agent inside each service instance or externally by a specialized component). That is, when demand grows that needs to be detected, a new instance can be provisioned. It takes time to provision a new instance, so it is important that the indicators are timely and even predictive to accommodate for that time. We discuss more details about monitoring in Chapter 7.
- Another possible technique is to use SLAs to control the number of instances. Each instance of the service guarantees through its SLAs that it is able to handle a certain number of requests with a specified latency. The clients of that service then know how many requests they can send and still receive a response within the specified latency. This technique has several constraints. First, it is likely that the requirements that a client imposes on your service will depend on the requirements imposed on the client, so there is a cascading effect up through the demand chain. This cascading will cause uncertainty in both the specification and the realization of the SLAs. A second constraint of the SLA technique is that each instance of your service may know how many requests it can handle, but the client has multiple available instances of your service. Thus, the provisioning component has to know how many instances currently exist of your service.

Mapping Among Architectural Elements

The final type of coordination decision that can be specified in the architecture is the mapping among architectural elements. We discuss two different types of mappings—work assignments and allocation. Both of these are decisions that are made globally.

- *Work assignments*. A single team may work on multiple modules, but having multiple development teams work on the same module requires a great deal of coordination among those development teams. Since coordination takes time, an easier structure is to package the work of a single team into modules and develop interfaces among the modules to allow modules developed by different teams to interoperate. In fact, the original definition of a module by David Parnas in the 1970s was as a work assignment of a team. Although not required, it is reasonable that each component (i.e., microservice) is the responsibility of a single development team. That is, the set of modules that, when linked, constitute a component are the output of a single development team. This does not preclude a single development team from being responsible for multiple components but it means that any coordination involving a component is settled within a single development team, and that any coordination involving multiple development teams goes across components. Given the set of constraints on the architecture we are describing, cross-team coordination requirements are limited.

- *Allocation.* Each component (i.e., microservice) will exist as an independent deployable unit. This allows each component to be allocated to a single (virtual) machine or container, or it allows multiple components to be allocated to a single (virtual) machine. The redeployment or upgrade of one microservice will not affect any other microservices. We explore this choice in Chapter 6.

4.3   Quality Discussion of Microservice Architecture

We have described an architectural style—microservice architecture—that reduces the necessity for inter-team coordination by making global architectural choices. The style provides some support for the qualities of dependability (stateless services) and modifiability (small services), but there are additional practices that a team should use to improve both dependability and modifiability of their services.

Dependability

Three sources for dependability problems are: the small amount of inter-team coordination, correctness of environment, and the possibility that an instance of a service can fail.

Small Amount of Inter-team Coordination

The limited amount of inter-team coordination may cause misunderstandings between the team developing a client and the team developing a service in terms of the semantics of an interface. In particular, unexpected input to a service or unexpected output from a service can happen. There are several options. First, a team should practice defensive programming and not assume that the input or the results of a service invocation are correct. Checking values for reasonableness will help detect errors early. Providing a rich collection of exceptions will enable faster determination of the cause of an error. Second, integration and end-to-end testing with all or most microservices should be done judiciously. It can be expensive to run these tests frequently due to the involvement of a potentially large number of microservices and realistic external resources. A testing practice called Consumer Driven Contract (CDC) can be used to alleviate the problem.

That is, the test cases for testing a microservice are decided and even co-owned by all the *consumers* of that microservice. Any changes to the CDC test cases need to be agreed on by both the consumers and the developers of the microservice. Running the CDC test cases, as a form of integration testing, is less expensive than running end-to-end test cases. If CDC is practiced properly, confidence in the microservice can be high without running many end-to-end test cases.

CDC serves as a method of coordination and has implications on how user stories of a microservice should be made up and evolve over time. Consumers and microservice developers collectively make up and own the user stories. CDC definition becomes a function of the allocation of functionality to the microservice, is managed by the service owner as a portion of the coordination that defines the next iteration, and, consequently, does not delay the progress of the current iteration.

Correctness of Environment

A service will operate in multiple different environments during the passage from unit test to post-production. Each environment is provisioned and maintained through code and a collection of configuration parameters. Errors in code and configuration parameters are quite common. Inconsistent configuration parameters are also possible. Due to a degree of uncertainty in cloud-based infrastructure, even executing the correct code and configuration may lead to an incorrect environment. Thus, the initialization portion of a service should test its current environment to determine whether it is as expected. It should also test the configuration parameters to detect, as far as possible, unexpected inconsistencies from different environments. If the behavior of the service depends on its environment (e.g., certain actions are performed during unit test but not during production), then the initialization should determine the environment and provide the settings for turning on or off the behavior. An important trend in DevOps is to manage all the code and parameters for setting up an environment just as you manage your application code, with proper version control and testing. This is an example of "infrastructure-as-code" as defined in Chapter 1 and discussed in more detail in Chapter 5. The testing of infrastructure code is a particularly challenging issue. We discuss the issues in Chapters 7 and 9.

Failure of an Instance

Failure is always a possibility for instances. An instance is deployed onto a physical machine, either directly or through the use of virtualization, and in large datacenters, the failure of a physical machine is common. The standard method through which a client detects the failure of an instance of a service is through the timeout of a request. Once a timeout has occurred, the client can issue a request again and, depending on the routing mechanism used, assume it is routed to a different instance of the service. In the case of multiple timeouts, the service is assumed to have failed and an alternative means of achieving the desired goal can be attempted.

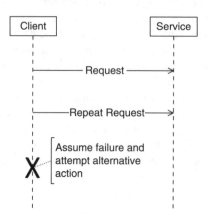

FIGURE 4.3   Time line in recognizing failure of a dependent service [Notation: UML Sequence Diagram]

Figure 4.3 shows a time line for a client attempting to access a failed service. The client makes a request to the service, and it times out. The client repeats the request, and it times out again. At this point, recognizing the failure has taken twice the timeout interval. Having a short timeout interval (failing fast) will enable a more rapid response to the client of the client requesting the service. A short time-out interval may, however, introduce false positives in that the service instance may just be slow for some reason. The result may be that both initial requests for service actually deliver the service, just not in a timely fashion. Another result may be that the alternative action is performed as well. Services should be designed so that multiple invocations of the same service will not introduce an error. *Idempotent* is the term for a service that can be repeatedly invoked with the same input and always produces the same output—namely, no error is generated.

Another point highlighted in Figure 4.3 is that the service has an alternative action. That is, the client has an alternative action in case the service fails. Figure 4.3 does not show what happens if there is no alternative action. In this case, the service reports failure to its client together with context information—namely, no response from the particular underlying service. We explore the topic of reporting errors in more depth in Chapter 7.

Modifiability

Making a service modifiable comes down to making likely changes easy and reducing the ripple effects of those changes. In both cases, a method for making the service more modifiable is to encapsulate either the affected portions of a likely change or the interactions that might cause ripple effects of a change.

Identifying Likely Changes

Some likely changes that come from the development process, rather than the service being provided, are:

- *The environments within which a service executes.* A module goes through unit tests in one environment, integration tests in another, acceptance tests in a third, and is in production in a fourth.
- *The state of other services with which your service interacts.* If other services are in the process of development, then the interfaces and semantics of those services are likely to change relatively quickly. Since you may not know the state of the external service, a safe practice is to treat, as much as possible, all communication with external services as likely to change.
- *The version of third-party software and libraries that are used by your service.* Third-party software and libraries can change arbitrarily, sometimes in ways that are disruptive for your service. In one case we heard, an external system removed an essential interface during the time the deployment process was ongoing. Using the same VM image in different environments will protect against those changes that are contained within the VM but not against external system changes.

Reducing Ripple Effects

Once likely changes have been discovered, you should prevent these types of changes from rippling through your service. This is typically done by introducing modules whose sole purpose is to localize and isolate changes to the environment, to other services, or to third-party software or libraries. The remainder of your service interacts with these changeable entities through the newly introduced modules with stable interfaces.

Any interaction with other services, for example, is mediated by the special module. Changes to the other services are reflected in the mediating module and buffered from rippling to the remainder of your service. Semantic changes to other services may, in fact, ripple, but the mediating module can absorb some of the impact, thereby reducing this ripple effect.

4.4 Amazon's Rules for Teams

As we mentioned in Chapter 1, Amazon has a rule that no team should be larger than can be fed with two pizzas; in the early years of this century they adopted an internal microservice architecture. Associated with the adoption was a list of rules to follow about how to use the services:

- "All teams will henceforth expose their data and functionality through service interfaces.
- Teams must communicate with each other through these interfaces.
- There will be no other form of inter-service/team communication allowed: no direct linking, no direct reads of another team's datastore, no shared-memory model, no backdoors whatsoever. The only communication allowed is via service interface calls over the network.
- It doesn't matter what technology they [other services] use.
- All service interfaces, without exception, must be designed from the ground up to be externalizable. That is to say, the team must plan and design to be able to expose the interface to developers in the outside world."

Each team produces some number of services. Every service is totally encapsulated except for its public interface. If another team wishes to use a service, it must discover the interface. The documentation for the interface must include enough semantic information to enable the user of a service to determine appropriate definitions for items such as "customer" or "address." These concepts can sometimes have differing meanings within different portions of an organization. The semantic information about an interface can be kept in the registry/load balancer that we described earlier, assuming that the semantic information is machine interpretable.

By making every service potentially externally available, whether or not to offer a service globally or keep it local becomes a business decision, not a technical one. External services can be hidden behind an application programming interface (API) bound through a library, and so this requirement is not prejudging the technology used for the interface.

A consequence of these rules is that Amazon has an extensive collection of services. A web page from their sales business makes use of over 150 services. Scalability is managed by each service individually and is included in its SLA in the form of a guaranteed response time given a particular load. The contract covers what the service promises against certain demand levels. The SLA binds both the client side and the service side. If the client's demand exceeds the load promised in the SLA, then slow response times become the client's problem, not the service's.

4.5   Microservice Adoption for Existing Systems

Although microservices reflect the small, independent team philosophy of DevOps, most organizations have large mission-critical systems that are not architected that way. These organizations need to decide whether to migrate their architectures to microservice architectures, and which ones to migrate. We discuss this migration somewhat in Chapter 10. Some of the things an architect thinking of adopting a microservice architecture should ensure are the following:

- Operational concerns are considered during requirements specification.
- The overarching structure of the system being developed should be a collection of small, independent services.
- Each service should be distrustful of both clients and other required services.
- Team roles have been defined and are understood.
- Services are required to be registered with a local registry/load balancer.
- Services must renew their registration periodically.
- Services must provide SLAs for their clients.
- Services should aim to be stateless and be treated as transient.
- If a service has to maintain state, it should be maintained in external persistent storage.
- Services have alternatives in case a service they depend on fails.
- Services have defensive checks to intercept erroneous input from clients and output from other services.
- Uses of external services, environmental information, and third-party software and libraries are localized (i.e., they require passage through a module specific to that external service, environment information, or external software or library).

However, adopting a microservice architecture will introduce new challenges. When an application is composed of a large number of network-connected microservices, there can be latency and other performance issues. Authentication and authorization between services need to be carefully designed so that they do not add intolerable overhead. Monitoring, debugging, and distributed tracing tools may need to be modified to suit microservices. As mentioned earlier, end-to-end testing will be expensive. Rarely can you rebuild your application from scratch without legacy components or existing data.

Migrating from your current architecture to a microservice architecture incrementally without data loss and interruption is a challenge. You may need to build interim solutions during this migration. We discuss these challenges and some solutions in the Atlassian case study in Chapter 13, wherein Atlassian describes the initial steps of their journey to a microservice architecture. An architect should have a checklist of things to consider when performing a migration.

4.6 Summary

The DevOps goal of minimizing coordination among various teams can be achieved by using a microservice architectural style where the coordination mechanism, the resource management decisions, and the mapping of architectural elements are all specified by the architecture and hence require minimal inter-team coordination.

A collection of practices for development can be added to the microservice architectural style to achieve dependability and modifiability, such as identifying and isolating areas of likely change.

Adopting a microservice architectural style introduces additional challenges in monitoring, debugging, performance management, and testing. Migrating from an existing architecture to a microservice architectural style requires careful planning and commitment.

4.7   For Further Reading

For more information about software architecture, we recommend the following books:

- *Documenting Software Architectures, 2nd Edition* [Clements 10]
- *Software Architecture in Practice, 3rd Edition* [Bass 13]

Service description, cataloguing, and management are discussed in detail in the *Handbook of Service Description* [Barros 12]. This book describes services that are externally visible, not microservices, but much of the discussion is relevant to microservices as well.

The microservice architectural style is described in the book *Building Microservices: Designing Fine-Grained Systems* [Newman 15].

Many organizations are already practicing a version of the microservice architectural development and DevOps, and sharing their valuable experiences.

- You can read more about the Amazon example here: http://apievangelist .com/2012/01/12/the-secret-to-amazons-success-internal-apis/ and http:// www.zdnet.com/blog/storage/soa-done-right-the-amazon-strategy/152
- Netflix points out some challenges in using microservice architecture at scale [Tonse 14].

The Netflix implementation of Eureka—their open source internal load balancer/registry—can be found at https://github.com/Netflix/eureka/wiki/ Eureka-at-a-glance

Consumer Driven Contracts (CDCs) are discussed in Martin Fowler's blog "Consumer-Driven Contracts: A Service Evolution Pattern," [Fowler 06].

5

Building and Testing

Testing leads to failure, and failure leads to understanding.
—Burt Rutan

5.1 Introduction

Although architects like to focus on design and implementation, the infrastructure that is used to support the development and deployment process is important for a number of reasons. This infrastructure should support the following requirements:

- Team members can work on different versions of the system concurrently.
- Code developed by one team member does not overwrite the code developed by another team member by accident.
- Work is not lost if a team member suddenly leaves the team.
- Team members' code can be easily tested.
- Team members' code can be easily integrated with the code produced by other members of the same team.
- The code produced by one team can be easily integrated with code produced by other teams.
- An integrated version of the system can be easily deployed into various environments (e.g., testing, staging, and production).
- An integrated version of the system can be easily and fully tested without affecting the production version of the system.
- A recently deployed new version of the system can be closely supervised.
- Older versions of the code are available in case a problem develops once the code has been placed into production.
- Code can be rolled back in the case of a problem.

The most important reason why practicing architects should probably be concerned about the development and deployment infrastructure is: Either they or the project managers are responsible for ensuring that the development infrastructure can meet the preceding requirements. There is nothing like being responsible for an outcome to focus attention.

None of the requirements are new, although the tools used to support these tasks have evolved and gained sophistication over the years. We organize this chapter using the concept of *deployment pipeline*. A deployment pipeline, as shown in Figure 5.1, consists of the steps that are taken between a developer committing code and the code actually being promoted into normal production, while ensuring high quality.

The deployment pipeline begins when a developer commits code to a joint versioning system. Prior to doing this commit, the developer will have performed a series of pre-commit tests on their local environment; failure of the pre-commit tests of course means that the commit does not take place. A commit then triggers an integration build of the service being developed. This build is tested by integration tests. If these tests are successful, the build is promoted to a quasi-production environment—the staging environment—where it is tested once more. Then, it is promoted to production under close supervision. After another period of close supervision, it is promoted to normal production. The specific tasks may vary a bit for different organizations. For example, a small company may not have a staging environment or special supervision for a recently deployed version. A larger company may have several different production environments for different purposes. We describe some of these different production environments in Chapter 6.

One way to define *continuous integration* is to have automatic triggers between one phase and the next, up to integration tests. That is, if the build is successful then integration tests are triggered. If not, the developer responsible for the failure is notified. *Continuous delivery* is defined as having automated triggers as far as the staging system. This is the box labeled UAT (user acceptance test)/staging/performance tests in Figure 5.1. We use the term *staging* for these various functions. *Continuous deployment* means that the next to last step (i.e., deployment into the production system) is automated as well. Once a service is deployed into production it is closely monitored for a period and then it is promoted into normal production. At this final stage, monitoring and testing still exist but the service is no different from other services in this regard. In this chapter, we are concerned with the building and testing aspects of this pipeline. Chapter 6 describes deployment practices, and Chapter 7 discusses monitoring methods.

We use the deployment pipeline as an organizing theme for this chapter. Then we discuss crosscutting concerns of the different steps, followed by sections on the pre-commit stage, build and integration testing, UAT/staging/performance tests, production, and post-production. Before moving to that discussion, however, we discuss the movement of a system through the pipeline.

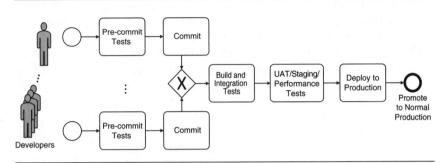

FIGURE 5.1   Deployment pipeline [Notation: BPMN]

5.2   Moving a System Through the Deployment Pipeline

Committed code moves through the steps shown in Figure 5.1, but the code does not move of its own volition. Rather, it is moved by tools. These tools are controlled by their programs (called *scripts* in this context) or by developer/operator commands. Two aspects of this movement are of interest in this section:

1. Traceability
2. The environment associated with each step of the pipeline

Traceability

Traceability means that, for any system in production, it is possible to determine exactly how it came to be in production. This means keeping track not only of source code but also of all the commands to all the tools that acted on the elements of the system. Individual commands are difficult to trace. For this reason, controlling tools by scripts is far better than controlling tools by commands. The scripts and associated configuration parameters should be kept under version control, just as the application code. A movement called *Infrastructure as Code* uses this rationale. Tests are also maintained in version control. Configuration parameters can be kept as files that are stored in version control or handled through dedicated configuration management systems.

Treating infrastructure-as-code means that this code should be subject to the same quality control as application source code. That is, this code should be tested, changes to it should be regulated in some fashion, and its different parts should have owners.

Keeping everything in version control and configuration management systems allows you to re-create the exact environments used anywhere, from local development to production. Not only is this very helpful in tracing issues, it also allows fast and flexible redeployment of your application in a new environment.

A complication to the requirement to keep everything in version control is the treatment of third-party software such as Java libraries. Such libraries can be bulky and can consume a lot of storage space. Libraries also change, so you must find a mechanism to ensure you include the correct version of third-party software in a build, without having multiple copies of the same version of the library on the servers running your system. Software project management tools like Apache Maven can go a long way to managing the complexities of library usage.

The Environment

An executing system can be viewed as a collection of executing code, an environment, configuration, systems outside of the environment with which the primary system interacts, and data. Figure 5.2 shows these elements.

As the system moves through the deployment pipeline, these items work together to generate the desired behavior or information.

- *Pre-commit.* The code is the module of the system on which the developer is working. Building this code into something that can be tested requires access to the appropriate portions of the version control repository that are being created by other developers. In Chapter 1, we discussed reducing coordination among teams. Pre-commit requires coordination within a team. The environment is typically a laptop or a desktop, the external systems are stubbed out or mocked, and only limited data is used for testing. Read-only external systems, for example, an RSS feed, can be

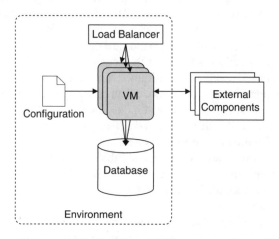

FIGURE 5.2   A sample environment [Notation: Architecture]

accessed during the pre-commit stage. Configuration parameters should reflect the environment and also control the debugging level.

- *Build and integration testing.* The environment is usually a continuous integration server. The code is compiled, and the component is built and baked into a VM image. The image can be either heavily or lightly baked (see the later section on packaging). This VM image does not change in subsequent steps of the pipeline. During integration testing, a set of test data forms a test database. This database is not the production database, rather, it consists of a sufficient amount of data to perform the automated tests associated with integration. The configuration parameters connect the built system with an integration testing environment.

- *UAT/staging/performance testing.* The environment is as close to production as possible. Automated acceptance tests are run, and stress testing is performed through the use of artificially generated workloads. The database should have some subset of actual production data in it. With very large data sets, it may not be possible to have a complete copy of the actual data, but the subset should be large enough to enable the tests to be run in a realistic setting. Configuration parameters connect the tested system with the larger test environment. Access to the production database should not be allowed from the staging environment.

- *Production.* The production environment should access the live database and have sufficient resources to adequately handle its workload. Configuration parameters connect the system with the production environment.

The configuration for each of these environments will be different. For instance, logging in the development environment is usually done in a much more detailed fashion than in the production environment. Doing so helps the developer find bugs, and the performance overhead created does not matter as much. Another example concerns credentials: The credentials for accessing production resources, such as the live customer database, should not be made available to developers. While some changes in configuration are unavoidable, it is important to keep these changes to a minimum to prevent affecting the behavior of the system. As such, testing with a vastly different configuration from the production system will not be helpful.

Wikipedia has a longer list of environments than we provide here because it enumerates more distinct testing environments. For the purposes of this chapter, the environments we enumerated are sufficient but, as noted, depending on the size of your organization, the regulatory environment, and other factors, more environments may be necessary. The Wikipedia list is:

- *Local*: Developer's laptop/desktop/workstation
- *Development*: Development server, a.k.a. sandbox
- *Integration*: Continuous integration (CI) build target, or for developer testing of side effects
- *Test/QA*: For functional, performance testing, quality assurance, etc.

- *UAT*: User acceptance testing
- *Stage/Pre-production*: Mirror of production environment
- *Production/Live*: Serves end-users/clients

Before we turn to the actual steps of the deployment pipeline we discuss the crosscutting aspects of testing.

5.3   Crosscutting Aspects

In this section, we discuss various crosscutting aspects of a deployment pipeline: test harnesses, negative tests, regression tests, traceability of errors, the size of components, and tearing down of environments.

- *Test harnesses*. A test harness is a collection of software and test data configured to test a program unit by running it under varying conditions and monitoring its behavior and output. Test harnesses are essential in order to automate tests. A critical feature of a test harness is that it generates a report. In particular it should, at a minimum, identify which tests failed. Most of the types of tests discussed in this chapter should be able to be automated and driven by the test harness.
- *Negative tests*. Most tests follow the "happy path" and check if the system behaves as expected when all assumptions about the environment hold and the user performs actions in the right order with the right inputs. It is also important to test if the system behaves in a defined way when these assumptions are not met. Tests that follow this purpose are collectively called negative tests. Examples are (simulated or actual) users performing actions in the wrong order (e.g., clicking buttons, calling commands, terminating the user interface (UI)/browser at an unexpected point in time, etc.) or simulated connectivity issues, such as external services becoming unavailable, connections being dropped at unexpected points in time, and so forth. The common expectation is that the application should *degrade* or *fail gracefully* (i.e., only degrade the functionality as necessitated by the actual problem), and, if failure is unavoidable, provide meaningful error messages and exit in a controlled manner.
- *Regression testing* is the core reason for maintaining and rerunning tests after they first passed. According to Wikipedia, regression testing "… seeks to uncover new software bugs, or *regressions*, in existing functional and non-functional areas of a system after changes such as enhancements, patches or configuration changes, have been made to them." Another use of regression testing is to ensure that any fixed bugs are not reintroduced later on. When fixing a bug in test-driven development, it is good practice to amend the test suite by adding a test that reproduces the bug. In the

current version, this test should fail. After the bug has been fixed, the test should pass. It is possible to automate the regression test creation: Failures detected at later points in the deployment pipeline (e.g., during staging testing) can be automatically recorded and added as new tests into unit or integration testing.

- *Traceability* of errors (also referred to as lineage or a form of provenance). If a bug occurs in production, you want to be able to find out quickly which version of the source code is running, so that you can inspect and reproduce the bug. We outline two options to handle this situation, both of which assume that you have a single mechanism for changing a system, be it through a configuration management system such as Chef, heavily baked images, and so forth. Regardless of the change mechanism, an assumption is made that every valid change uses that mechanism. Deviations from that practice are in principle possible, whether done inadvertently or maliciously, and you want to have mechanisms in place to detect or prevent them.

  - The first option to enable traceability is to associate identifying tags to the packaged application, such as the commit ID of various pieces of software and scripts that specify the provenance. In Java and .NET environments, packages can be enriched with metadata, where the commit ID can be added. Containers or VM images can be enriched in a similar fashion. The information can be added to log lines, and these can (selectively) be shipped to a central log repository. By doing so, a failing VM does not destroy the information necessary for analyzing the failure.
  - Another option is to have an external configuration management system that contains the provenance of each machine in production. One example for this is Chef, which keeps track of all changes it applies to a machine. The virtue of this approach is that the provenance information is at a known location for any application that needs to access that list. The drawback is that, when not using an existing system which offers this functionality, keeping a centralized list up to date can be a complex undertaking.

- *Small components*. We mentioned in Chapter 1 that small teams mean small components. In Chapter 4, we discussed microservices as a manifestation of small components. It is also the case that small components are easier to test individually. A small component has fewer paths through it and likely has fewer interfaces and parameters. These consequences of smallness mean that small components are easier to test, with fewer test cases necessary. However, as mentioned in Chapter 1, the smallness also introduces additional challenges in integration and requires end-to-end tests due to the involvement of more components.

- *Environment tear down.* Once an environment is no longer being used for a specific purpose, such as staging, it should be dismantled. Freeing resources associated with the environment is one rationale for tearing down an environment; avoiding unintended interactions with resources is another. The case study in Chapter 12 makes tear down an explicit portion of the process. It is easy to lose track of resources after their purpose has been achieved. Every VM must be patched for security purposes, and unused and untracked resources provide a possible attack surface from a malicious user. We discuss an example of an exploitation of an unused VM in Chapter 8.

We will discuss testing in more detail later in the chapter. For now, you should understand that different environments allow for different kinds of tests, and the more tests are completed successfully, the more confidence you should have in a version's quality.

5.4 Development and Pre-commit Testing

All tasks prior to the commit step are performed by individual developers on their local machines. Code development and language choice is out of scope here. We cover the general topics of versioning and branching, feature toggles, configuration parameters, and pre-commit testing.

Version Control and Branching

Even small development projects are nowadays placed into systems for *version control*—also called *revision control* or *source control*. Such systems date from the 1950s as manual systems. CVS (Concurrent Versions System) dates from the 1980s, and SVN (Subversion) dates from 2000. Git (released in 2005) is currently a popular version control system. Core features of version control are: the ability to identify distinct versions of the source code, sharing code revisions between developers, recording who made a change from one version to the next, and recording the scope of a change.

CVS and SVN are centralized solutions, where each developer checks out code from a central server and commits changes back to that server. Git is a distributed version control system: Every developer has a local clone (or copy) of a Git repository that holds all contents. Commits are done to the local repository. A set of changes can be synchronized against a central server, where changes from the server are synchronized with the local repository (using the *pull* command) and local changes can be forwarded to the server (using the *push* command). Push can only be executed if the local repository is up-to-date, hence a push is usually preceded by a pull. During this pull, changes to the same files (e.g., to the same Java class) are merged automatically. However, this merge can fail, in which case the developer has to resolve any conflicts locally. The resulting changes from an (automatic or semi-manual) merge are committed locally and then pushed to the server.

Almost all version control systems support the creation of new branches. A branch is essentially a copy of a repository (or a portion) and allows independent evolution of two or more streams of work. For example, if part of the development team is working on a set of new features while a previous version is in production and a critical error is discovered in the production system, the version currently in production must be fixed. This can be done by creating a branch for the fix based on the version of the code that was released into production. After the error has been fixed and the fixed version has been released into production, the branch with the fix is typically merged back into the main branch (also called the trunk, mainline, or master branch).

This example is useful in highlighting the need for traceability that we discussed previously. In order to fix the error, the code that was executing needs to be determined (traceability of the code). The error may be due to a problem with the configuration (traceability of the configuration) or with the tool suite used to promote it into production (traceability of the infrastructure).

Although the branch structure is useful and important, two problems exist in using branches.

1. You may have too many branches and lose track of which branch you should be working on for a particular task. Figure 5.3 shows a branch structure with many branches. Determining within this structure on which branch a particular change should be made can be daunting. For this reason, short-lived tasks should not create a new branch.
2. Merging two branches can be difficult. Different branches evolve concurrently, and often developers touch many different parts of the code. For instance, a few developers might make changes to the version currently in production in order to fix bugs, shield the version from newly discovered vulnerabilities, or support urgently required changes. At the same time, several groups of developers might be working toward a new release, each group working on a separate feature branch. Toward the end of the development cycle, you need to merge all feature branches and include the changes resulting from maintenance of the previous release.

An alternative to branching is to have all developers working on the trunk directly. Instead of reintegrating a big branch, a developer deals with integration issues at each commit, which is a simpler solution, but requires more frequent action than using branches. Paul Hammant discussed how Google uses this technique. Development at Google is trunk-based and at full scale: 15,000 developers committing to trunk, with an average of 5,500 submissions per day and 75 million test cases run per day.

Branches

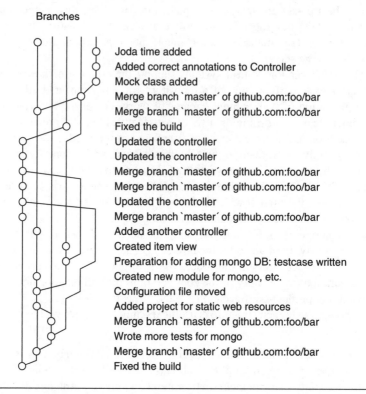

Joda time added
Added correct annotations to Controller
Mock class added
Merge branch `master´ of github.com:foo/bar
Merge branch `master´ of github.com:foo/bar
Fixed the build
Updated the controller
Updated the controller
Merge branch `master´ of github.com:foo/bar
Merge branch `master´ of github.com:foo/bar
Updated the controller
Merge branch `master´ of github.com:foo/bar
Added another controller
Created item view
Preparation for adding mongo DB: testcase written
Created new module for mongo, etc.
Configuration file moved
Added project for static web resources
Merge branch `master´ of github.com:foo/bar
Wrote more tests for mongo
Merge branch `master´ of github.com:foo/bar
Fixed the build

FIGURE 5.3   Git history of a short-lived project with 20 developers showing many merges (Adapted from http://blog.xebia.com/2010/09/20/git-workflow/) [The straight lines represent distinct branches and the diagonal lines represent either forks or merges.]

The problem with doing all of the development on one trunk is that a developer may be working on several different tasks within the same module simultaneously. When one task is finished, the module cannot be committed until the other tasks are completed. To do so would introduce incomplete and untested code for the new feature into the deployment pipeline. Solving this problem is the rationale for feature toggles.

Feature Toggles

A *feature toggle* (also called a *feature flag* or a *feature switch*) is an "if" statement around immature code. Listing 5.1 shows an example. A new feature that is not ready for testing or production is disabled in the source code itself, for example, by setting a global Boolean variable. Once the feature is ready, the toggle is flipped and the respective code is enabled. Common practice places the switches

LISTING 5.1   Pseudo-code sample use of feature toggle

```
If (Feature_Toggle) then
      new code
    else
      old code
    end;
```

for features into configuration, which is the subject of the next section. Feature toggling allows you to continuously deliver new releases, which may include unfinished new features—but these do not impact the application, since they are still switched off. The switch is toggled in production (i.e., the feature is turned on) only once the feature is ready to be released and has successfully passed all necessary tests.

We will discuss another use for feature toggles in Chapter 6.

There are, however, certain dangers in feature toggles. Recall the case of Knight Industries discussed in Chapter 1. The issue that led to a loss of more than (US) $440 million in about 45 minutes included wrong treatment of a feature toggle: The name of a toggle from years earlier was reused in the latest version, but it meant something else in the previous version. Since one of the production servers was still running the old version when the toggle was switched on, (US) $440 million was lost. Lesson 1: Do not reuse toggle names. Lesson 2: Integrate the feature and get rid of the toggle tests as soon as is timely.

When there are many feature toggles, managing them becomes complicated. It would be useful to have a specialized tool or library that knows about all of the feature toggles in the system, is aware of their current state, can change their state, and can eventually remove the feature toggle from your code base.

Configuration Parameters

A configuration parameter is an externally settable variable that changes the behavior of a system. A configuration setting may be: the language you wish to expose to the user, the location of a data file, the thread pool size, the color of the background on the screen, or the feature toggle settings. As you can see, the list of potential configuration parameters is endless.

For the purposes of this book, we are interested in configuration settings that either control the relation of the system to its environment or control behavior related to the stage in the deployment pipeline in which the system is currently run.

The number of configuration parameters should be kept at a manageable level. More configuration parameters usually result in complex connections between them, and the set of compatible settings to several parameters will only be known to experts in the configuration of the software. While flexibility is an admirable goal, a configuration that is too complex means you are essentially creating a specialized programming language. For instance, the SAP Business Suite had tens of thousands of configuration parameters at one point. While that flexibility allows many companies to use the software in their environments, it also implies that only a team of experts can make the right settings.

Nowadays there are good libraries for most programming languages to provide relatively robust configuration handling. The actions of these libraries include: checking that values have been specified (or default values are available) and are in the right format and range, ensuring that URLs are valid, and even checking whether settings are compatible with multiple configuration options.

You can split configuration parameters into groups according to usage time, for example, whether they are considered at build time, deployment, startup, or runtime. Any important option should be checked before its usage. URLs and other references to external services should be rechecked during startup to make sure they are reachable from the current environment.

One decision to make about configuration parameters is whether the values should be the same in the different steps of the deployment pipeline. If the production system's values are different, you must also decide whether they must be kept confidential. These decisions yield three categories.

1. Values are the same in multiple environments. Feature toggles and performance-related values (e.g., database connection pool size) should be the same in performance testing/UAT/staging and production, but may be different on local developer machines.
2. Values are different depending on the environment. The number of virtual machines (VMs) running in production is likely bigger than that number for the testing environments.
3. Values must be kept confidential. The credentials for accessing the production database or changing the production infrastructure must be kept confidential and only shared with those who need access to them—no sizeable organization can take the risk that a development intern walks away with the customer data.

Keeping values of configuration parameters confidential introduces some complications to the deployment pipeline. The overall goal is to make these values be the current ones in production but keep them confidential. One technique is to give meta-rights to the deployment pipeline and restrict access to the pipeline. When, for instance, a new VM is deployed into production, the deployment pipeline can give it rights to access a key store with the credentials required to operate in production. Another technique is for the deployment pipeline to set the network configuration in a virtual environment for a machine such that it gets to access the production database servers, the production configuration server, and so forth, if the machine is to be part of the production environment. In this case, only the deployment pipeline should have the right to create machines in the production portion of the network.

Testing During Development and Pre-commit Tests

Two types of testing processes occur during development. The first is a design philosophy—test-driven development—and the second is unit testing.

- *Test-driven development*. When following this philosophy, before writing the actual code for a piece of functionality, you develop an automated test for it. Then the functionality is developed, with the goal of fulfilling the test. Once the test passes, the code can be refactored to meet higher-quality standards. A virtue of this practice is that happy or sunny day path tests are created for all of the code.
- *Unit tests*. Unit tests are code-level tests, each of which is testing individual classes and methods. The unit test suite should have exhaustive coverage and run very fast. Typical unit tests check functionality that relies solely on the code in one class and should not involve interactions with the file system or the database. A common practice is to write the code in a way that complicated but required artifacts (such as database connections) form an input to a class—unit tests can provide mock versions of these artifacts, which require less overhead and run faster.

While these tests can be run by the developer at any point, a modern practice is to enforce *pre-commit tests*. These tests are run automatically before a commit is executed. Typically they include a relevant set of unit tests, as well as a few smoke tests. Smoke tests are specific tests that check in a fast (and incomplete) manner that the overall functionality of the service can still be performed. The goal is that any bugs that pass unit tests but break the overall system can be found long before integration testing. Once the pre-commit tests succeed, the commit is executed.

5.5   Build and Integration Testing

Build is the process of creating an executable artifact from input such as source code and configuration. As such, it primarily consists of *compiling* source code (if you are working with compiled languages) and *packaging* all files that are required for execution (e.g., the executables from the code, interpretable files like HTML, JavaScript, etc.). Once the build is complete, a set of automated tests are executed that test whether the integration with other parts of the system uncovers any errors. The unit tests can be repeated here to generate a history available more broadly than to a single developer.

Build Scripts

The build and integration tests are performed by a continuous integration (CI) server. The input to this server should be scripts that can be invoked by a single command. In other words, the only input from an operator or the CI server to create a build is the command "build"; the rest of the action of the continuous integration server is controlled by the scripts. This practice ensures that the build is repeatable and traceable. Repeatability is achieved because the scripts can be rerun, and traceability is achieved because the scripts can be examined to determine the origin of the various pieces that were integrated together.

Packaging

The goal of building is to create something suitable for deployment. There are several standard methods of packaging the elements of a system for deployment. The appropriate method of packaging will depend on the production environment. Some packaging options are:

- *Runtime-specific packages*, such as Java archives, web application archives, and federal acquisition regulation archives in Java, or .NET assemblies.
- *Operating system packages*. If the application is packaged into software packages of the target OS (such as the Debian or Red Hat package system), a variety of well-proven tools can be used for deployment.
- *VM images* can be created from a template image, to include the changes from the latest revision. Alternatively, a new build can be distributed to existing VMs. These options are discussed next. At any rate, VM images can be instantiated for the various environments as needed. One downside of their use is that they require a compatible hypervisor: VMware images require a VMware hypervisor; Amazon Web Services can only run Amazon Machine Images; and so forth. This implies that the test environments must use the same cloud service. If not, the deployment needs to be adapted accordingly, which means that the deployment to test environments does not necessarily test the deployment scripts for production.
- *Lightweight containers* are a new phenomenon. Like VM images, lightweight containers can contain all libraries and other pieces of software necessary to run the application, while retaining isolation of processes, rights, files, and so forth. In contrast to VM images, lightweight containers do not require a hypervisor on the host machine, nor do they contain the whole operating system, which reduces overhead, load, and size. Lightweight containers can run on local developer machines, on test servers owned by the organization, and on public cloud resources—but they require a compatible operating system. Ideally the same version of the same operating system should be used, because otherwise, as before, the test environments do not fully reflect the production environment.

There are two dominant strategies for applying changes in an application when using VM images or lightweight containers: *heavily baked* versus *lightly baked images*, with a spectrum between the extreme ends. Baking here refers to the creation of the image. Heavily baked images cannot be changed at runtime. This concept is also termed *immutable servers*: Once a VM has been started, no changes (other than configuration values) are applied to it. If the baking automatically takes place during the build phase, then the same server image is used in all subsequent test phases and at production. An image that has passed all tests gives a strong guarantee: Minus some configuration values, the servers spun off this image will face the same conditions in production as in testing. Heavily baked images do not only encapsulate changes to the application, but also to the installed packages. Whenever changes to the packages are required, a new image is baked and tested. This increases trust in the image and removes uncertainty and delay during launch/ runtime of new VMs, since no software updates get in the way of either. Chapter 6 discusses how to roll out new revisions based on heavily baked images.

Lightly baked images are fairly similar to heavily baked images, with the exception that certain changes to the instances are allowed at runtime. For example, it might be overkill to bake a new image, launch new VMs based on it, and retire all existing VMs every time a PHP-based application changes. In this case it should be sufficient to stop the web application server, check out the new PHP code from version control, and restart the web application server. While doing so may inspire less confidence than heavily baked images, it can be more efficient in terms of time and money.

The artifact resulting from the build (e.g., a binary executable), which is tested (and found to be of acceptable quality) should be the one that is deployed into production. In other words: if your executable code is in a language that needs to be compiled, like Java, C, etc., do not recompile after the build phase. We have seen a bug that depended on the version of the compiler being used. The bug existed in one version of a compiler and was repaired in the next version. Recompiling during passage through the deployment pipeline introduces the possibility of changing the behavior of the application as a result of a compiler bug.

Whatever packaging mechanism is used, the build step in the deployment pipeline should consist of compiling, packaging or baking an image, and archiving the build in a build repository.

Continuous Integration and Build Status

Once building is set up as a script callable as a single command, continuous integration can be done as follows:

- The CI server gets notified of new commits or checks periodically for them.
- When a new commit is detected, the CI server retrieves it.
- The CI server runs the build scripts.
- If the build is successful, the CI server runs the automated tests—as described previously and in the next section.
- The CI server provides results from its activities to the development team (e.g., via an internal web page or e-mail).

An important concept in CI is called *breaking the build*. A commit is said to break the build if the compilation/build procedure fails, or if the automatic tests that are triggered by it violate a defined range of acceptable values for some metrics. For instance, forgetting to add a new file in a commit but changing other files that assume the presence of a new file will break the build. Tests can be roughly categorized into critical (a single failure of a test would result in breaking the build) and less critical (only a percentage of failed tests larger than a set threshold would result in breaking the build).

All metrics can be summarized into a binary result: Is your build good (enough)? (i.e., a nonbroken or green build); or is your build not good (enough)? (i.e., a broken or red build).

Breaking the build means that other team members on the same branch can also not build. Thus, continuous integration testing is effectively shut down for much of the team. Fixing the build becomes a high-priority item. Some teams have an "I broke the build" hat that a team member must wear until the build is fixed as a means of emphasizing the importance of not breaking the build.

Test status can be shown in a variety of ways. Some teams use electronic widgets (such as lava lamps), or have big, visible monitors showing red/green lights for each component. Other teams use desktop notifications, particularly when they are located at a client's site, where the client might get nervous if a big red light shows up.

Finally, if your project is split into multiple components, these components can be built separately. In version control, they may be kept as one source code project or as several. In either case, the components can be built separately into distinct executables (e.g., separate JARs in Java). If that is the case, it makes sense to have a dedicated build step that combines all components into one package. This adds flexibility in the deployment pipeline (e.g., in how to distribute the components). It also enables decentralized building: The CI server can distribute build jobs to several machines, such as idle developer machines. However, one challenge of building components separately is to ensure that only compatible versions of the components are deployed. These and related considerations will be discussed in Chapter 6.

Integration Testing

Integration testing is the step in which the built executable artifact is tested. The environment includes connections to external services, such as a surrogate database. Including other services requires mechanisms to distinguish between production and test requests, so that running a test does not trigger any actual transactions, such as production, shipment, or payment. This distinction can be achieved by providing mock services, by using a test version provided by the owner of the service, or—if dealing with test-aware components—by marking test messages as such by using mechanisms built into the protocol used to communicate with that service. If mock versions of services are used, it is good practice to separate the test network from the real services (e.g., by firewall rules) to make absolutely sure no actual requests are sent by running the tests. Much worse than breaking the build is affecting the production database during test. We return to this topic when we discuss incidents in Section 5.8.

As with all of the tests we discussed, integration tests are executed by a test harness, and the results of the tests are recorded and reported.

5.6   UAT/Staging/Performance Testing

Staging is the last step of the deployment pipeline prior to deploying the system into production. The staging environment mirrors, as much as possible, the production environment. The types of tests that occur at this step are the following:

- User acceptance tests (UATs) are tests where prospective users work with a current revision of the system through its UI and test it, either according to a test script or in an exploratory fashion. This is done in the UAT environment, which closely mirrors production but still uses test or mock versions of external services. Furthermore, some confidential data may be removed or replaced in the UAT environment, where test users or UAT operators do not have sufficient levels of authorization. UATs are valuable for aspects that are hard or impossible to automate, such as consistent look and feel, usability, or exploratory testing.
- Automated acceptance tests are the automated version of repetitive UATs. Such tests control the application through the UI, trying to closely mirror what a human user would do. Automation takes some load off the UATs, while ensuring that the interaction is done in exactly the same way each time. As such, automated acceptance tests enable a higher rate of repetition than is possible with relatively expensive human testers, at odd times of the day or night. Due to the relatively high effort to automate acceptance tests, they are often done only for the most important checks, which need to be executed repetitively and are unlikely to require a lot of maintenance. Typically these tests are specified in and executed by specialized test suites, which should not trip over minor changes in the UI, such as moving a button a few pixels to the right. Automated acceptance tests are relatively slow to execute and require proper setup.
- Smoke tests, mentioned earlier, are a subset of the automated acceptance tests that are used to quickly analyze if a new commit breaks some of the core functions of the application. The name is believed to have originated in plumbing: A closed system of pipes is filled with smoke, and if there are any leaks, it is easy to detect them. One rule of thumb is to have a smoke test for every user story, following the happy path in it. Smoke tests should be implemented to run relatively fast, so that they can be run even as part of the pre-commit tests.

- Nonfunctional tests test aspects such as performance, security, capacity, and availability. Proper performance testing requires a suitable setup, using resources comparable to production and very similar every time the tests are run. This ensures that changes from the application, not background noise, are measured. As with the setup of other environments, virtualization and cloud technology make things easier. However, especially when it comes to public cloud resources, one needs to be careful in that regard because public clouds often exhibit performance variability.

5.7   Production

Deploying a system to production does not mean that observing its behavior or running tests is completed. We discuss early release testing, error detection, and live testing.

Early Release Testing

There are several forms of early release testing. Chapter 6 discusses how to release the application to achieve early release testing; here we focus on the testing method.

- The most traditional approach is a beta release: A selected few users, often subscribed to a beta program, are given access to a prerelease (beta) version of the application. Beta testing is primarily used for on-premises use of software.
- Canary testing is a method of deploying the new version to a few servers first, to see how they perform. It is the cloud equivalent of beta testing. Analogous to using canary birds in underground coal mining, where distress signals from the birds indicated the presence of toxic gases, these first few servers are monitored closely to detect undesired effects from the upgrade. One (or a few) of the application servers are upgraded from the current version to a stable and well-tested release candidate version of the application. Load balancers direct a small portion of the user requests to the candidate version, while monitoring is ongoing. If the candidate servers are acceptable in terms of some metrics (e.g., performance, scalability, number of errors, etc.) the candidate version is rolled out to all servers.
- A/B testing is similar to canary testing, except that the tests are intended to determine which version performs better in terms of certain business-level key performance indicators. For example, a new algorithm for recommending products may increase revenue, or UI changes may lead to more click-throughs.

Error Detection

Even systems that have passed all of their tests may still have errors. These errors can be either functional or nonfunctional. Techniques used to determine nonfunctional errors include monitoring of the system for indications of poor behavior. This can consist of monitoring the timing of the response to user requests, the queue lengths, and so forth. Netflix reports they have 95 different metrics that they monitor and compare with historical data. Deviations from the historical data trigger alerts to the operator, the developers, or both.

Once an alert has been raised, tracking and finding its source can be quite difficult. Logs produced by the system are important in enabling this tracking. We discuss this in Chapter 7, but for the purposes of this chapter, it is important that the provenance of the software causing the alert and the user requests that triggered the alert all can be easily obtained. Enabling the diagnosis of errors is one of the reasons for the emphasis on using automated tools that maintain histories of their activities.

In any case, once the error is diagnosed and repaired, the cause of the error can be made one of the regression tests for future releases.

Live Testing

Monitoring is a passive form of testing. That is, the systems run in their normal fashion and data is gathered about their behavior and performance. Another form of testing after the system has been placed in production is to actually perturb the running system. This form is called *live testing*. Netflix has a set of test tools called the Simian Army. The elements of the Simian Army are both passive and active. The passive elements examine running instances to determine unused resources, expired certificates, health checks on instances, and adherence to best practices.

The active elements of the Simian Army inject particular types of errors into the production system. For example, the Chaos Monkey kills active VMs at random. Recall in Chapter 2 that we discussed the fact that failure is common in the cloud. If a physical server fails then all of the VMs hosted on that machine abruptly terminate. Consequently, applications should be resilient to that type of failure. The Chaos Monkey simulates that type of failure. An instance is killed, and overall metrics such as response time are monitored to ensure that the system is not affected by that failure. Of course, you would not want to kill too many instances at once.

Another active element of the Simian Army is the Latency Monkey. The Latency Monkey injects delays into messages. Networks become busy and are unexpectedly slow. The Latency Monkey simulates slow networks by artificially delaying messages from one service to another. As with the Chaos Monkey, this testing is done carefully to avoid impacting customers.

5.8   Incidents

No matter how well you test or organize a deployment, errors will exist once a system gets into production. Understanding potential causes of post-deployment errors helps to more quickly diagnose problems. We do not have a taxonomy or relative frequency of various types of post-deployment errors. What we have instead are several anecdotes we have heard from IT professionals.

- A developer connected test code to a production database. We have heard this example multiple times. One time it was an inexperienced developer, and another time it was a developer who opened an SSH through a tunnel into the production environment.
- Version dependencies existing among the components. When dependencies exist among components, the order of deployment becomes important and it is possible if the order is incorrect that errors will result. In Chapter 6, we discuss the use of feature toggles to avoid this problem.
- A change in a dependent system coincided with a deployment. For instance, a dependent system removed a service on which an application depended, and this removal happened after all of the staging tests had been passed. The discussion about "baking" in this chapter relates to this problem. If the dependent system had been baked into an image then subsequent changes to it would not have been incorporated. If the dependent system is external to the image then the characteristics of building an executable image will not affect the occurrence of this error.
- Parameters for dependent systems were set incorrectly. That is, queues overflowed or resources were exhausted in dependent systems. Adjusting the configurations for the dependent systems and adding monitoring rules were the fixes adopted by the affected organization.

5.9   Summary

Having an appropriate deployment pipeline is essential for rapidly creating and deploying systems. The pipeline has at least five major steps—pre-commit, build and integration testing, UAT/staging/performance tests, production, and promoting to normal production.

Each step operates within a different environment and with a set of different configuration parameter values—although this set should be limited in size as much as possible. As the system moves through the pipeline, you can have progressively more confidence in its correctness. Even systems promoted to normal production, however, can have errors and can be improved from the perspective of performance or reliability. Live testing is a mechanism to continue to test even after placing a system in production or promoting it to normal production.

Feature toggles are used to make code inaccessible during production. They allow incomplete code to be contained in a committed module. They should be removed when no longer necessary because otherwise they clutter the code base; also, repurposed feature toggles can cause errors.

Tests should be automated, run by a test harness, and report results back to the development team and other interested parties. Many incidents after placing a system in production are caused by either developer or configuration errors.

An architect involved in a DevOps project should ensure the following:

- The various tools and environments are set up to enable their activities to be traceable and repeatable.
- Configuration parameters should be organized based on whether they will change for different environments and on their confidentiality.
- Each step in the deployment pipeline has a collection of automated tests with an appropriate test harness.
- Feature toggles are removed when the code they toggle has been placed into production and been judged to be successfully deployed.

5.10 For Further Reading

For a more detailed discussion of many of the issues covered in the chapter, see the book: *Continuous Delivery: Reliable Software Releases through Build, Test, and Deployment Automation* [Humble 10].

Carl Caum discusses the difference between continuous delivery and continuous deployment in his blog [Puppet Labs 13].

Much of the basic conceptual information in this chapter comes from Wikipedia.

- Revision control systems are discussed in general at http://en.wikipedia .org/wiki/Revision_control. Specific systems such as Git have their own entries.
- Test harnesses are discussed in http://en.wikipedia.org/wiki/Test_harness
- Regression testing is discussed in http://en.wikipedia.org/wiki/ Regression_testing
- Different types of types of environments (or server tiers) are listed in http:// en.wikipedia.org/wiki/Development_environment

Paul Hammant discusses branch versus trunk-based approaches in [DZone 13].

The argument between heavily baked and lightly baked images can be sampled at [Gillard-Moss 13]

The topic of performance variation in public clouds has been investigated in several scientific publications, such as "Runtime Measurements in the Cloud: Observing, Analyzing, and Reducing Variance" [Schad 10].

The Simian Army is defined and discussed in [Netflix 15].

6

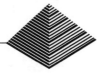

Deployment

Error Code 725: It works on my machine.
—RFC for HTTP Status Code 7XX: Developer Errors

6.1 Introduction

Deployment is the process of placing a version of a service into production. The initial deployment of a service can be viewed as going from no version of the service to the initial version of the service. Because an initial deployment happens only once for most systems and new versions happen frequently, we discuss upgrading a service in this chapter. If it is the initial version then some of the issues we discuss (such as downtime of the currently deployed version) are not relevant. The overall goal of a deployment is to place an upgraded version of the service into production with minimal impact to the users of the system, be it through failures or downtime.

There are three reasons for changing a service—to fix an error, to improve some quality of the service, or to add a new feature. For simplicity in our initial discussion, we assume that deployment is an all-or-nothing process—at the end of the deployment either all of the virtual machines (VMs) running a service have had the upgraded version deployed or none of them have. Later in this chapter, we see that there are places for partial deployments, but we defer this discussion for now.

Figure 6.1 shows the situation with which we are concerned. This is a refinement of Figure 4.1 where microservice 3 is being upgraded (shown in dark gray). Microservice 3 depends on microservices 4 and 5, and microservices 1 and 2 (i.e., clients of microservice 3) depend on it. For now, we assume that any VM runs exactly one service. This assumption allows us to focus on services— their design and their relationships—and to equate deployment of services with deployment of VMs. We discuss other options later in this chapter.

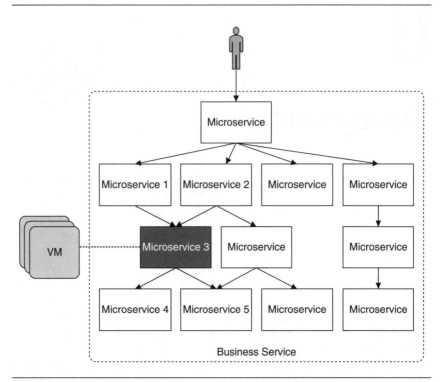

FIGURE 6.1   Microservice 3 is being upgraded. (Adapted from Figure 4.1.)
[Notation: Architecture]

Figure 6.1 also shows the multiple VMs on which the service is running. The number of VMs for a particular service depends on the workload experienced by that service and may grow into the hundreds or even thousands for VMs that must provide for many clients. Each active VM has a single version of the service being deployed, but not all VMs may be executing the same version.

The goal of a deployment is to move from the current state that has N VMs of the old version, A, of a service executing, to a new state where there are N VMs of the new version, B, of the same service in execution.

6.2   Strategies for Managing a Deployment

There are two popular strategies for managing a deployment—blue/green deployment and rolling upgrade. They differ in terms of costs and complexity. The cost may include both that of the VM and the licensing of the software running inside the VM. Before we discuss these strategies in more detail, we need to make the following two assumptions:

1. Service to the clients should be maintained while the new version is being deployed. Maintaining service to the clients with no downtime is essential for many Internet e-commerce businesses. Their customers span the globe and expect to be able to transact business around the clock. Certainly, some periods of a day are going to be busier than others, but service must be available at all times. Organizations that have customers primarily localized in one geographic area can afford scheduled downtime—but why have downtime if it is avoidable? Scheduled off-hours during downtime requires system administrators and operators to work in the off-hours. This is another reason to avoid downtime.

2. Any development team should be able to deploy a new version of their service at any time without coordinating with other teams. This may certainly have an impact on client services developed by other teams. We have previously discussed the relationship between synchronous coordination of development teams and the time to release new features. Allowing a development team or individual developer to release a new version of their service without coordinating with teams developing client services removes one cause for synchronous coordination. It may, however, cause logical problems, which we discuss in Section 6.3.

In addition, the placement of a new VM with a version into production takes time. In order to place an upgraded VM of a service into production, the new version must be loaded onto a VM and be initialized and integrated into the environment, sometimes with dependency on placements of some other services first. This can take on the order of minutes. Consequently, depending on how parallel some actions can be and their impact on the system still serving clients, the upgrade of hundreds or thousands of VMs can take hours or, in extreme cases, even days.

Blue/Green Deployment

A *blue/green deployment* (sometimes called *big flip* or *red/black deployment*) consists of maintaining the N VMs containing version A in service while provisioning N VMs of virtual machines containing version B. Once N VMs have been provisioned with version B and are ready to service requests, then client requests can be routed to version B. This is a matter of instructing the domain name server (DNS) or load balancer to change the routing of messages. This routing switch can be done in a single stroke for all requests. After a supervisory period, the N VMs provisioned with version A are removed from the system. If anything goes wrong during the supervisory period, the routing is switched back, so that the requests go to the VMs running version A again. This strategy is conceptually simple, but expensive in terms of both VM and software licensing costs.

Long-running requests and stateful data during the switch-over and rollback require special care.

The provisioning of the N VMs containing version B prior to terminating all version A VMs is the source of the cost. First, the new VMs must all be provisioned. The provisioning can be done in parallel, but the total time for provisioning hundreds of VMs can still be time-consuming. There will be an additional N VMs allocated beyond what is necessary to provide service to clients for the duration of the whole process, including initial provisioning of version B and the supervisory time after fully switching to version B. For this period of time, therefore, the VM-based cost doubles.

A variation of this model is to do the traffic switching gradually. A small percentage of requests are first routed to version B, effectively conducting a canary test. We mentioned canary testing in Chapter 5 and discuss it in more detail in the section "Canary Testing." If everything goes well for a while, more version B VMs can be provisioned and more requests can be routed to this pool of VMs, until all requests are routed to version B. This increases confidence in your deployment, but also introduces a number of consistency issues. We discuss these issues in Section 6.3.

Rolling Upgrade

A *rolling upgrade* consists of deploying a small number of version B VMs at a time directly to the current production environment, while switching off the same number of VMs running version A. Let us say we deploy one version B VM at a time. Once an additional version B VM has been deployed and is receiving requests, one version A VM is removed from the system. Repeating this process N times results in a complete deployment of version B. This strategy is inexpensive but more complicated. It may cost a small number of additional VMs for the duration of the deployment, but again introduces a number of issues of consistency and more risks in disturbing the current production environment.

Figure 6.2 provides a representation of a rolling upgrade within the Amazon cloud. Each VM (containing exactly one service for the moment) is decommissioned (removed, deregistered from the elastic load balancer (ELB), and terminated) and then a new VM is started and registered with the ELB. This process continues until all of the VMs containing version A have been replaced with VMs containing version B. The additional cost of a rolling upgrade can be low if you conduct your rolling upgrade when your VMs are not fully utilized, and your killing of one or a small number of VMs at a time still maintains your expected service level. It may cost a bit if you add a small number of VMs before you start the rolling upgrade to mitigate the performance impact and risk of your rolling upgrade.

During a rolling upgrade, one subset of the VMs is providing service with version A, and the remainder of the VMs are providing service with version B. This creates the possibility of failures as a result of mixed versions. We discuss this type of failure in the next section.

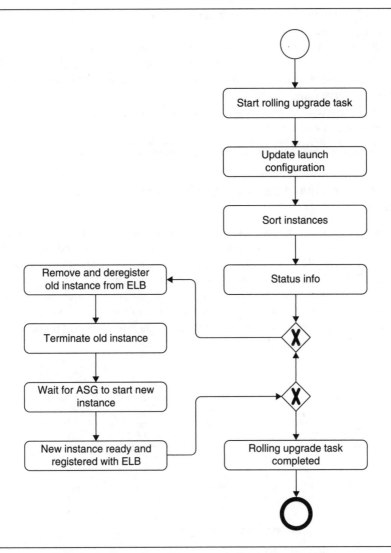

FIGURE 6.2 Representation of a rolling upgrade [Notation: BPMN]

6.3 Logical Consistency

Assuming that the deployment is done using a rolling upgrade introduces one type of logical inconsistency—multiple versions of the same service will be simultaneously active. This may also happen with those variants of the blue/green deployment that put new versions into service prior to the completion of the deployment.

Revisiting Figure 6.1 and assuming that a service is being deployed without synchronous coordination with its client or dependent services, we can see a second possible source of logical inconsistency—inconsistency in functionality between a service and its clients.

A third source of logical inconsistency is inconsistency between a service and data kept in a database.

We now discuss these three types of inconsistencies.

Multiple Versions of the Same Service Simultaneously Active

Figure 6.3 shows an instance of an inconsistency because of two active versions of the same service. Two components are shown—the client and two versions (versions A and B) of a service. The client sends a message that is routed to version B. Version B performs its actions and returns some state to the client. The client then includes that state in its next request to the service. The second request is routed to version A, and this version does not know what to make of the state, because the state assumes version B. Therefore, an error occurs. This problem is called a *mixed-version race condition*.

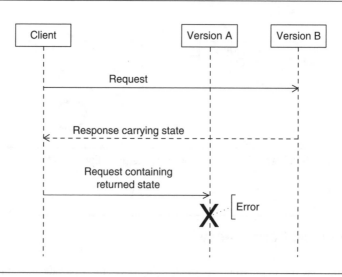

FIGURE 6.3 Mixed-version race condition, leading to an error [Notation: UML Sequence Diagram]

Several different techniques exist to prevent this situation.

- Make the client version aware so that it knows that its initial request was serviced by a version B VM. Then it can require its second request to be serviced by a version B VM. In Chapter 4, we described how a service is registered with a registry/load balancer. This registration can contain the version number. The client can then request a specific version of the service. Response messages from the service should contain a tag so that the client is aware of the version of the service with which it has just interacted.
- Toggle the new features contained in version B and the client so that only one version is offering the service at any given time. More details are given below.
- Make the services forward and backward compatible, and enable the clients to recognize when a particular request has not been satisfied. Again, more details are given below.

These options are not mutually exclusive. That is, you can use feature toggles within a backward compatible setting. Suppose for example, you make a major reorganization of a service and add new features to it. Within a rolling upgrade you will have installed some VMs of the new version with its reorganization while still not having activated the new features. This requires the new version to be backward compatible.

We begin by discussing feature toggling. Feature toggling was introduced in Chapter 5 as a means for deploying partially completed code without it impacting the testing process. Here we use the same mechanism for activating new capabilities in an upgrade.

Feature Toggling

If services are developed by a single small team, the features of the services will be limited. This means that features are likely to span multiple services. In turn, this means that you must coordinate the activation of the feature in two directions. First, all of the VMs for the service you just deployed must have the service's portion of the feature activated. And second, all of the services involved in implementing the feature must have their portion of the feature activated.

Feature toggles, as described in Chapter 5, can be used to control whether a feature is activated. A feature toggle, to repeat, is a piece of code within an *if* statement where the *if* condition is based on an externally settable feature variable. Using this technique means that the problems associated with activating a feature are (a) determining that all services involved in implementing a feature have been sufficiently upgraded and (b) activating the feature in all of the VMs of these services at the same time.

Both of these problems are examples of synchronizing across the elements of a distributed system. The primary modern methods for performing such synchronization are based on the Paxos or ZAB algorithms. These algorithms are difficult to implement correctly. However, standard implementations are available in systems such as ZooKeeper, which are not difficult to use.

Let us look at how this works from the service's perspective. For simplicity of description, we assume the service being deployed implements a portion of a single feature, *Feature X*. When a VM of the service is deployed, it registers itself as being interested in *FeatureXActivationFlag*. If the flag is false, then the feature is toggled off; if the flag is true, the feature is toggled on. If the state of the *FeatureXActivationFlag* changes, then the VM is informed of this and reacts accordingly.

An agent external to any of the services in the system being upgraded is responsible for setting *FeatureXActivationFlag*. This agent can be a human gatekeeper, or it can be automated. The flag is maintained in ZooKeeper and thus kept consistent across the VMs involved. As long as all of the VMs are informed simultaneously of the toggling, then the feature is activated simultaneously and there is no version inconsistency that could lead to failures. The simultaneous information broadcast is performed by ZooKeeper. This particular use of ZooKeeper for feature toggling is often implemented in other tools. For example, Netflix's Archaius tool provides configuration management for distributed systems. The configuration being managed can be feature toggles or any other property.

The agent is aware of the various services implementing *Feature X* and does not activate the feature until all of these services have been upgraded. Thus, there is no requirement that the services involved be upgraded in any particular order or even in temporal proximity to each other. It could be a matter of days or even weeks before all of the services involved have been modified to implement *Feature X*.

One complication comes from deciding when the VMs have been "sufficiently upgraded." VMs may fail or become unavailable. Waiting for these VMs to be upgraded before activating the feature is not desirable. The use of a registry/ load balancer as described in Chapter 4 enables the activation agent to avoid these problems. Recall that each VM must renew its registration periodically to indicate that it is still active. The activation agent examines the relevant VMs that are registered to determine when all VMs of the relevant services have been upgraded to the appropriate versions.

Backward and Forward Compatibility

Using feature toggles to coordinate the various services involved in a new feature is one option for preventing failures as a result of multiple versions. Another option is to ensure forward and backward compatibility of services.

- A service is backward compatible if the new version of the service behaves as the old version. For requests that are known to the old version of a service, the new version provides the same behavior. In other words, the external interfaces provided by version B of a service are a superset of the external interfaces provided by version A of that service.
- Forward compatibility means that a client deals gracefully with error responses indicating an incorrect method call. Suppose a client wishes to utilize a method that will be available in version B of a service but the

method is not present in version A. Then if the service returns an error code indicating it does not recognize the method call, the client can infer that it has reached version A of the service.

Requiring backward compatibility might seem at first to preclude many changes to a service. If you cannot change an interface, how can you add new features or, for example, refactor your service? In fact, maintaining backward compatibility can be done using the pattern depicted in Figure 6.4.

The service being upgraded makes a distinction between internal and external interfaces. External interfaces include all of the existing interfaces from prior versions as well as, possibly, new ones added with this version. Internal interfaces can be restructured with every version. In-between the external interfaces and the internal interfaces is a translation layer that maps the old interfaces to the new ones. As far as a client is concerned, the old interfaces are still available for the new version. If a client wishes to use a new feature, then a new interface is available for that feature.

One consequence of using this pattern is that obsolete interfaces may be maintained beyond the point where any clients use them. Determining which clients use which interfaces can be done through monitoring and recording all service invocations. Once there are no usages for a sufficiently long time, the interface can be deprecated. The deprecating of an interface may result in additional maintenance work, so it should not be done lightly.

Forward and backward compatibility allows for independent upgrade for services under your control. Not all services will be under your control. In particular, third-party services, libraries, or legacy services may not be backward compatible. In this case, there are several techniques you can use, although none of them are foolproof.

- *Discovery.* In Chapter 4, we described how services register so that clients can find them. This registration should involve the version number of the service.

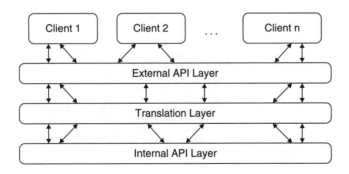

FIGURE 6.4 Maintaining backward compatibility for service interfaces [Notation: Architecture]

The clients can request that they be connected to particular versions of services or versions satisfying some constraint. If no existing service satisfies the constraint then the client either executes a fall-back action or reports failure. This requires the client to be aware of the version of the service that they require and that the service conforms to the architecture by registering its version number. There is an ongoing discussion in the standards community as to whether version numbers should be included as a portion of service interfaces.

- *Exploration.* Discovery assumes that a service registers with a registry. Libraries and many third-party software systems do not perform such a registration. In this case, using introspection on the library or third-party system enables the client to determine the version number. Introspection requires that the library or third-party software makes their version number accessible at runtime, either through an interface or through other mechanisms such as recording the version number on a file. Introspection also assumes that the client is aware of the version of the service that it requires.
- *Portability layer.* Figure 6.5 shows the concept of a portability layer. A portability layer provides a single interface that can be translated into the interfaces for a variety of similar systems. This technique has been used to port applications to different operating systems, to allow multiple different devices to look identical from the application perspective, or to allow for the substitution of different database systems. In Chapter 4, we identified the requirement that interactions with external systems from a component be localized into a single module. This module acts as a portability layer. One requirement is that the interface defined for the portability layer be adequate to manage all versions of the external system. Two variants of this pattern exist depending on whether the two versions of the external system need to coexist. If the two versions need to coexist, the portability layer must decide at runtime which version of the external system to use and the service must provide some basis to allow the portability layer to choose. Managing devices with different protocols falls into this category. If the two versions do not need to coexist, then the decision

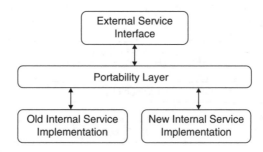

FIGURE 6.5   Portability layer with two versions of the external system coexisting [Notation: Architecture]

can be made at build time and the correct version of the portability layer can be incorporated into the service. Figure 6.5 shows the two versions coexisting.

Compatibility with Data Kept in a Database

In addition to maintaining compatibility among the various services, some services must also be able to read and write to a database in a consistent fashion. Suppose, for example, that the data schema changes: In the old version of the schema, there is one field for customer address; in the new version, the address is broken into street, city, postal code, and country. Inconsistency, in this case, might mean that a service intends to write the address as a single field using the schema that has the address broken into portions. Inconsistencies are triggered by a change in the database schema. Note that a schema can be either explicit such as in relational database management systems (RDBMSs) or implicit such as in various NoSQL database management systems.

The most basic solution to such a schema change is not to modify existing fields but only to add new fields or tables, which can be done without affecting existing code. The use of the new fields or tables can be integrated into the application incrementally. One method for accomplishing this is to treat new fields or tables as new features in a release. That is, either the use of the new field or table is under the control of a feature toggle or the services are forward and backward compatible with respect to database fields and tables.

If, however, a change to the schema is absolutely required you have two options:

1. Convert the persistent data from the old schema to the new one.
2. Convert data into the appropriate form during reads and writes. This could be done either by the service or by the database management system.

These options are not mutually exclusive. You might perform the conversion in the background and convert data on the fly while the conversion is ongoing. Modern RDBMSs provide the ability to reorganize data from one schema to another online while satisfying requests—although at a storage and performance cost. See Sockut and Iyer cited in Section 6.10 for a discussion of the issues and the techniques used. NoSQL database systems typically do not provide this capability, and so, if you use them, you have to engineer a solution for your particular situation.

6.4 Packaging

We now turn from consistency of services during runtime to consistency of the build process in terms of getting the latest versions into the services. Deciding that components package services and that each service is packaged as exactly

one component, as we discussed in Chapter 4, does not end your packaging decisions. You must decide on the binding time among components residing on the
same VM and a strategy for placing services into VMs. Packaging components
onto a VM image is called *baking* and the options range from *lightly baked* to
heavily baked. We discussed these options in Chapter 5. What we add to that discussion here is the number of processes loaded into each VM.

A VM is an image that is running on top of a hypervisor that enables sharing a single bare metal processor, memory, and network among multiple tenants
or VMs. The image of the VM is loaded onto the hypervisor from which it is
scheduled.

A VM image could include multiple independent processes—each a service. The question then is: Should multiple services be placed in a single VM
image? Figure 6.6 shows two options. In the top option, a developer commits a
service for deployment, which is embedded into a single VM image. For example, Netflix claims they package one service per VM. In the bottom option, different developers commit different services into a single VM image. The emergence
of lightweight containers often assumes one service per container, but with the
possibility to have multiple containers per VM.

One difference in these two options is the number of times that a VM image
must be baked. If there is one service per VM, then that VM image is created
when a change in its service is committed. If there are two services per VM, then
the VM image must be rebaked whenever a change to either the first or second
service is committed. This difference is minor.

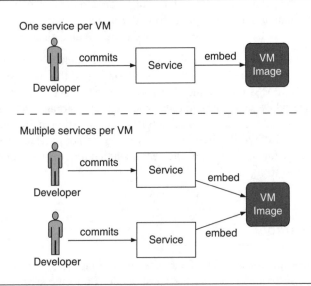

FIGURE 6.6   Different options for packaging services [Notation: Architecture]

A more important difference occurs when service 1 sends a message to service 2. If the two are in the same VM, then the message does not need to leave the VM to be delivered. If they are in different VMs, then more handling and, potentially, network communication are involved. Hence, the latency for messages will be higher when each service is packaged into a single VM.

On the other hand, packaging multiple services into the same VM image opens up the possibility of deployment race conditions. The race conditions arise because different development teams do not coordinate over their deployment schedules. This means that they may be deploying their upgrades at (roughly) the same time. Our examples below assume the upgraded services are included in the deployed portion of the VM (heavily baked) and not loaded later by the deployed software.

We see one possibility in Figure 6.7. Development team 1 creates a new image with a new version (v_{m+1}) of service 1 (S1) and an old version of service 2 (S2). Development team 2 creates a new image with an old version of service 1 and a new version (v_{n+1}) of service 2. The provisioning processes of the two teams overlap, which causes a deployment race condition. We see another version of the same problem in Figure 6.8. In this example, development team 1 builds their image after development team 2 has committed their changes. The result is similar in that the final version that is deployed does not have the latest version of both service 1 and service 2.

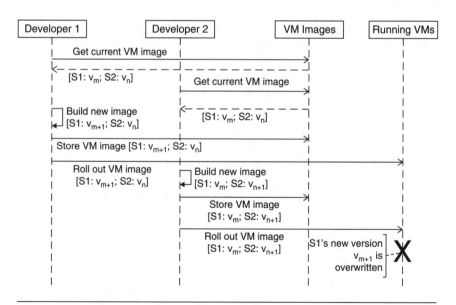

FIGURE 6.7 One type of race condition when two development teams deploy independently [Notation: UML Sequence Diagram]

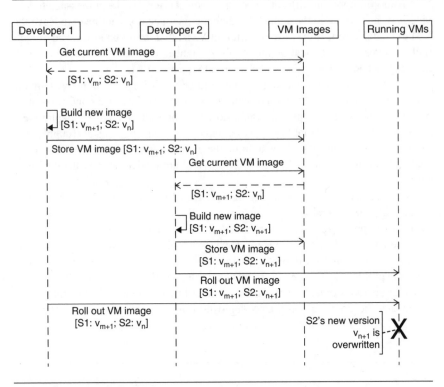

FIGURE 6.8 A different type of race condition when two development teams deploy independently [Notation: UML Sequence Diagram]

The tradeoff for including multiple services into the same VM is between reduced latency and the possibility of deployment race conditions.

6.5 Deploying to Multiple Environments

You may wish to deploy some of your services to one environment such as VMware and other services to a different environment such as Amazon EC2. As long as services are independent and communicate only through messages, such a deployment is possible basically with the design we have presented. The registry/load balancer that we discussed in Chapter 4 needs to be able to direct messages to different environments.

There will also be a performance penalty for messages sent across environments. The amount of this penalty needs to be determined experimentally so that the overall penalty is within acceptable limits.

Business Continuity

In Chapter 2, we briefly discussed the need for and the concepts associated with business continuity. Recall that business continuity is the ability for a business to maintain service when facing a disaster or serious outages. Now we can begin to see how business continuity is achieved. Fundamentally, it is achieved by deploying to sites that are physically and logically separated from each other. We differentiate between deploying to a public cloud and a private cloud, although the essential element, the management of state, is the same. We discuss more about disaster recovery in Chapter 10 and in the case study in Chapter 11.

Public Cloud

Public clouds are extremely reliable in the aggregate. They consist of hundreds of thousands of physical servers and provide extensive replication and failover services. Failures, however, do occur. These failures can be to particular VMs of your system or to other cloud services.

- A failure to a VM is not a rare occurrence. Cloud providers achieve economies of scale partially by purchasing commodity hardware. Any element of the hardware can fail—memory, disk, motherboard, network, or CPU. Failures may be total or partial. A partial failure in the underlying hardware can make your VM run slowly although it is still executing. In either case, you must architect your system to detect VM failures and respond to them. This is outside the scope of this chapter.
- A failure to the cloud infrastructure is a rare but not impossible occurrence. A quick search on "public cloud outages" can give you information about the latest high-profile outages that have occurred. Other outages are lower-profile but do still occur. You can survive many outages by choosing how you deploy your VMs.

Amazon EC2 has multiple regions (nine as of this writing) scattered around the globe. Each region has multiple availability zones. Each availability zone is housed in a location that is physically distinct from other availability zones and that has its own power supply, physical security, and so forth. If you deploy VMs of your system to different availability zones within the same region, you have some measure of protection against a cloud outage. If you deploy VMs of your system to different regions, then you have much more protection against outages, since some of the services such as elastic load balancing are per-region. Two considerations that you must keep in mind when you deploy to different availability zones or regions are state management and latency.

1.   *State management.* Making services stateless has several advantages, as discussed, for example, in Chapter 4. If a service is stateless then additional VMs can be created at any time to handle increased workload. Additional VMs can also be created in the event of a VM failure. With appropriate

infrastructure, the creation or deletion of VMs of a stateless service is transparent to the client. The disadvantages of stateless services are that state must be maintained somewhere in the system and latency may increase when the service needs to obtain or change this state. One consequence of increased latency is that services may cache state locally. This means that you may be required to purge the cache in certain circumstances. Small amounts of state can be maintained in various services such as Memcached, which is designed for caching (as indicated by the name). Large amounts of state should be maintained in a persistent repository. Deploying to different availability zones or regions requires that your persistent repositories be kept consistent. MRDMSs can be configured to provide this service automatically. Some of the NoSQL database systems also provide replication across multiple VMs of the repository. Public cloud providers typically offer specific services for this purpose, although in the case of Amazon, the replication between Amazon RDS replicas is only offered across availability zones.

One problem with making services stateless is that the service may be provided by third-party software that does maintain state, is outside of your control, and does not provide replication services. Migrating from such software to a different supplier is one of the tradeoffs that you must consider when making your business continuity plans.

2. *Latency*. Sending messages from one availability zone to another adds a bit of latency; messages sent from one region to another adds more latency to your system. One set of measurements puts the additional latency at 1.35ms across availability zones within the EU region and 231ms between the EU and the eastern United States. The additional latency is another one of the tradeoffs that you must consider with respect to business continuity.

Private Cloud

Many organizations may be required or may decide to maintain private datacenters rather than utilizing the public cloud. These datacenters are located in distinct physical locations, for example, ~100 miles apart, and with a high-speed link between them. We have seen many organizations with two datacenters but none with three. Having three datacenters adds 50% to the cost of maintaining business continuity, and the possibility of a double failure is usually judged to be highly unlikely. This is a risk management decision a particular organization must make.

From a software architectural perspective, the only difference between using two datacenters and two availability zones in the public cloud is the choice of hardware within the datacenter. In the public cloud, you can specify which sort of (virtual) hardware you wish to have allocated. In the private cloud, a solution to the problem of disparate hardware is to make the hardware identical across both datacenters. Then services can be deployed into either datacenter without making the services or the deployment tools aware of the datacenter. Virtualization provides some measure of hardware independence, but hardware features such as the number of physical cores or the use of blades impact the operating system and the performance. If the two datacenters have hardware features that impact the operating system and these features are visible to VMs, then a VM cannot be directly moved from one environment to another. If performance is impacted by the differing hardware, the deployment tools need to cater to that, for example, by provisioning 50% more virtual machines per service in the second datacenter, because the machines are slower by that much.

A further advantage of having two identical datacenters is that one can be used for pre-production testing during periods when the expected load on that datacenter is low.

6.6 Partial Deployment

Up to this point, our discussion has been focused on all-or-nothing deployments. Now we discuss two types of partial deployments—canary testing and A/B testing. We introduced these briefly in Chapter 5; here we elaborate on how to achieve these types of partial deployments.

Canary Testing

A new version is deployed into production after having been tested in a staging environment, which is as close to a production environment as possible. There is still a possibility of errors existing in the new version, however. These errors can be either functional or have a quality impact. Performing an additional step of testing in a real production environment is the purpose of canary testing. A canary test is conceptually similar to a beta test in the shrink-wrapped software world.

One question is to whom to expose the canary servers. This can be a random sample of users. An alternative is to decide the question based on the organization a user belongs to, for example, the employees of the developing organization, or particular customers. The question could also be answered based on geography, for example, such that all requests that are routed to a particular datacenter are served by canary versions.

The mechanism for performing the canary tests depends on whether features are activated with feature toggles or whether services are assumed to be forward or backward compatible. In either case, a new feature cannot be fully tested in production until all of the services involved in delivering the feature have been partially deployed.

Messages can be routed to the canaries by making the registry/load balancer canary-aware and having it route messages from the designated testers to the canary versions. More and more messages can be routed until a desired level of performance has been exhibited.

If new features are under the control of feature toggles, then turning on the toggle for the features on the canary versions activates these features and enables the tests to proceed.

If the services use forward and backward compatibility, then the tests will be accomplished once all of the services involved in a new feature have been upgraded to the new version. In either case, you should carefully monitor the canaries, and they should be rolled back in the event an error is detected.

A/B Testing

We introduced A/B testing in Chapter 5. It is another form of testing that occurs in the production environment through partial deployment. The "A" and "B" refer to two different versions of a service that present either different user interfaces or different behavior. In this case, it is the behavior of the user when presented with these two different versions that is being tested.

If either A or B shows preferable behavior in terms of some business metric such as orders placed, then that version becomes the production version and the other version is retired.

Implementing A/B testing is similar to implementing canaries. The registry/ load balancer must be made aware of A/B testing and ensure that a single customer is served by VMs with either the A behavior or the B behavior but not both. The choice of users that are presented with, say, version B may be randomized, or it may be deliberate. If deliberate, factors such as geographic location, age group (for registered users), or customer level (e.g., "gold" frequent flyers), may be taken into account.

6.7   Rollback

For some period after deployment, the new version of a service is on probation. It has gone through testing of a variety of forms but it still is not fully trusted. Recognition of the potential untrustworthiness of a new version is contained in the release plan that we discussed in Chapter 1 where testing the rollback plan is one of the dictates of the plan. Rolling back means reverting to a prior release. It is also possible to roll forward—that is, correct the error and generate a new release with the error fixed. Rolling forward is essentially just an instance of upgrading, so we do not further discuss rolling forward.

Because of the sensitivity of a rollback and the possibility of rolling forward, rollbacks are rarely triggered automatically. A human should be in the loop who decides whether the error is serious enough to justify discontinuing the current deployment. The human then must decide whether to roll back or roll forward.

If you still have VMs with version A available, as in the blue/green deployment model before decommissioning all version A VMs, rolling back can be done by simply redirecting the traffic back to these. One way of dealing with the persistent state problem is to keep version A VMs receiving a replicated copy of the requests version B has been receiving during the probation period.

However, if you are using a rolling upgrade model or you cannot simply replace version B by version A as a whole, you have to replace a version B VM with a version A VM in more complicated ways. The new version B can be in one of four states during its lifetime: uninstalled, partially installed, fully installed but on probation, or committed into production.

Two of these states have no rollback possibilities. If version B has not yet been installed then it cannot be rolled back. Once it has been committed, it also cannot be rolled back—although the old version could be treated as a new deployment and be redeployed. As we said in Chapter 5, if version B has been committed then removal of all of the feature toggles that have been activated within version B should be put on the development teams' list of activities to perform.

The remaining two states—namely, version B is partially installed or fully installed but on probation—have rollback possibilities. The strategy for rolling back depends on whether feature toggles are being used and have been activated. This pertains to both of the remaining two states.

- *Not using feature toggles.* Rolling back VMs in this case is a matter of disabling those VMs and reinstalling VMs running version A of the service.
- *Using feature toggles.* If the features have not been activated, then we have the prior version. Disable VMs running version B and reinstall version A. If the feature toggles have been activated, then deactivate them. If this prevents further errors, then no further action is required. If it does not, then we have the situation as if feature toggles were not present.

The remaining case deals with persistent data and is the most complicated. Suppose all of the version B VMs have been installed and version B's features activated, but a rollback is necessary. Rolling back to the state where version B is installed but no features activated is a matter of toggling off the new features, which is a simple action. The complications come from consideration of persistent data.

A concern when an error is detected is that incorrect values have been written into the database. Dealing with erroneous database values is a delicate operation with significant business implications. We present a general approach here but it should be used with caution. You certainly do not want to make the situation worse.

Our general approach is to roll back those requests that were processed by versions of the service where new features were activated and replay them with an older, working version. We first discuss what is necessary to accomplish the rollback, and then we discuss potential problems that can occur.

In order to roll back potentially questionable transactions, they need to be identified. This can be accomplished by maintaining a pedigree for each data item. The pedigree includes the version number of the service that wrote the data item and an identification of the request that triggered the writing of the data item. It also involves logging requests with sufficient information so that you can recover a causal chain from initial request to writing the data.

When a rollback is triggered, the versions of the services involved in implementing that feature are identified. This enables you to identify the data items that were written by those versions, which, in turn, enables the identification of the requests to be replayed. Removing the identified data items and restoring any overwritten items purges the database of potentially erroneous directly written values. Restoring overwritten items requires keeping a history of data fields and their values. It is possible that an erroneous data value could have cascaded through the triggering of dependent actions. Worse, it is possible that an erroneous data value could have external effects. For example, a customer may have been shown a much reduced fare and purchased a ticket.

Tracking the cascading of actions and determining which data values are potentially erroneous and which have escaped the system can be done by maintaining a pedigree of the data items. If the pedigree of a data item includes the data items on which it depends then those dependent data items that are saved in the database can be located and removed. For those dependent actions that are externally visible, logging the source of any externally visible data item enables you to determine the consequences of the erroneous feature, but correction becomes a business matter. Some of the incorrect externally visible data may not have a severe impact, others do. Determining the consequences of externally visible erroneous data requires special handling and must be done in conjunction with business decision makers.

Once the offending data is removed, the specified requests can be replayed with older versions of the services. This regenerates the data that has been removed, but in a non-erroneous fashion. A problem with this strategy is that the requests may depend on the features that have been removed. In this case, the replay should trigger an error indication from one of the services. The replay mechanism must know what to do with these errors.

As you may have gathered, identifying and correcting incorrect values in the database is a delicate and complicated operation requiring the collection of much metadata.

6.8 Tools

A large number of tools exist to manage deployment. One method for categorizing tools is to determine whether they directly affect the internals of the entity being deployed. As mentioned in Chapter 5, if a VM image contains all the required software including the new version, you can replace a whole VM of the old version with a whole VM of the new version. This is called using a *heavily baked* deployment approach. Alternatively, you can use tools to change the internals of a VM, so as to deploy the new version by replacing the old version without terminating the VM. Even if you terminate the VM with the old version, you can start a new *lightly baked* VM but then access the machine from the inside to deploy the new version at a later stage of the deployment process.

Netflix Asgard, for example, is an open source, web-based tool for managing cloud-based applications and infrastructure. Asgard is not interested in the contents of these VMs. It uses a VM image that contains the new version and creates VMs for these images. One of the features of Asgard is that it understands deployment processes such as rolling upgrade. It allows specification of the number of VMs to be upgraded in a single cycle. Infrastructure-as-a-Service (IaaS) vendors also provide specific tools for coordinated VM provisioning, which is used as a part of a deployment. For example, Amazon allows users to use CloudFormation scripts as a parameterized, declarative approach for deployment of VMs. CloudFormation scripts understand dependencies and rollback.

Chef and Puppet are two examples of tools that manage the items inside a virtual machine. They can replace a version of a piece of software inside a VM and ensure that configuration settings conform to a specification.

One emerging trend is the use of lightweight container tools, such as Docker, in deployment. A lightweight container is an OS-level virtualization technique for running multiple isolated OSs on a single host (VM or physical machine). They are like VMs, but they are smaller and start much faster.

Image management and testing tools such as Vagrant and Test Kitchen help control both VMs and items inside the VMs. A developer can spin up production-like environments for pre-commit testing and integration testing to reveal issues that would only surface in production.

6.9 Summary

Strategies for deploying multiple VMs of a service include blue/green deployment and rolling upgrade. A blue/green deployment does not introduce any logical problems but requires allocating twice the number of VMs required to provide a service. A rolling upgrade is more efficient in how it uses resources but introduces a number of logical consistency problems.

- Multiple different versions of a single service can be simultaneously active. These multiple versions may provide inconsistent versions of the service.
- A client may assume one version of a dependent service and actually be served by a different version.
- Race conditions can exist because of the choice of packing multiple and dependent services and multiple development teams performing concurrent deployment. Choosing the number of services to be packed into a single VM is often a tradeoff among resource utilization, performance, and complexity of deployment.

Solutions to the problems of logical consistency involve using some combination of feature toggles, forward and backward compatibility, and version awareness.

Deployments must occasionally be rolled back. Feature toggles support rolling back features, but the treatment of persistent data is especially sensitive when rolling back a deployment.

Deployment also plays an important role for achieving business continuity. Deploying into distinct sites provides one measure of continuity. Having an architecture that includes replication allows for a shorter time to repair and to resume processing in the event of an unexpected outage.

A variety of tools exist for managing deployment. The emergence of lightweight containers and image management tools is helping developers to deploy into small-scale production-like environments more easily for testing.

6.10 For Further Reading

To learn more about the peril of doing an upgrade, you can find an empirical study on the topic at [Dumitras 09].

The Paxos algorithm is difficult to understand and implement. That is why we recommend the use of libraries or tools that have already implemented it and provide higher-level features. But if you do want to have a better understanding of the algorithm, have a look at the latest, supposedly simple, explanation of it from the Turing Award–winning author, Leslie Lamport [Lamport 14].

ZooKeeper is based on the ZAB algorithm, and is arguably used much more widely than Paxos. You can find more about ZooKeeper and some links to higher-level tools at http://zookeeper.apache.org. For a comparison of Paxos and ZooKeeper's ZAB, see [Confluence 12].

Whether it be for a schema change or a rollback of erroneous upgrade, you can find more about the reorganization of a live database at [Sockut 09].

To read more about the pros and cons of the heavily baked and the lightly baked approach for VM images, see [InformationWeek 13].

You can find more about latency between services involving multiple regions/VMs at the links:

http://www.smart421.com/cloud-computing/amazon-web-services-inter-az-latency-measurements/

http://www.smart421.com/cloud-computing/which-amazon-web-services-region-should-you-use-for-your-service/

As for tooling, you can find more information about the various tools we mentioned here:

- Netflix Asgard: https://github.com/Netflix/asgard
- Amazon CloudFormation: http://aws.amazon.com/cloudformation/
- Chef: http://docs.opscode.com/chef_overview.html
- Puppet: http://puppetlabs.com/puppet/what-is-puppet
- Docker: https://www.docker.com/whatisdocker/
- Vagrant: https://www.vagrantup.com/

PART THREE

CROSSCUTTING CONCERNS

Part Two described the facets of a deployment pipeline. This is a functional perspective that focuses on the parts of the pipeline. In this part, we focus on those topics that crosscut the pipeline. There are four such chapters in Part Three.

In Chapter 7, we discuss the collection, processing, and interpretation of data during the execution of a system. Such data is vital for several purposes including error detection and recovery, forecasting, and the identification of performance problems.

In Chapter 8, we discuss security from several different perspectives. One perspective is that of the auditor who must evaluate the extent to which the security of your application or environment complies with its requirements. We also discuss securing the deployment pipeline. In either case, our discussion includes both malicious attempts to breach your security and accidental breaches committed by your personnel who mean no harm.

In addition to security, several other quality attributes are important to DevOps. We discuss these in Chapter 9. We show how qualities such as traceability, performance, reliability, and repeatability are important to the successful execution of a deployment pipeline.

Finally, in Chapter 10, we focus on business. An organization cannot adopt many DevOps practices without buy-in from other portions of the business including management. This chapter discusses how you could develop a business plan for DevOps, including the types of measurements you should take and how you can approach an incremental adoption of DevOps practices.

7

Monitoring

With Adnene Guabtni and Kanchana Wickremasinghe

> *First get your facts;*
> *then you can distort them at your leisure.*
> —Mark Twain

7.1 Introduction

Monitoring has a long history in software development and operation. The earliest monitors were hardware devices like oscilloscopes, and such hardware devices still exist in the monitoring ecosystem. We are going to ignore this history, however, and focus on software monitoring in this chapter. Software monitoring comprises myriad types of monitoring and the considerations that come with them. Activities as varied as collecting metrics at various levels (resources/OS/middleware/application-level), graphing and analyzing metrics, logging, generating alerts concerning system health status, and measuring user interactions all are a portion of what is meant by monitoring.

As Richard Hamming said: "The purpose of computing is insight, not numbers." The insights available from monitoring fall into five different categories.

1. Identifying failures and the associated faults both at runtime and during postmortems held after a failure has occurred.
2. Identifying performance problems of both individual systems and collections of interacting systems.
3. Characterizing workload for both short- and long-term capacity planning and billing purposes.

4. Measuring user reactions to various types of interfaces or business offerings. We discussed A/B testing in Chapters 5 and 6.
5. Detecting intruders who are attempting to break into the system.

We use the term *monitoring* to refer to the process of observing and recording system state changes and data flows. State changes can be expressed by direct measurement of the state or by logs recording updates that impact part of the state. Data flows can be captured by logging requests and responses between both internal components and external systems. The software supporting such a process is called a *monitoring system*.

When we speak of monitoring a workload, we are including the tools and infrastructure associated with operations activities. All of the activities in an environment contribute to a datacenter's workload, and this includes both operations-centric and monitoring tools.

In this chapter, we focus on new aspects of monitoring and challenges that arise with the advent of the DevOps movement. DevOps' continuous delivery/deployment practices and strong reliance on automation mean that changes to the system happen at a much higher frequency. Use of a microservice architecture also makes monitoring of data flows more challenging. We discuss these and other challenges in more detail in Section 7.6. Some examples of the new challenges are

- Monitoring under continuous changes is difficult. Traditional monitoring relies heavily on anomaly detection. You know the profile of your system during normal operation. You set thresholds on metrics and monitor to detect abnormal behavior. If your system changes, you may have to readjust them. This approach becomes less effective if your system is constantly changing due to continuous deployment practices and cloud elasticity. Setting thresholds based on normal operation will trigger multiple false alarms during a deployment. Disabling alarms during deployments will, potentially, miss critical errors when a system is already in a fairly unstable state. Multiple deployments can simultaneously occur as we discussed in Chapter 6, and these deployments further complicate the setting of thresholds.
- The cloud environment introduces different levels from application programming interface (API) calls to VM resource usage. Choosing between a top-down approach and a bottom-up approach for different scenarios and balancing the tradeoffs is not easy.
- When adopting the microservice architecture we introduced in Chapter 4, monitoring requires attention to more moving parts. It also requires logging more inter-service communication to ensure a user request traversing through a dozen services still meets your service level agreements. If anything goes wrong, you need to determine the cause through analysis of large volumes of (distributed) data.
- Managing logs becomes a challenge in large-scale distributed systems. When you have hundreds or thousands of nodes, collecting all logs centrally becomes difficult or prohibitively expensive. Performing analysis on huge collections of logs is challenging as well, because of the sheer volume of logs, noise, and inconsistencies in logs from multiple independent sources.

Monitoring solutions must be tested and validated just as other portions of the infrastructure. Testing a monitoring solution in your various environments is one portion of the testing, but the scale of your non-production environments may not approach the scale of your production—which implies that your monitoring environments may be only partially tested prior to being placed into production. We have heard how a feature toggle involving monitoring brought down a major Internet service for 45 minutes. This reinforces not only the importance of testing monitoring software but also the importance of maintaining control of feature toggles.

We organize this chapter by describing what to monitor, how to monitor, when to monitor, and how to interpret the monitoring data. We provide pointers to tools, further discuss the challenges just described, and provide an example of interpreting monitoring data.

7.2   What to Monitor

The data to be monitored for the most part comes from the various levels of the stack. Table 7.1 lists the insights you might gain from the monitoring data and the portions of the stack where such data can be collected. Notice that the whole stack is involved in most of the purposes for which you will do monitoring. We emphasize that tools supporting operations are applications that contribute to the workload, have failures, and should be monitored. In Chapter 6, we pointed out the failures that can come from race conditions during deployment. Monitoring changes to configurations and resource specification files enables the detection of such errors.

The fundamental items to be monitored consist of inputs, resources, and outcomes. The resources can be hard resources such as CPU, memory, disk, and network—even if virtualized. They can also be soft resources such as queues, thread pools, or configuration specifications. The outcomes include items such as transactions and business-oriented activities.

We now discuss the monitoring goals from Table 7.1.

TABLE 7.1   Goals of Monitoring by Level of the Stack

Goal of Monitoring	Source of Data
Failure detection	Application and infrastructure
Performance degradation detection	Application and infrastructure
Capacity planning	Application and infrastructure
User reaction to business offerings	Application
Intruder detection	Application and infrastructure

Failure Detection

Any element of the physical infrastructure can fail. The cause can be anything from overheating to mice eating the cables. Total failures are relatively easy to detect: No data is flowing where data used to flow. It is the partial failures that are difficult to detect, for instance: a cable is not firmly seated and degrades performance; before a machine totally fails because of overheating it experiences intermittent failure; and so forth.

Detecting failure of the physical infrastructure is the datacenter provider's problem. Instrumenting the operating system or its virtual equivalent will provide the data for the datacenter.

Software can also fail, either totally or partially. Total failure, again, is relatively easy to detect. Partial software failures have myriad causes, just as partial hardware failures do. The underlying hardware may have a partial failure; a downstream service may have failed; the software, or its supporting software, may have been misconfigured, and so forth.

Detecting software failures can be done in one of three fashions.

1. The monitoring software performs health checks on the system from an external point.
2. A special agent inside the system performs the monitoring.
3. The system itself detects problems and reports them.

Partial failures may also manifest as performance problems, which we now discuss.

Performance Degradation Detection

Detecting performance degradations is, arguably, the most common use of monitoring data. Degraded performance can be observed by comparing current performance to historical data—or by complaints from clients or end users. Ideally your monitoring system catches performance degradation before users are impacted at a notable strength.

Performance measures include latency, throughput, and utilization.

Latency

Latency is the time from the initiation of an activity to its completion. It can be measured at various levels of granularity. At a coarse grain, latency can refer to the period from a user request to the satisfaction of that request. At a fine grain, latency can refer to the period from placing a message on a network to the receipt of that message.

Latency can also be measured at either the infrastructure or the application level. Measuring latency within a single physical computer can be done by reading the clock prior to initiating an activity, reading the clock subsequent to the activity, and calculating the difference. Measuring latency across different physical computers is more problematic because of the difficulty of synchronizing clocks. We discuss this problem in more detail later.

It is important when reporting latency numbers to associate them with the activity that they are measuring. Furthermore, latency is cumulative in the sense that the latency of responding to a user request is the sum of the latency of all of the activities that occur until the request is satisfied, adjusted for parallelism. It is useful when diagnosing the cause of a latency problem to know the latency of the various subactivities performed in the satisfaction of the original request.

Throughput

Throughput is the number of operations of a particular type in a unit time. Although throughput could refer to infrastructure activities (e.g., the number of disk reads per minute), it is more commonly used at the application level. For example, the number of transactions per second is a common reporting measure.

Throughput provides a system-wide measure involving all of the users, whereas latency has a single-user or client focus. High throughput may or may not be related to low latency. The relation will depend on the number of users and their pattern of use.

A reduction in throughput is not, by itself, a problem. The reduction in throughput may be caused by a reduction in the number of users. Problems are indicated through the coupling of throughput and user numbers.

Utilization

Utilization is the relative amount of use of a resource and is, typically, measured by inserting probes on the resources of interest. For example, the CPU utilization may be 80%. High utilization can be used as either an early warning indicator of problems with latency or throughput, or as a diagnostic tool used to find the cause of problems with latency or throughput.

The resources can either be at the infrastructure or application level. Hard resources such as CPU, memory, disk, or network are best measured by the infrastructure. Soft resources such as queues or thread pools can be measured either by the application or the infrastructure depending on where the resource lives.

Making sense of utilization frequently requires attributing usage to activities or applications. For example, *app1* is using 20% of the CPU, disk compression is using 30%, and so on. Thus, connecting the measurements with applications or activities is an important portion of data collection.

Capacity Planning

We distinguish between long- and short-term capacity planning. Long-term capacity planning involves humans and has a time frame on the order of days, weeks, months, or even years. Short-term capacity planning is performed automatically and has a time frame on the order of minutes.

Long-Term Capacity Planning

Long-term capacity planning is intended to match hardware needs, whether real or virtualized, with workload requirements. In a physical datacenter, it involves ordering hardware. In a virtualized public datacenter, it involves deciding on the number and characteristics of the virtual resources that are to be allocated. In both cases, the input to the capacity planning process is a characterization of the current workload gathered from monitoring data and a projection of the future workload based on business considerations and the current workload. Based on the future workload, the desired throughput and latency for the future workload, and the costs of various provisioning options, the organization will decide on one option and provide the budget for it.

Short-Term Capacity Planning

In the context of a virtualized environment such as the cloud, short-term capacity planning means creating a new virtual machine (VM) for an application or deleting an existing VM. A common method of making and executing these decisions is based on monitoring information collected by the infrastructure. In Chapter 4, we discussed various options for controlling the allocation of VM instances based on the current load. Monitoring the usage of the current VM instances was an important portion of each option.

Monitoring data is also used for billing in public clouds. Charging for use is an essential characteristic of the cloud as defined by the U.S. National Institute of Science and Technology and discussed in Chapter 2. In order to charge for use, the use must be determined, and this is accomplished through monitoring by the cloud provider.

User Interaction

User satisfaction is an important element of a business. Besides the utility and quality of the application itself, user satisfaction depends on four elements that can be monitored.

1. *The latency of a user request.* Users expect decent response times. Depending on the application, seemingly trivial variations in response can have a large impact. Google reports that delaying a search results page by 100ms to 400ms has a measurable impact on the number of searches that users perform. Amazon reports a similar effect.
2. *The reliability of the system with which the user is interacting.* We discussed failure and failure detection earlier.
3. *The effect of a particular business offering or user interface modification.* We discussed A/B testing in Chapters 5 and 6. The measurements collected

from A/B testing must be meaningful for the goal of the test, and the data must be associated with variant A or B of the system.

4. *The organization's particular set of metrics.* Every organization has a set of metrics that it uses to determine the effectiveness of their offerings and their support services. If you run a photo gallery website, you may be interested specifically in metrics like photo upload rates, photo sizes, photo processing times, photo popularity, advertisement click-through rates, and levels of user activity. Other organizations will have different metrics, but they should all be important indicators of either user satisfaction or the effectiveness of the organization's computer-based services.

There are generally two types of user interaction monitoring.

1. *Real user monitoring (RUM).* RUM essentially records all user interactions with an application. RUM data is used to assess the real service level a user experiences and whether server side changes are being propagated to users correctly. RUM is usually passive in terms of not affecting the application payload without exerting load or changing the server-side application.
2. *Synthetic monitoring.* Synthetic monitoring is similar to developers performing stress testing on an application. Expected user behaviors are scripted either using some emulation system or using actual client software (such as a browser). However, the goal is often not to stress test with heavy loads, but again to monitor the user experience. Synthetic monitoring allows you to monitor user experience in a systematic and repeatable fashion, not dependent on how users are using the system right now. Synthetic monitoring may be a portion of the automated user acceptance tests that we discussed in Chapter 5.

Intrusion Detection

Intruders can break into a system by subverting an application, for example, through incorrect authorization or a man-in-the-middle attack. Applications can monitor users and their activities to determine whether the activities are consistent with the users' role in the organization or their past behavior. For instance, if user John has a mobile phone using the application, and the phone is currently in Australia, any log-in attempts from, say, Nigeria should be seen as suspicious.

An intrusion detector is a software application that monitors network traffic by looking for abnormalities. These abnormalities can be caused either by attempts to compromise a system by unauthorized users or by violations of an organization's security policies.

Intrusion detectors use a variety of different techniques to identify attacks. They frequently use historical data from an organization's network to understand what is normal. They also use libraries that contain the network traffic patterns observed during various attacks. Current traffic on a network is compared to the expected (from an organization's history) and the abnormal (from the attack history) to decide whether an attack is currently under way.

Intrusion detectors can also monitor traffic to determine whether an organization's security policies are being violated without malicious intent. For example, a current employee may attempt to open a port for external traffic for experimental purposes. The organization may have a policy disallowing external traffic on particular ports. The intrusion detector can detect such violations.

Intrusion detectors generate alerts and alarms as we discuss in Section 7.5. Problems with false positives and false negatives exist with intrusion detectors as they do with all monitoring systems.

Determining whether a particular data anomaly reflects an intrusion is not an easy task. We discuss an example in more detail in Section 7.8.

7.3   How to Monitor

Monitoring systems typically interact with the elements being monitored, as shown in Figure 7.1. The system to be monitored (Systems 1, 2, ... in Figure 7.1) can be as broad as a collection of independent applications or services, or as narrow as a single application. If the system is actively contributing to the data being monitored (the arrow labeled "agentless") then the monitoring is intrusive and affects the system design. If the system is not actively contributing to the data being monitored (the arrow labeled "agent-based") then the monitoring is nonintrusive and does not affect the system design. A third source of data is indicted by the arrow labeled "health checks." External systems can also monitor system or application-level states through health checks, performance-related requests, or transaction monitoring.

The data collected either through agents or through agentless means is eventually sent to a central repository ("Monitoring data storage" in Figure 7.1). The central repository is typically distributed—so it is logically but not physically central. Each step from the initial collection to the central repository can do filtering and aggregation. The considerations in determining the amount of filtering and aggregation are: the volume of data being generated, the potential failure of local nodes, and the granularity of the necessary communication. Retrieving the data from local nodes is important because the local node may fail and the data become unavailable. Sending all of the data directly to a central repository may introduce congestion to the network. Thus, selecting the intermediate steps from the local nodes to the central repository and the filtering and aggregation done at each step are important architectural decisions when setting up a monitoring framework.

One strategy for making the filtering/consolidation decision is to consider the effect of the loss of data. Some data represents instantaneous readings that

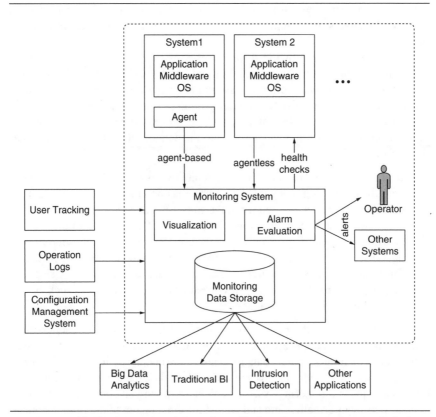

FIGURE 7.1 Monitoring system interacting with the elements being monitored [Notation: Architecture]

are shortly to be superseded by another set of instantaneous readings. Loss of one set of readings may not affect the overall monitoring or the triggering of alarms.

Once monitoring data is collected, you can do many things. Alarms can be configured to trigger alerts that notify operators or other systems about major state changes. Graphing and dashboards can be used to visualize system state changes for human operators. A monitoring system also allows operators to drill down into detailed monitoring data and logs, which is important for error diagnosis, root cause analysis, and deciding on the best reaction to a problem.

So far we have presented a traditional view of the monitoring system, but this view is increasingly being challenged by new interactions between the monitoring system and other systems. We show these outside of the dotted areas in Figure 7.1.

You can perform stream processing and (big) data analytics on monitoring data streams and historical data. Not only can you gain insights into system characteristics using system-level monitoring data, you may also gain insights into user behaviors and intentions using application- and user-level monitoring data.

Because of these growing different uses of monitoring data, many companies are starting to use a unified log and metrics-centric publish-subscribe architecture for both the monitoring system and the overall application system. More and more types of data, including nontraditional log and metrics data, are being put into a unified storage, where various other systems (whether monitoring-related or not) can subscribe to the data of interest. Several implications of the unified view are

- It significantly reduces the coupling of any two systems. Systems interact with the unified log in a publish-subscribe fashion that makes publishers ignorant of the specific identity of the subscriber and vice versa.
- It simplifies the integration of multiple sources of data. Much of the analysis of monitoring data involves the correlation of multiple sources of data. We have mentioned relating business metrics to performance metrics. The sources of these measurements are not going to be the same. Using a central log store allows data to be correlated based on attributes such as time stamps rather than their source.

The line between the monitoring system and the system to be monitored is getting blurred when application and user monitoring data are treated the same as system-level monitoring data—data from anywhere and at any level could contribute to insights about both systems and users. Thus, the architecture presented here is no longer just a monitoring system architecture when you consider all the other systems putting information into and getting information out of the central storage.

We now discuss several aspects of the architecture in more detail, namely, the method of retrieving monitoring data, monitoring operations, and data collection and storage.

Agent-Based and Agentless Monitoring

In some situations, the system to be monitored already has internal monitoring facilities that can be accessed through a defined protocol. For example, the Simple Network Management Protocol (SNMP) is a common mechanism for gathering metrics from servers and network equipment. It is especially useful on network equipment because that equipment often comes as a closed system and you cannot install monitoring agents. Windows Management Instrumentation (WMI) provides access to management data for Windows systems. You can use protocols like Secure Shell (SSH) to remotely access a system and retrieve available data. Agentless monitoring is particularly useful when you cannot install agents, and it can simplify the deployment of your monitoring system. In Section 7.2, we discussed applications that contributed information to the monitoring system.

Application Response Measurement (ARM) is an industry standard that provides ways for an application to trigger actions such as requesting an external ARM-supported system to start or stop tracking a transaction and correlating times spent in different systems for a single transaction.

The agent-based and agentless approaches both have their strengths and weaknesses. The agentless approach is better in terms of deployment and maintenance effort. However, it is less secure if the collection repository is outside of your network because more ports need to be opened and firewall rules relaxed to allow different layers of a system to communicate its data to the external world. In contrast, an agent on a host can communicate with the OS and applications locally and send all collected information over a single channel. This also allows an agent-based approach to optimize network traffic and processing overhead.

In addition to collecting monitoring data from inside a system, you can collect information from an external viewpoint. You can set up health checks to periodically check a system or conduct performance monitoring from an external user's point of view.

As we mentioned earlier, multiple types of information are considered monitoring information or at least as contributing to monitoring data analysis. Questions to be considered when designing a system include: Where does this information come from? How does this information fit into the application and monitoring architecture? What are the quality implications?

Monitoring Operation Activities

Some operations tools, such as Chef, monitor resources such as configuration settings to determine whether they conform to prespecified settings. We also mentioned monitoring resource specification files to identify changes. Both of these types of monitoring are best done by agents that periodically sample the actual values and the files that specify those values.

Treating infrastructure-as-code implies that infrastructure should contribute monitoring information in the same fashion as other applications. This can be through any of the means that we have discussed: agents, agentless, or external.

In Chapter 14, we discuss how to perform fine-grained monitoring of the behavior of operations tools and scripts. This can include assertions over monitoring data. For instance, during a rolling upgrade a number of VMs are taken out of service to be replaced with VMs running a newer version of the application. Then you can expect the average CPU utilization of the remaining machines to increase by a certain factor.

Collection and Storage

The core of monitoring is recoding and analyzing time series data, namely, a sequence of time-stamped data points. These data points are typically acquired at successive intervals in time and represent certain aspects of states and state changes. In addition, the system being monitored will generate time-stamped event notifications at various levels of severity. These notifications are typically output as logs. The monitoring system can conduct direct measurement or collect existing data, statistics, or logs and then turn them into metrics, which have a set of properties usually indicating time and space. The data is then transferred to a repository using a predefined protocol. The incoming data streams often need to be further processed into a time series and stored in a time series database. Three key challenges are: collating related items by time, collating related items by context, and handling the volume of monitoring data.

- *Collating related items by time*. Time stamps in a distributed system are not going to be consistent. Different nodes in a single cluster may differ in their clocks by several microseconds. Different nodes across multiple clusters may differ by much more. Thus, using time stamps to decide that two items are related in time or even if they are sequential is problematic. Using time intervals to determine relation rather than exact measurements is one technique, although it may miss some relationships if the time difference between two related measurements is greater than the window defined as determining a relationship.
- *Collating related items by context*. The context for a message is often as important as the message. Suppose you are performing a rolling upgrade and replacing two instances in each wave of the upgrade. Different nodes may produce log messages about the state of the instance upgrade. Without being able to determine that two messages refer to the same instance, it is very difficult to reconstruct a sequence of events to diagnose a problem. This same problem occurs when monitoring data flows. A particular message from an instance of a system is in direct response to the input to that instance and in indirect response to a user request or an external event. Identifying both the direct and indirect triggers for a particular message is important to enable analysis of performance problems or failures.
- *The volume of monitoring data*. You may need a retention policy to cope with the volume of data collected. A simple retention time for your monitoring data may be suboptimal: you may be interested in storing finer-grained monitoring data for the recent past and increasingly course-grained data aggregates for a more distant past. Your varying policies may also be related to your current remaining storage capacity and the criticality of the metrics. For fast processing of queries or display, you may also choose to process the basic data into special views with indexing.

One popular time series database is the Round-Robin Database (RRD), which is designed for storing and displaying time series data with good retention policy configuration capabilities. As we are moving into the big data age, big data storage and processing solutions are increasingly used for monitoring data. You can treat your monitoring data as data streams feeding into streaming systems for real-time processing, combined with (big) historical data. You can load all your data into big data storage systems such as Hadoop Distributed File System (HDFS) or archive it in relatively inexpensive online storage systems such as Amazon Glacier.

7.4 When to Change the Monitoring Configuration

Monitoring is either time- or event-based. Time-based monitoring is based on a reporting interval but the interval does not need to be a constant interval for all applications and throughout the execution of an application. Timing frequency and generation of events should all be configurable and changed in response to events occurring in the datacenter. Some examples of events that could change the monitoring configuration are:

- *An alert.* We discuss alarms and alerts in detail in the next section. One consequence of an alert could be that the frequency of sampling is increased. The frequency could be decreased if the alert does not turn into an alarm.
- *Deployment.* Any of the deployment scenarios we discussed in Chapter 6 can trigger changes to monitoring. These include

  - *Canary deployment.* Since the purpose of a canary deployment is to test new versions, these new versions should be monitored more closely.
  - *Rolling upgrade.* We discussed several possible race conditions depending on your packaging of services into VMs. Closer monitoring will help detect the occurrence of a race condition more quickly.
  - *Feature activation or deactivation.* Activating or deactivating features will change the behavior of services. Such changes should trigger changes in the monitoring configuration.

- *Changes to any infrastructure software including DevOps tools.* Changes to infrastructure software can affect the behavior or performance of applications just as changes to the applications themselves.
- *Changes to any configuration parameters.* One of the major sources of errors in modern distributed systems is incorrect parameters. More detailed monitoring in the wake of changes to parameters can help detect problems more quickly.

7.5 Interpreting Monitoring Data

Now assume that the monitoring data (both time- and event-based) has been collected in a central repository. This data is being added and examined continually, by both other systems and humans. We begin by describing some general principles about the content of log messages.

Logs

A log is a time series of events, since it is a sequence of records ordered by time. Records are typically appended to the end of the log. Rather than directly recording the states, logs usually record the actions performed that may result in a state change of the system. The changed value itself may not be included in the log.

Logs play an important role in monitoring, especially in DevOps settings. In development, programmers are familiar with application logging, where they print out system states and actions to assist their development, testing, and debugging activities. Most logging will then be turned off or removed for production deployment, so that only warnings and critical information will be logged and displayed. Logs written by the developers are frequently for the developers' use rather than for operators. One of the motivations of the DevOps movement has been to treat operators as first-class stakeholders, and this means writing logs that they can use. The sources of these logs are not only applications. Web servers, database systems, and the DevOps pipeline all produce logs. Another type of important log is composed of the log lines printed by operations tools. When a system is being upgraded by an upgrade tool, migrated by a migration tool, or reconfigured by a configuration management tool, logs about the operations or change histories are recorded—these are very important for error detection and diagnosis of any operation, including those triggered by the DevOps pipeline.

Logs are used during operations to detect and diagnose problems. Logs are used during debugging to detect errors. Logs are used during post-problem forensics to understand the sequence that led to a particular problem. Some general rules about writing logs are

- Logs should have a consistent format. This is not always possible since some logs are produced by third-party systems out of your control. The log production that is within your control should be consistent, however.
- Logs should include an explanation for why this particular log message was produced. Tags such as "error condition detected" or "tracing of code" can be used.
- Log entries should include context information. Context is more than date and time; it also includes information to support tracking the log entry such as:
  - Source of the log entry within the code
  - Process ID for the process executing when the log entry was produced
  - Request ID for the request that caused that process to execute this log producer
  - VM ID for the VM that produced this message
- Logs should provide screening information. Log messages are collected in a repository that is accessed through queries. Severity levels are an example of screening information, alert levels are another.

Graphing and Display

Once you have all relevant data, it is useful to visualize it in various ways. Most monitoring data is time series data, which is amenable to plotting. A flexible system should allow you to have full control over what to plot and how. Some monitoring systems have strong visualization capabilities embedded. There are also specialized systems just for visualization and querying, such as Graphite, which support real-time graphing of large amounts of data.

You can set up a dashboard showing important real-time aspects of your system and its components at an aggregated level. You can also dive into the details interactively or navigate through history when you detect an issue. An experienced operator will use visual patterns of graphs to discern problems. The graphs may show spikes, bursts, cyclic variation, steadily trending up/down, or sparse events, all of which need to be understood in the context of characteristics of the state being monitored and the environment. In a virtualized environment running on shared physical resources or in a continuous deployment setting, there will be a large number of legitimate changes going on, such as resource scaling, resource migration, and rolling upgrade. Therefore, visual abnormalities may not always indicate problems. It is becoming increasingly challenging for human operators to look at the graphs and figure out which interactions in a complex setup lead to the perceived graphs. This naturally leads to challenges for alerting systems and alarm configuration.

Alarms and Alerts

Monitoring systems inform the operator of significant events. This information can be in the form of either an alarm or an alert. Technically, alerts are raised for purposes of informing and may be in advance of an alarm (e.g., the datacenter temperature is rising), whereas alarms require action by the operator or another system (e.g., the datacenter is on fire). Alarms and alerts are generated based on configurations set by the operators. Alarms and alerts can be triggered by events (e.g., a particular physical machine is not responding), by values crossing a threshold (e.g., the response time for a particular disk is greater than an acceptable value), or by sophisticated combinations of values and trends.

In an ideal world, every alarm generated by the monitoring system represents a real issue that needs attention and every issue that needs attention generates an alarm. When an alarm is triggered, the alerts should provide information to enable further diagnosis of the situation and provide guidance as to the remedial action. Unfortunately, we do not live in an ideal world. The typical issues therefore are

- How do you configure your monitoring system to reduce false positives (alarms without the necessity for action) and false negatives (the necessity for action without an alarm being raised)?
- How do you configure your monitoring system so that the alerts provide necessary information to diagnose an alarm?

In a monitoring system with many metrics covering many aspects of the system, generating an alert or an alarm can pose very tricky tradeoffs. A problem for operators is receiving false positive alarms or a flood of alerts from different channels about the same event. Under such conditions, operators will quickly get "alert fatigue" and start ignoring alerts or simply turn some of them off. On the other hand, if you try to reduce false positives, you may risk missing important events, which increases false negatives. If your alarms are very specific in their triggering conditions, you may be informed about some subtle errors early in their occurrence—but you may risk rendering your alarms less effective when the system undergoes changes over time, or when the system momentarily exhibits interference of legitimate but previously unknown operations. Continuous deployment and cloud elasticity exacerbate the problem. As you can see, determining the correct configurations for a monitoring system is nontrivial and will vary depending on the environment and the severity of problems you might uncover.

Some general rules to improve the usefulness of alerts and alarms are

- Introduce context to your alarms. This could be as simple as disabling certain alerts during specific times or actions; for example, when replacing a physical computer it does not make sense to raise alarms about the computer's health. Other more complex contexts could be related to external events or interfering operations.
- Alarms can not only go off if something happens, they can also be set to go off if an *expected* event did *not* happen. This helps with drills and testing of your alarms since you can set an alarm to go off when an event that you know is not going to happen does not, in fact, happen.
- Aggregate different alerts that are likely referring to the same events.
- Set clear severity levels and urgency levels so people or systems receiving the alerts can act accordingly.

Diagnosis and Reaction

Operators often use monitoring systems to diagnose the causes and observe the progress of mitigation and recovery. However, monitoring systems are not designed for interactive or automated diagnosis. Thus, operators, in ad hoc ways, will try to correlate events, dive into details and execute queries, and examine logs. Concurrently, they manually trigger more diagnostic tests and recovery actions (such as restarting processes or isolating problematic components) and observe their effects from the monitoring system.

We discussed reliability engineers in an earlier chapter. The essence of the skill of a reliability engineer is the ability to diagnose a problem in the presence of uncertainty. Once the problem has been diagnosed, frequently the reaction is clear although, at times, possible reactions have different business consequences.

If there are business consequences of the reactions to a problem, the escalation procedures of an organization should indicate who makes the decision.

Monitoring DevOps Processes

DevOps processes should be monitored so that they can be improved and problems can be detected. In Chapter 3, we discussed the improvement of processes. Such improvement depends on gathering information.

Damon Edwards lists five things that are important to monitor:

1.   A business metric
2.   Cycle time
3.   Mean time to detect errors
4.   Mean time to report errors
5.   Amount of scrap (rework)

Observe that the raw data for these five values will come from multiple sources and multiple reporting systems. As we said earlier, being able to correlate data from multiple sources is important in interpreting monitoring data.

7.6   Challenges

In this section, we discuss the four challenges mentioned in Section 7.1 in more detail. These challenges arise due to DevOps practices and modern computing environments.

Challenge 1: Monitoring Under Continuous Changes

A problem in the operations context is signaled by a deviation from normal behavior. Normal behavior assumes the system is relatively stable over time. However, in a large-scale complex environment, *changes are the norm.* We are not talking about varying workloads or dynamic aspects of your application, which are often well anticipated. The new challenges come from both cloud elasticity, making infrastructure resources more volatile, and the automated DevOps operations, which trigger various sporadic operations (such as upgrade, reconfiguration, or backups). Sporadic operations and continuous deployment and deployment practices make software changes more frequent. As we have seen, deploying a new version into production multiple times a day is becoming a common practice. Each deployment is a change to the system and may impact monitoring. Furthermore, these changes may be happening simultaneously in different portions of an application or the infrastructure.

To what extent can you use the past monitoring data of your system to do performance management, capacity planning, anomaly detection, and error diagnosis for the new system? In practice, operators may turn off monitoring during scheduled maintenance and upgrades as a work-around to reduce false positive alerts triggered by those changes. When change is the norm, this can lead to no monitoring—for example, flying blind.

One technique is to carefully identify the non-changing portions of the data. For example, use dimensionless data (i.e., ratios). You may find that although individual variables change frequently, the ratio of two variables is relatively constant. Another technique is to focus monitoring on those things that have changed.

We also discussed, in Chapter 6, the merits of canary testing as a way of monitoring a small rollout of a new system for issues in production. One technique is to compare performance of the canaries with historical performance. Changes that cannot be rationalized because of feature changes may indicate problems.

Another challenge related to monitoring under continuous changes is the specification of monitoring parameters. When your system is not overly complex and relatively stable, specifying what needs to be monitored, setting thresholds, and defining the alerting logic can be done manually. In the past, large-scale monitoring reconfiguration usually happened during major infrastructure changes and migration to new infrastructure, for example, to a virtualized environment or the cloud. A new software release came in every few months, and there was ample time left for tweaking the monitoring part. Even in such an environment, the complexity of setting up and *maintaining* a monitoring system during occasional changes is still often mentioned as the number one challenge identified by monitoring experts.

Continuous changes in the system infrastructure and the system itself complicate the setting of monitoring parameters. On the infrastructure side, we mentioned in Chapter 5 that there can be significant variation in performance even if you are requesting exactly the same VM type. This variance is due to factors beyond your control, such as the CPU type you get. Your monitoring may need to be adjusted for this, or you may configure your scaling controller to replace VMs that are performing slowly with new VMs, in the hope of being luckier with the next ones.

As a consequence, it makes sense to automate the configuration of alarms, alerts, and thresholds as much as possible. The monitoring configuration process is just another DevOps process that can and should be automated. When you provision a new server, a part of the job is to register this server in the monitoring system automatically. When a server is terminated, a de-registration process should happen automatically.

We discussed changing configurations as a result of changes, but the assumption in that discussion was that the rules for changing the configurations would be manually set. Some thresholds can be automatically derived from underlying changes. Other thresholds can be automatically learned over time. For example, the monitoring results during canary testing for a small set of servers can be the new baseline for the full system and populated automatically.

Challenge 2: Bottom-Up vs. Top-Down and Monitoring in the Cloud

One major goal of monitoring is to detect faults, errors, or small-scale failures as soon as possible, so you can react to them early. In order to fulfil this goal, it is natural to monitor in a bottom-up fashion: Ideally, errors in lower layers and in *individual* components can be detected early, before they propagate and affect upper-layer application servers or applications themselves in terms of *aggregated* values. There are two challenges here.

First, there is usually a lot more to be monitored at the individual component level and other low levels. You may have a single application that is composed of several components deployed on hundreds of servers, which are in turn supported by networks and storage components. A single root cause may trigger noticeable phenomena across many components. It can be very tricky to correlate these phenomena and identify the root cause in a real-world environment.

A second challenge is related to continuous change caused by cloud elasticity and automation. In the cloud, lower-layer infrastructure and servers come and go for both legitimate reasons, (e.g., termination for preventing server drifts, scaling out/in, and rolling upgrades) as well as illegitimate reasons (e.g., instance failures or resource sharing uncertainty). It is a nontrivial task to discern the illegitimate reasons from the legitimate ones.

Adopting a more top-down approach for monitoring cloud-based and highly complex systems is an attempt to solve these problems. You monitor the top level or aggregated data and only dive into the lower-level data in a smart way if you notice issues at the top level. The lower-level data must still be collected but not systematically monitored for errors. The collection of lower-level data is only done to the degree that performance, storage, and shipping overhead allow. This is not a "silver bullet," for a number of reasons. First, you are sacrificing the opportunity to notice issues earlier, and it might already be too late to prevent a bigger impact once you notice that something is wrong at the top level. The second and even more problematic issue is how to dive down to the lower-level data. The time between the moment you detected the higher-level issues and the moment the lower-level root cause happened may be fairly long. Modern distributed systems have built-in fault tolerance to mask faults and errors, preventing them from manifesting at the system level and affecting end user experience. Essentially, it may take a variable amount of time from when an initial fault takes place until it propagates through the system to become apparent. You cannot simply rely on the time stamp of your high-level error detection. Also, you cannot assume the metrics and logs related to the original problem are still there: They may have disappeared together with a dead node or region of your network. Trying to ship all relevant data to a safer location all the time poses a major challenge in a large-scale system with millions of external and internal requests per second.

There is no easy solution. Bottom-up and top-down monitoring are both important and should be combined in practice. Context information is usually much more important than just time stamps. As already mentioned, incorporating operations knowledge about changes into your monitoring data is an important way of correlating events better.

Challenge 3: Monitoring a Microservice Architecture

In earlier chapters, we discussed that one consequence of DevOps on architecture is the adoption of a microservice architecture, which enables having an independent team for each microservice. However, this turns your system into a *fanout* system or a *deep-hierarchy* system. Every external request may potentially travel through a large number of internal services before an answer is returned. If any of the services is slow to respond, the overall response time will suffer. In a large-scale system, one part or another may experience some slowdown at any given time, which may consequently lead to a negative impact on an unacceptable portion of the overall requests. We described long-tail responses in Chapter 2. Micropartitions and selective replication enable easier migration, which can be used to move services away from problematic parts of the network. Monitoring multiple requests for the same service and determining that only one response is necessary becomes quite a challenge.

Another challenge that microservice architectures raise is how to identify and fix "slow" nodes. We mentioned the difficulty of determining sporadic performance problems earlier. In a microservice architecture with many nodes, determining slow but still performing nodes becomes more of an issue. The questions are: What is "slow"? How do you choose appropriate thresholds? We discuss some solutions in the case study in Chapter 13.

Challenge 4: Dealing with Large Volumes of Distributed (Log) Data

In a large-scale system, monitoring everything will incur a considerable overhead in terms of performance, transmission, and storage. A large-scale system can easily generate millions of events, metric measurements, and log lines per minute. Some considerations about this volume of data are

1. The performance overhead of collecting metrics at a small time interval might be significant. Operators should use varied and changeable intervals rather than fixed ones, depending on the current situation of the system. If there are initial signs of an anomaly or when a sporadic operation is starting, you may want finer-grained monitoring, and you may return

to bigger time intervals when the situation is resolved or the operation completed.

2. You should use a modern distributed logging or messaging system for data collection, rather than building one yourself. A distributed logging system such as Logstash can collect all kinds of logs and conduct a lot of local processing before shipping the data off. This type of system allows you to reduce performance overhead, remove noise, and even identify errors locally. LinkedIn developed Kafka, a high-performance distributed messaging system, largely for log aggregation and monitoring data collection. It adopts an event-oriented architecture and decouples the incoming stream and the processing.

3. With the emergence of big data analytics, researchers are starting to use advanced machine learning algorithms to deal with noisy, inconsistent, and voluminous data. This is a space to watch.

7.7 Tools

There are many monitoring systems and tools available, both from the open source community and from commercial players. Due to an overloading of the term *monitoring*, it is often difficult to compare them. We list a few typical ones.

- *Nagios*: Nagios is probably the most widely used monitoring tool due to its large number of plug-ins. The plug-ins are basically agents that collect metrics you are interested in. A large and active community maintains plug-ins for many metrics and systems. However, Nagios' core is largely an alerting system with limited features. Nagios also has limitations in dealing with a cloud environment where servers come and go.

- *Sensu and Icinga*: There are several systems that try to improve over Nagios. Sensu is a highly extensible and scalable system that works well in cloud environments. Incinga is a fork of Nagios. It focuses on a more scalable distributed monitoring architecture and easy extension. Inciga also has a stronger internal reporting system than Nagios. Both systems can reuse Nagios's large plug-in pool.

- *Ganglia*: Ganglia was originally designed to collect cluster metrics. It is designed to have node-level metrics replicated to nearby nodes to prevent data loss and over-chattiness to the central repository. Many IaaS providers support Ganglia.

- *Graylog2, Logstash, and Splunk*: These three are distributed log management systems, tailored for processing large amounts of text-based logs. There are front ends for integrative exploration of logs and powerful search features.

- *CloudWatch and the like*: If you are using a public cloud, the cloud provider will usually offer some solution for monitoring. For example, AWS offers CloudWatch, which allows hundreds of metrics to be collected at a fixed interval.
- *Kafka*: As mentioned earlier, due to the significant challenges in collecting a large amounts of logs and metrics for real-time, multiple uses by other systems, specialized systems were designed for the collection and dissemination part. Kafka is a publish-subscribe messaging system used not only for monitoring but also for other purposes.
- *Stream processing tools (Storm, Flume, S4)*: If you are collecting a large number of logs and metrics continuously, you are effectively creating monitoring data streams. Thus, stream processing systems can be used for processing monitoring data, even in a real-time fashion.

Apdex (Application Performance Index) is an open standard developed by an alliance of companies. It defines a standard method for reporting and comparing the performance of software applications in computing. Its purpose is to convert measurements into insights about user satisfaction, by specifying a uniform way to analyze and report on the degree to which measured performance meets user expectations.

7.8   Diagnosing an Anomaly from Monitoring Data—the Case of Platformer.com

Two of the reasons we identified for monitoring are to identify performance problems and to detect intruders in the system. In this section, we explore a small case study with some data from Platformer.com that demonstrates three aspects:

- Distinguishing between these two causes of an anomaly in performance data is not always straightforward.
- Deciding whether monitoring the performance of an application is a Dev responsibility or an Ops responsibility is not straightforward.
- Lack of coordination between different organizational entities incurs costs.

We begin by presenting the context for the data collection we are going to discuss. We then discuss the data that was observed and how it was analyzed. We conclude this section by reflecting on the implications of this incident on DevOps and responsibilities.

Context

Platformer.com is an Australian Platform as a Service (PaaS) provider. It provides a marketplace of applications, such as content management solutions, customer relationship management, and so forth, as well as databases and other underlying systems. Through their interface, the customer can specify when and how the system should scale, how disaster recovery should be implemented, and so forth. The value comes from providing services at a higher level of abstraction than IaaS, so that customers can get similar benefits without having to deal with all the complexity of understanding and managing IaaS services. It also allows customers to avoid being locked into a specific cloud vendor because the same interfaces suffice for multiple cloud providers.

Platformer.com's customers have three options for infrastructure services:

1. *Access third-party cloud providers.* AWS, Microsoft Azure, Rackspace, and OrionVM are among the third-party providers supported by Platformer .com. Customers access the third-party cloud providers through a Platformer.com portal.
2. *Access on the customers' private cloud.* This option places Platformer.com software on the customers' private cloud.
3. *Access on the customers' private datacenter.* This option is similar to using the customers' private cloud but does not require the customer to have adopted a cloud solution.

Platformer.com provides its services using a layered architecture, as shown in Figure 7.2. The salient portions of the architecture are the API that provides a customer with a common view of Platformer.com services, regardless of the

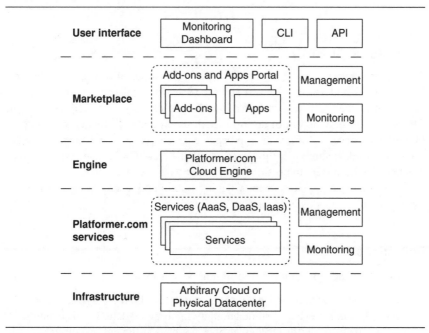

FIGURE 7.2   Platformer.com architecture [Notation: Architecture]

delivery mechanism, and the dashboard that is used to display monitoring information back to the customer.

The sample customer using Platformer.com in this discussion is called PhotoPNP. They are a not-for-profit organization that offers online services for the exhibition, education, and publication of photography. They rely on Platformer.com's services to provision the web content management solution Joomla, integrated with an e-commerce application.

Data Collection

When providing a single API that is implemented on disparate platforms, a PaaS provider such as Platformer.com must either provide the least common denominator of the platforms they support (services that all of the platforms support) or simulate services available on some platforms with services available on others.

In the case of monitoring, Platformer.com provides measurements of CPU, disk, memory, and networking performance. These measures serve the Platformer.com needs of load balancing activities, the provisioning of new VMs, if required, or the de-provisioning of existing VMs. The measurements are reported to Platformer.com's customers through a dashboard.

Because of the variety of platforms supported by Platformer.com, a variety of measurement tools are used, depending on the underlying platform. Table 7.2 provides a list of the underlying platforms and the monitoring solution used in each platform.

Detecting an Anomaly

PhotoPNP's servers have a normal CPU utilization of about 5%, but on September 17 and 18, it spiked to around 17%. This spike was correlated with variations in the other resources for which metrics were collected. A spike in CPU load is one symptom of an intruder in the system—in this case, in one of PhotoPNP's servers. Platformer.com became concerned and investigated why the spike occurred. It subsequently turned out that PhotoPNP had an opening night to introduce the system to potential users and this caused the spike. This observation was confirmed by subsequently having PhotoPnNP check Google Analytics for user-level metrics over the period in question.

Reflections

This example leads to a number of different conclusions.

- One question within the DevOps community is who the first responder should be in the event of some anomaly in observed data. In this example, we see that the platform provider does not have sufficient insight to

TABLE 7.2   Monitoring Solutions Associated with Platforms

Infrastructure Provisioning	Management Solutions	Monitoring Solutions
Public IaaS Provider		
Amazon Web Services	AWS management API	AWS CloudWatch
Rackspace	Rackspace management API	Rackspace cloud monitoring & alerting
OrionVM	OrionVM API	Nagios or AlienVault
Microsoft Azure	Azure management API	Azure monitoring & alerting
IBM/SoftLayer (public)	SoftLayer management API	SoftLayer comprehensive monitoring & alerting
DigitalOcean	DigitalOcean management API	Nagios or AlienVault
Private IaaS Provider		
IBM SoftLayer (private)	SoftLayer management API	SoftLayer comprehensive monitoring & alerting
Telkomsigma	(CloudSigma) VMware management API	Nagios, AlienVault
On-Premise IT		
Physical servers (Linux)	Non-virtualized servers are set up and managed utilizing tools such as Puppet and Chef	Nagios or AlienVault
	Virtualized servers are built and managed utilizing virt-manager utilities and/or OpenStack API	
Physical servers (Windows)	Non-virtualized servers are set up and managed utilizing Microsoft SMS	Nagios, AlientVault
	Virtualized servers are set up and managed utilizing VMware API and/or OpenStack API	

attribute the anomaly to a normal application-level demand. Consequently, if the development team had been the first responder, then the confusion would not have happened. On the other hand, if the spike in CPU usage had actually been caused by an intruder, having the application developers be the first responders would have delayed an adequate response. Furthermore, requiring the application developers to be able to detect an intruder is asking them to have a level of expertise far beyond their application.

- The suggestion that an intruder might have penetrated PhotoPNP's servers came from an examination of the CPU utilization, but the attribution of the load required application-level metrics rather than just system-level metrics.

   Earlier we discussed using log management systems to correlate logs or metrics taken from diverse sources. In the case of Platformer.com, the application-level metrics were not available because their visibility was limited to basic system-level metrics.

- If PhotoPNP had informed Platformer.com that they were planning an event that would generate additional load, then the suspicion of a potential intruder would not have occurred. In the Platformer.com case, the business-level entity was in another organization—but this type of local communication could just as easily have happened within the same organization, so this could easily become an example of the lack of coordination between business and IT entities.

7.9 Summary

Monitoring is done for at least five purposes: detecting failure, diagnosing performance problems, planning capacity, obtaining data for insights into user interactions, and detecting intrusion. Each of these purposes requires different data and different means of interpreting that data.

Many monitoring systems exist, and a common structure allows one to take advantage of both time- and event-based collection. A common structure also caters to applications that are monitoring-aware and those that are not. The monitoring pipeline typically results in monitoring data being in a central repository where it can be queried and used to generate alarms, alerts, and visualizations. Correlating data from multiple sources is important in performing analysis.

Continuous deployment practices increase the frequency of change—to applications and to underlying infrastructure. There is less time for observing and adjusting your monitoring solution to these changes. This suggests automating the monitoring configuration process itself, including automated smart, dynamic adjustments to alarm thresholds. The cloud environment makes some parts of the system more opaque and introduces constant changes at the infrastructure level. Monitoring tools need to be designed for such an environment.

Systems are increasing in complexity, degree of distribution, and size. The sheer volumes of the metrics and logs demand new generations of infrastructure to support the collection, transfer, and storage for monitoring data. And once you have collected a lot of monitoring data, big data analytics has the potential for enabling insight from it. These insights are no longer just about system health and performance, but about your business and customers.

7.10 For Further Reading

The book *Effective Monitoring and Alerting* [Ligus 13] goes into the details of many of the topics we discussed in this chapter.

Ganglia is one of the monitoring tools we mentioned and is the subject of the book *Monitoring with Ganglia* [Massie 12].

The microservice architectural style is described in *Building Microservices: Designing Fine-Grained Systems* [Newman 15].

The idea of the log as a unifying mechanism comes from a LinkedIn page [Kreps 13].

The research into the impact of delaying a response to a Google query comes from a Google research blog [Brutlag 09].

Damon Edwards provides the types of monitoring of DevOps processes in [Edwards 14].

As always, we rely on Wikipedia for many descriptions:

- Real user monitoring: http://en.wikipedia.org/wiki/Real_user_monitoring
- Synthetic monitoring: http://en.wikipedia.org/wiki/Synthetic_monitoring
- Apdex: http://en.wikipedia.org/wiki/Apdex

The tools that we mentioned can be found at the following links:

- RRDtool: http://oss.oetiker.ch/rrdtool/
- Application Response Measurement: https://collaboration.opengroup.org/tech/management/arm/
- Logstash: http://logstash.net/
- Nagios: http://www.nagios.org/
- Sensu: http://sensuapp.org/
- Icinga: https://www.icinga.org/
- Graylog: http://graylog2.org/
- Splunk:http://www.splunk.com/
- CloudWatch: http://aws.amazon.com/cloudwatch/
- Kafka: http://kafka.apache.org
- Storm: http://storm.incubator.apache.org/
- Flume: http://flume.apache.org/
- S4: http://incubator.apache.org/s4/

8

Security and Security Audits

To err is human;
to really screw up you need the root password.
—Anonymous

An initial reaction to discussing security in a DevOps context is to assume that security practices are not agile and can actually hinder improving the time between a code commit and acceptance into normal production. We believe that this reaction is totally backward. Discussing adoption of DevOps practices without considering security makes the security team a critic of these practices and dooms the adoption of these practices in many enterprises. In our case study in Chapter 12, we see an approach that advocates integrating the security team into the adoption process. Other DevOps activities that are candidates for the discussion of security are

- *Security audits.* When a security audit is imminent, coordination between Dev and Ops becomes quite important.
- *Securing the deployment pipeline.* The deployment pipeline itself is an attractive target for malicious attackers.
- *Microservice architectures.* The adoption of a microservice architecture introduces new security challenges.

Security audits are a fact of life for financial organizations, organizations dealing with health records or other private information, or organizations that have internal controls over financial transactions (i.e., almost all organizations). Security audits examine all aspects of an organization, from its policies to its implementation. One of the catchphrases in DevOps is "infrastructure-as-code," which means treating scripts and DevOps process specifications as code, and applying the same quality control practices as you do with code. Security policies, governance rules, and configurations can be naturally embedded in the infrastructure code and automation for easier auditing. The automation can also help generate audit outputs and detect noncompliance. We return to this idea when we discuss specific aspects of security.

A security audit verifies that a set of requirements on the organization has been met. These requirements provide an umbrella over all of the policies and practices of the organization, both the IT and non-IT sides. This means that whatever practices a development group follows, these practices must conform to these requirements.

We organize this chapter by first discussing what is meant by security, then we discuss threats to security. At that point, we present the organizational roles to determine who is supposed to be doing what to counter those threats. We discuss techniques to counter the threats and explain what happens during a security audit. We then cover the security issues from an application development perspective, and we close by discussing the security of the deployment pipeline.

8.1   What Is Security?

Security is easily remembered by the acronym CIA, which stands for confidentiality, integrity, and availability. Confidentiality means that no unauthorized people are able to access information; integrity means that no unauthorized people are able to modify information; and availability means that authorized people are able to access information.

Authorization is an essential part of these definitions. The most secure system has no users but also no utility. It is difficult to allow access by authorized people and deny access by unauthorized people. Authorization has two elements that answer the following questions: Who is trying to access or modify information and do they have the right to perform the operation they requested? Both of these elements are supported by a variety of techniques. In a DevOps context, the information and operation here refer to the application and, equally important, to the deployment pipeline (e.g., source code, build servers, and specific pipeline operations). Furthermore, these techniques have been incorporated into widely available software packages. One of the strong recommendations from security experts is "Do not roll your own." The errors that may creep in can be subtle. You may not detect subtle errors, but they could provide an avenue for an attacker to compromise your system.

One of the assumptions that security professionals make is that any single means of protection can be circumvented. Consequently, security professionals advocate "defense in depth," which means that an attacker must circumvent numerous different defenses to compromise your system. Consider the case of how sensitive information on paper is protected in a typical spy story: There is a fence around an isolated estate, guard dogs inside the fence, a security system at the house, locked doors inside of the house, and a safe inside that contains the sensitive paper. This analogy points out that the amount of security you need is a result of a cost/benefit analysis. How much your organization is willing to spend on security will depend on how big the loss can be if your system is compromised. Equivalently, how much an attacker is willing to spend on compromising your system will depend on the benefit achieved from the compromise.

Defense in depth also raises the idea that your system can be compromised. In this case, you will need mechanisms to detect what has happened and to give you the ability to recover. Thus, associated with CIA is also a property of nonrepudiation: Individuals cannot deny the operations they performed on the data in your system. This is important for auditing.

Another concept is that of the life cycle of an attack. Attacks can be prevented, detected while they are occurring, or detected after they have succeeded. In the security world, measures to minimize security risks are called "security controls." Controls can be preventive, detective, or corrective depending on their use within the life cycle of an attack.

Finally, controls can be additionally categorized by who is responsible for their implementation. Technical controls such as encryption are implemented within the application or the infrastructure. Organizational controls such as applying security patches within 24 hours of their release by the vendor are implemented through policies and procedures developed by the organization. These two types of controls can be complementary, and an action may require both types. For example, not only should security patches be installed promptly (organizational), but the system should be able to respond to queries about its patch level (technical).

8.2 Threats

The point of view of an attacker provides one perspective for you to take when designing your system or subsystem. Microsoft has introduced the acronym STRIDE for a threat model. See Figure 8.1. STRIDE stands for

- *Spoofing identity.* An example of identity spoofing is illegally accessing and then using another user's authentication information, such as username and password.
- *Tampering with data.* Data tampering involves the malicious modification of data.
- *Repudiation.* Repudiation threats are associated with users who deny performing an action without other parties having a way to prove otherwise.
- *Information disclosure.* Information disclosure threats involve the exposure of information to individuals who are not supposed to have access to it.

Spoofing identity

Tampering with data

Repudiation

Information disclosure

Denial of service

Elevation of privilege

FIGURE 8.1   The STRIDE model

- *Denial of service.* Denial of service (DoS) attacks target the service availability to valid users—for example, by making a web server temporarily unavailable or unusable.
- *Elevation of privilege.* In this type of threat, an unprivileged user gains privileged access and thereby has sufficient access to compromise or destroy the entire system.

Notice how these threats relate to the CIA definitions. Spoofing circumvents authentication; tampering violates the integrity of data; repudiation is an explicit statement of what should happen in the event of a breach or attempted breaking of the rules; information disclosure is the negative of confidentiality; denial of service compromises availability; and elevation of privilege is a technique to allow compromise of any of the CIA properties.

During an audit, you should be prepared to demonstrate how the controls in your system, in conjunction with other organizational and platform controls, reduce the likelihood of any of these threats succeeding.

Insiders pose one source of threats that should be mentioned here. The Software Engineering Institute (SEI) defines an insider as "a current or former employee, contractor, or business partner who has or had authorized access to an organization's network, system or data." An attack by an insider means that the insider has misused that access to intentionally violate one of the CIA properties.

Verizon reports that approximately 15% of data breaches are from insiders. Thus, insider attacks are significant and should be considered in an organization's security analysis.

Both Verizon and the SEI loosely characterize the motives behind an attack as being

- *Financial*. Financially motivated attacks involve the theft of money or of items that can be sold. Markets exist for items such as credit card numbers, and tracking those markets can enable you to gain some understanding of the extent of the breaches that have occurred.
- *Intellectual property*. Many attacks attempt to gain intellectual property such as trade secrets from commercial organizations or classified information from government organizations.
- *Sabotage*. This category of attacks includes denial-of-service attacks and modifying customer-facing information such as websites as well as out-and-out destruction of sensitive data by disgruntled employees.

Finally, it is important to note that many problems can be caused by security-related mistakes rather than intentional attacks, as we highlighted in the chapter quotation—"To err is human; to really screw up you need the root password."

8.3   Resources to Be Protected

Of the elements of security, C and I refer to "information." Information is one of the key resources to be protected. Information can be at rest, in use, or in transit. This includes information related to DevOps activities such as source code, test data, logs, updates, and who placed a version into production.

- *Information at rest* is stored on persistent storage. It can be accessed either through the software systems under the control of one of the actors or through physical possession of the persistent storage. As an example of the former, a legitimate user logs in and receives credentials allowing him or her to access certain data. The software that can be accessed understands the credentials and knows how to retrieve, display, and modify the data. As an example of the latter, a copy of sensitive data is kept on a laptop that is stolen from the trunk of your car. In the DevOps context, in addition to protecting persistent application-related data, you should consider whether the information you put inside plain-text log lines is sensitive, whether your test data (which could be an early snapshot of sensitive production databases) is well protected, and whether the security around your source code is enough. The tradeoff is between protecting everything through encryption and subsequent decryption and the resulting performance costs of this encryption and decryption. As we will see, the smallness of microservices may make it easier to enforce service-specific security policies.
- *Information in use* is being used by an information system. It may be displayed to the user, it may be stored in a cache for performance or reliability

reasons, or it may be stored in a virtual machine (VM), also for performance or reliability reasons. This data is available to users who can access the portion of the information system where it currently exists. In the DevOps context, many advocate a much shorter server life span (as a result of using phoenix or ephemeral servers, where any change means replacing the old set of VMs through a set of new VMs) for reliability reasons and to prevent server drift. This practice also adds to security in terms of destroying any sensitive information accumulating in the server over time. Information in use may also be internally encrypted and only decrypted for display. This may have the effect of rendering caching proxies less effective and usage more cumbersome.

- *Information in transit* is being moved from one location to another. If the movement is over a network, then the data is available through access to the network. Network access can be through one of the endpoints of the transit or through an intermediate point. Legitimate reasons exist for accessing data at an intermediate point. For example, monitoring network traffic or using a firewall to filter certain information are both legitimate reasons and rely on network access at an intermediate point of the transfer of information. If the data is being moved from one VM to another on the same physical host or from one process to another through a socket, then it is accessed by either the endpoints or the transmission mechanism. There are many techniques to encrypt the data during movement and authenticate both ends. This adds more complexity in certificate and key management and incurs an additional performance penalty for both authentication/authorization and encryption/decryption. We discuss this later in a microservice architecture context.

Computational resources also need to be protected. This is the A in CIA. Authorized users should be able to access the resources they need. Again, this includes DevOps resources such as the build server. Resources can become unavailable to an authorized user for multiple reasons, including:

- The simplest reason is that you have forgotten your password or misplaced your keys. We all use multiple systems with different keys and requirements for password length and composition. We also are exhorted not to reuse passwords and have specific keys for specific purposes. In such a situation, forgetting a particular password or mismanaging a key is not uncommon. Systems should provide a means to recover or revoke a password or key.
- Your password, key, or certificate could also have been maliciously reset or compromised. If an attacker succeeds in compromising your certificate, the attacker may pretend to be you and act maliciously. Systems should have a means to verify and alert users when a change has happened and provide corrective means quickly. Managing, monitoring, and replacing

compromised certificates are complicated processes that take a significant amount of time, often amid downtime.
- The system you are attempting to access may be the subject of a denial-of-service attack. Such an attack is an orchestrated series of requests to a system to consume resources responding to these requests and keep the resources unavailable for authorized users. Installing gateway filters based on IP addresses is one method for preventing a denial-of-service attack from being successful. An application programming interface (API) key is another popular method for limiting access rate and user abuse, whether intentional or not.

Not every intruder will compromise one of the CIA properties. Suppose an unauthorized student is using your system to do homework. This user's demands on the system are low, and so the use does not compromise availability. The student does not access or modify information so the student's use does not compromise C or I. This use, however, is still illegitimate and is an indication that your computational resources are not well protected.

A final concern about resource protection comes from the special nature of the cloud, especially in a DevOps context. Developers have the ability to easily create new VM images (e.g., for using a heavily baked deployment approach) and instances of them. It is easy to lose track of both images and instances, particularly when there is no charge for usage, such as in a private cloud. *VM image sprawl* is the term used to describe the proliferation of VM images to the point where the management systems lose track of them. The images take up significant storage, and losing track of which image is used in what instances also introduces additional security problems. For example, lost images or instances are not patched as a portion of the normal patching process and, consequently, are more vulnerable to attacks than patched systems. A recent example of a successful attack because of VM sprawl comes from BrowserStack: An old unutilized VM was unpatched and was compromised by Shellshock. The unutilized VM contained some credentials that were then used to compromise active VMs.

Lost instances may also incur additional cost. Mechanisms should be in place to track both VM images and instances. For example, Netflix's Simian Army tool suite includes a Janitor Monkey that finds unused resources and removes them. A Security/Conformity Monkey also finds security violations or vulnerabilities. Some operating systems vendors provide specific tools, such as Red Hat's Spacewalk, to help you check if the latest patches have been applied to your (virtual) machines. As said earlier, enforcing a shorter lifetime for a VM, meaning terminating and replacing it after a fixed amount of time even when healthy, is a technique for preventing VM sprawl. This not only prevents configuration drifting and encourages better fault tolerance, but also improves security in terms of reducing attack profile, helping tracking and removing sensitive information traces.

8.4   Security Roles and Activities

We identify four different roles related to security, and we will refer to these roles when we discuss the various activities that are involved in achieving a secure environment. The people performing these roles may belong to the same organization or to different organizations.

1.   *Security architect.* A security architect is responsible for the design of an organization's network to achieve security for the network. The security architect is also responsible for overseeing the implementation of the network.

2.   *Solution architect.* A solution architect is responsible for the design of systems to support the organization's business functions. Developers implement these designs.

3.   *IT staff.* The organization's IT staff is responsible for monitoring and tracing any events related to potential security attacks. The IT staff is also responsible for the implementation of the architecture designed by the security architect.

4.   *Platform provider.* The platform provider is responsible for securing the perimeter of the computing platforms used by an organization, ensuring isolation among the customers of the platform, and ensuring that the customers get adequate resources when they require them. The platform provider also provides services used by the security architect.

You can see a set of dependencies among these roles. The platform provider provides a base potentially usable by many teams and business units within many organizations, the security architect designs security for the whole organization using the services provided by the platform, the IT staff implements and monitors the design provided by the security architect, and the solution architect designs systems within the security architecture and the platform.

In a DevOps context, the activities performed by these roles can be embedded in tools. As always, the use of these tools needs to be logged and kept for future examination by the auditor. There is also a debate on the developers' role in implementing network- and infrastructure-related security through infrastructure-as-code, subsuming some of the responsibilities of IT staff. With security vendors starting to expose APIs and allowing more automation, and with the emergence of software-defined networks (SDNs), this is becoming a reality. The most important question is perhaps not whether Devs or Ops plays a role in implementing a particular layer of security design, but whether these layers are implemented, tracked, automated, and auditable.

The security community has been active in identifying and publicizing the types of controls that an organization should adopt to manage the risks to information security and privacy. Two different widely used lists are published by the National Institute of Standards and Technology (NIST 800-53) and by the International Organization for Standardization/International Electrotechnical Commission (ISO/IEC 27001). These two organizations collaborate, and their lists cross-reference each other, so the two lists are very similar. We will base our discussion on NIST 800-53 because it is freely available over the Internet.

One method of organizing controls is by functionally related categories. The categories of NIST 800-53 are: access control, awareness and training, audit and accountability, security assessment and authorization, configuration management, contingency planning, identification and authentication, incident response, maintenance, media protection, physical and environmental protection, planning, personnel security, risk assessment, system and services acquisition, system and communication protection, system and information integrity, and program management.

As you can see, these categories span a wide range of supporting activities by a wide collection of actors within an organization. Enumerating all of these controls takes over 200 pages. The controls differentiate between activities that are performed by the organization (e.g., the organization establishes and manages cryptographic keys for required cryptography employed within the information system) and those performed by the information system (e.g., the information system implements organization-defined cryptographic uses and types of cryptography required for each use in accordance with applicable federal laws, executive orders, directives, policies, regulations, and standards).

The controls are mainly specified in terms of outcomes, not in terms of methods. For example, one control states, "The information system uniquely identifies and authenticates [*Assignment: organization-defined specific and/or types of devices*] before establishing a [*Selection (one or more): local; remote; network*] connection." There is no discussion of how the system identifies and authenticates, only that these processes occur. Conformance to these controls should be implemented, tested, and monitored. For implementation, it is a matter of having manual or automatic means to enforce the control. You will rely on existing security mechanisms in a platform, service, or library to realize security features like authorization, authentication, and encryption. Some of these mechanisms can be automated by code invoking a security product's APIs. Then the code becomes an important piece of evidence during auditing. For testing, this means that security-related testing is integrated into the continuous deployment pipeline, which may result in static analysis in an integrated development environment (IDE) before commit or security-related test cases in the build and test server. This continuous and integrated nature of security testing becomes another evidence for auditing. Finally, for monitoring, production environment security monitoring and conformance checking can be implemented to detect and correct any security violations. Thus, DevOps processes and tools that implement a control can be used without compromising an organization's ability to pass an audit and, in many cases, can improve the organization's ability.

From an auditor's perspective, the method for assessing an organization's security controls begins with the policies adopted by the organization. An auditor initially attempts to answer the question: Are an organization's policies adequate to meet the security requirements for the system or systems under assessment? The organizational controls enumerated by NIST 800-53 or a derivative provide a starting place for the assessment. Different domains have used NIST 800-53 as a starting point and added their own domain-specific requirements. These domain-specific variants have names more familiar than NIST 800-53. Names such as HIPAA for health information, PCI for credit card information, and security profiles for the electric grid are familiar to those in these respective industries. The auditor then moves on to the controls chosen to implement a particular policy and attempts to answer the questions: Are the chosen controls adequate to implement the policy?; Are they implemented correctly?; and Are they operating as intended? Again, the implementation controls enumerated by NIST 800-53 or its derivatives provide a starting place for determining whether the controls are adequate. The correct implementation and the operation as intended are determined by the auditor based on evidence provided by the organization.

We focus on the technical controls—those, at least partially, that the software architect has some input or control over. Three categories exist for the technical controls:

- *"Within channels" controls*. These are the controls that allow legitimate users access to the network, authenticate users, and authorize users to access information or resources. These controls support and should be applied to activities involved in the application itself, in the deployment pipeline, and in other operations. For example, modifying a script should involve authentication and authorization and be tracked in a version control system.
- *"Outside of channels" controls*. These are the controls intended to prevent access through nonapproved channels. For example, side channel attacks exploit timing, power consumption, and sound and electrometric leaks to gain useful information. Information can be at rest, in use, or in transit and should be protected in any case. Resources should not be used outside of normal channels, and side channels should be evaluated.
- *Auditing*. A record should be kept of various activities within the system such as use of resources, accesses to data, and modification of data. The auditing controls are intended to ensure that such a record is created and maintained. Again, in the DevOps context, this means a number of different things: 1) the use of automated tools and infrastructure-as-code to record security testing results; 2) the integration of security testing in the DevOps pipeline; and 3) the security of the DevOps pipeline and other operations themselves. All these provide good evidence in a security audit.

8.5 Identity Management

Unless an application is available to all users without restriction, identifying users is a prerequisite to determining whether a particular use is legitimate. Identity management refers to all tasks required to create, manage, and delete user identities. During the lifetime of a user account this will include adding or removing access to specific systems, resetting lost passwords/keys, and enforcing periodic password/key changes. All activities within the identity management task should be logged for audit purposes—not only human-initiated activities but also activities performed by tools or scripts. Invocations among (micro)services also need to be authenticated.

Identity management relates to the roles of platform provider and security architect. The platform provider provides the means to manage the identity of all of the users of the platform, and the security architect does the same for all users of an organization's systems. Given that the organization's systems are executing on a platform from the platform provider, the organization's users are also users of the platform. The same identity management can be used for accessing applications, development activities, and deployment pipelines. We return to this concept when we discuss authorization.

A wide variety of commercial identity management tools exist. Identity management controls are categorized under the identification and authentication category of NIST 800-53. Identity management tools as well as authentication tools are under the control of the security architect and operated by the IT staff.

Authentication

Authentication controls are intended to verify that you are who you say you are. That is, they protect against a spoofing attack. The "you" here also covers a service invoking another service. We focus on authenticating an individual here and will discuss authentication among services later.

Authenticating an individual gets complicated for a number of reasons.

- "You" may not mean you, but may mean a system operating on your behalf.
- "You" may not be uniquely identified by the system, but instead "you" may be a role.
- Your authentication mechanism (e.g., password or certificate) may have been compromised.
- You may no longer be an employee or authorized user of the system.

In the security world, there are three methods of authenticating you as an individual. These are something you know (e.g., a password), something you have (e.g., a smart card), or something you are, (e.g., fingerprints). Some systems require you to use two of these three categories. For example, your ATM card has a magnetic strip (something you have) as well as requiring a PIN (something you know). Other systems require you to know multiple things. For example, you need to know both a password and the answer to a secret question. The system can authenticate itself to you prior to asking for something you know. For example, systems show a picture you have preselected to identify to you that you have arrived at the correct location before you enter a password. This technique is an attempt to avoid having your password compromised. A certificate-based approach is more secure in some aspects but requires more complicated infrastructure setup.

In the remainder of this discussion we elaborate on the different types of authentication controls.

Controls Relating to a System Operating on Your Behalf

The considerations for hardware and software differ, and we divide the discussion accordingly.

Hardware

A strong method for ensuring only legitimate devices can connect to your system is to require devices to be preregistered. This prevents man-in-the-middle attacks. A weaker form is for your system to leave state (e.g., a cookie) on an external system that identifies that system as having previously accessed your system. If the external system does not have such state then additional questions may be asked.

Maintenance is one scenario where the strong method becomes important. That is, your system has a physical component (e.g., an ATM machine), and maintenance is performed via utilization of a specialized computer. Registering the specialized computer prevents the use of a fraudulent maintenance computer to compromise the system.

Software

We mentioned that your system may access resources through a platform. Your system has users, and your system is a user of the platform. Requiring the user to log on first to your system and second to the platform is undesirable for several reasons:

- Users resist having to log in several times to the same system. Although you know that, in reality, there are multiple systems, from a user's perspective it should appear as a single system.
- The platform resources accessed may be shared across several users, and exposing the same password to multiple users violates authentication controls. Requiring each user to have an account on the platform as well as on your system becomes cumbersome. Deleting an account, for example, requires coordination between your system and the platform that is difficult to manage.

Two fundamental techniques exist to allow one system to access another system with user credentials. One is single sign-on and the other is separate, system-managed credentials.

- Single sign-on relies on a distinct credential providing service. Multiple different versions of this capability have been developed, but the best known is perhaps Kerberos. The initial sign-on generates a Kerberos ticket-granting ticket. This ticket is used to sign on to other systems that accept Kerberos tickets.
- System-managed credentials means that your system maintains a set of credentials suitable for access to platforms or other systems. Your system utilizes these credentials on behalf of your users to authenticate use of the platform. The issue you must consider is how to protect these credentials from unauthorized access. This is the subject of a distinct set of controls in NIST 800-53 called "System and Communications Protection." Certificates also have an expiration date, and one common cause for inability to communicate with external systems is the use of expired certificates. One of the members of Netflix's Simian Army is a Security Monkey, among whose responsibilities is checking for expired certificates.

Role-Based Authentication

Role-based authentication (RBA) is a technique for assigning identifications based on roles rather than on identity. For example, you may log in as super user using the root password. Super user is a role you are assuming; it is not your identity. RBA simplifies some problems since once a role is identified, the access privileges associated with the role can be automatically assigned. The problem with RBA is that there is no traceability. A problem may be traced to "super user" but not to an individual. We discuss how to rectify this problem in the next section on authorization.

Controls to Prevent Compromising Passwords

Passwords can be compromised in several different ways:

- *An attacker breaks an individual's password through various forms of brute force attacks.* Controls specify minimum password length, password lifetime, and limits on password reuse.
- *A user allows her or his password to be determined through social engineering means.* There are controls about security education for users, but perhaps the most notorious use of social engineering to determine a password comes from the Stuxnet worm. This worm exploited the fact that some system passwords were hard coded in the software being attacked. In addition, these passwords were available on the Internet. One of the controls to prevent this type of attack is to require that default passwords be changed before a system goes into production.
- *An authorized user changes roles or leaves the organization.* We defer the discussion of role change to the next section on authorization, but when an employee leaves the organization, a control specifies that their account privileges are deleted within a short time frame.

- *Your system is compromised, allowing determination of passwords.*
  Controls specify that passwords must be stored in an encrypted form using
  an approved piece of cryptographic software. The data is difficult to decrypt
  if it is encrypted in a sufficiently strong manner. Furthermore, the software
  that provides encryption and decryption should be approved, meaning it has
  been tested by an authorized testing organization.

Authorization

Once a user is identified then it becomes possible to control access to resources
based on the privileges granted to that user. The most relevant control in NIST
800-53 is "AC-3, Access Enforcement":

> *Control: The information system enforces approved authorizations for*
> *logical access to information and system resources in accordance with*
> *applicable access control policies.*

As with authentication, authorizations can be logged, whether the resources
are accessed manually, through scripts, or through tools, along with who was
responsible for the authorization.

Techniques to Control Access to Resources

There are two fundamental techniques used to control access to resources: access
control lists (ACLs) and capabilities.

- *ACLs*. An ACL is a list of users or roles and allowed operations attached
  to a resource such as a file system or database field. When a user asks for
  access to the resource to perform a particular operation, the list is examined
  to determine whether that user or role has the right to perform that
  operation on the resource.
- *Capability*. A capability is a token that grants particular rights on a
  resource. A good analogy is a key and a lock. The capability is the key; the
  resource maintains the lock. When access is requested, the resource will
  verify that the token provided with the access request contains sufficient
  privileges for the provider of that token to be granted access.

Regardless of the technique used to control access, the least possible privileges should be granted to a user or role to enable them to perform their required
tasks.

Role-Based Access Control

We discussed RBA and pointed out that assigning privileges to roles simplifies managing large number of users. Now we discuss how that translates into
access control. Every user should have a unique identity as far as the system is

concerned, but users may change roles and, consequently, have different access privileges. Consider, for example, the root password. Suppose an operator gets promoted to a position that does not require root access. The options are: leave the root password as is, resulting in an unauthorized individual knowing the root password; change the root password, resulting in all of the remaining operators having to learn a new password; or use role-based access control (RBAC).

RBAC is based on a mapping between individuals and roles. A role is allowed certain access privileges, and the identity management system maintains a mapping between users and roles. It also maintains a mapping between roles and privileges. Then, when a user changes roles, the mapping between users and roles is changed as well and the authorization system is provided with the information appropriate to the new role. Thus, our hypothetical operator who gets promoted will be removed from the operator role and assigned a new role, and the identity management system will provide the appropriate new privileges to that individual while removing root access. This transition is also logged for auditing purposes.

In large organizations, RBAC becomes complicated because it assumes a uniform definition of roles across the organization. Many large organizations have similar, but different, roles in different portions of the organization. Defining roles uniformly may involve moving responsibilities from one role to another in certain places within the organization. Suppose, for example, one portion of an organization has adopted continuous deployment practices and another has not. To what role do you assign "can authorize deployment to production?"

Let us use a deployment pipeline example to illustrate this. In the popular Jenkins continuous integration tool, there are alternative ways of providing authorization to a deployment pipeline. You usually want to have different authorization to different parts of the pipeline. For example, developers may not be authorized to trigger certain types of quality assurance (QA) jobs or deploy to a production environment. You can use the Jenkins Role Strategy plug-in to define different roles that have authorization to different parts of the pipeline. Then you can link jobs to roles. At the moment, this is done through regular expression on job names, which can be complicated to manage especially if you have many jobs. An alternative approach is to use the Jenkins Matrix Authorization plug-in where you organize all your jobs into different folders. You can then define authorizations at the folder level by mapping them to users or roles.

8.6 Access Control

Identity management controls are intended to prevent spoofing, tampering, information disclosure, and elevation of privilege for those users who have gone through authentication and authorization channels. Tampering and information disclosure are still threats from those who do not go through authentication and authorization channels, and are discussed in this section. We discuss the remaining elements of STRIDE—nonrepudiation and denial of service—in the next section.

We begin by discussing controls intended to prevent tampering and information disclosure. The spy analogy that we used in the beginning of this chapter is relevant here. Prevent access and then, if that does not work, make what the intruder finds not usable.

Preventing Access

Working from outside in, the boundary of the system or the organization's software system must be defined. That is, the resources to be protected must be clearly identified. Resources may have different levels of protection, for example, available for reading by unauthenticated users (a website open to the Internet) or not available for reading by unauthenticated users (an internal website).

Defining Boundaries

The organization's network can be partitioned into subnets, each with its own boundary. Each subnet represents a collection of resources that have the same level of protection. Using a microservice architecture provides more flexibility in determining the boundaries. Once the boundaries are defined, then communication from outside of a boundary to inside of the boundary or vice versa can be controlled. Access from the Internet is treated differently from mobile access, which, in turn, is different from internal access. There should be firewalls, gateways, routers, guards, malicious code analysis, and virtualization systems or encrypted tunnels protecting each subnet. This overall structure is within the domain of the security architect.

Tools that live outside of a subnet—such as deployment tools—must have permissions granted so that they can deploy into the subnet. These permissions can be inherited from the invoker of the tool. A special subnet called the Demilitarized Zone is open to Internet access and restricted in accessing the internal network. External-facing websites are typically placed in this subnet. With this type of boundary protection, external access must go through a firewall or gateway that can restrict port usage, maintain blacklisted IP addresses, and perform other checking. An attacker that wishes to gain unauthorized access to data or resources must first go through perimeter checking at the boundary.

Isolation

Isolation is a technique related to perimeter checking. Isolation means that logically distinct functions are kept apart, either physically or logically. Physical separation has historically been used—do not connect resources you wish to protect to the Internet and restrict physical access to these resources. In the modern world, physical separation is appropriate in very few cases, typically in a process control context, but is not feasible when the main means of accessing systems is over the Internet.

Isolation, in the modern context, can be interpreted as separation. You can separate computational functions, for example, based on their security sensitivity. Then a boundary can be established and credentials can be required for data or a process to cross that boundary. Sensitive personal data can be separated from other data. Then access can be allowed, with one set of credentials, to the set of attributes, with a different set of credentials to the personal data, and with a third set of credentials to both.

When resources are shared, such as two VMs sharing a single physical machine, then isolation is enforced by the system software executing on the physical machine. Memory, disk, and networks can all be shared in a cloud environment. Isolation of memory is performed using virtual memory techniques, isolation of disk is performed using partitioning of disks, and isolation of network usage is performed by the network protocols used.

Encryption

In order to prevent an attacker from gaining access to data, whether at rest or in transit, encryption is used to protect that data. Many of the controls in NIST 800-53 describe the use of cryptographic algorithms and software. The algorithm and the software must be certified to be both strong and correct in order to pass an auditing process.

Data in use can only be reached by breaking the isolation of processes. Data in use is typically not encrypted both for performance and human reasons. It takes time to encrypt and decrypt data—this is the performance reason. Humans have difficulty reading encrypted data—this is the human reason.

Observe how the different techniques are complementary. Isolation identifies boundaries, boundary controls prevent unauthorized access, and encryption means that once an attacker reaches data, it cannot be interpreted.

Other Considerations

Three other considerations are relevant in terms of preventing access. These are: decommissioning data, patching, and change management.

1. Data that is no longer useful still might remain on the system. This data could be available for an attacker. Some controls deal with how to decommission data. This may involve removal from all of the locations where it has been stored, but it can also involve keeping copies of the data for auditing purposes.
2. Systems have vulnerabilities. Vendors repair vulnerabilities through patches. These patches must be applied. Controls specify that patches must be applied promptly and that systems must be able to report their patch level upon request.
3. Tracking the versions and patch levels of all of the software on your system is important, not only when performing root cause analysis but also from a security perspective. Which potential vulnerabilities in your system have been patched is something that is important to know. Not only the versions

of the software but also the versions of the configuration specifications and the deployment specifications are important to track for the purposes of being able to prove that your system can withstand particular types of attacks. The existence of a set of configuration management controls is of particular importance to DevOps. Not only is changing a configuration directly without going through the normal process bad practice, it also may violate security controls and cause a problem during a security audit.

Let us use a service authentication example to illustrate all this. The communication between different services or between services and browsers may need to be authenticated and also encrypted to prevent eavesdropping or man-in-the-middle attacks. One way of doing this is the use of HTTPS to encrypt the traffic. With it, the client service also gains a strong guarantee on the server-side service being who it claims to be. A problem with this is that the organization needs to manage the HTTPS certification issuing and revoking processes, the automation of which is nontrivial. If you have many microservices and servers, this can become a significant overhead for the teams and the deployment pipeline. There are also performance penalties due to the many authentications among microservices and the encryption rendering reverse proxies (e.g., Squid) unusable. You may want to have strong security at the boundary so that you can choose not to use encryption inside your secured network, and only use it when you communicate past the boundary.

Who Is Responsible for the Prevention Controls?

We have identified three roles that are relevant for the prevention of unauthorized access—security architect, solution architect, and platform provider. Border protection is the responsibility of the owner of the system just inside the border. That is, the platform provider is responsible for protecting access to the platform's resources, the security architect is responsible for protecting access to the organization's resources, and the solution architect is responsible for protecting access to particular systems. Defensive programming and lack of trust in incoming messages are two of the design practices that characterize secure development principles.

The same concept of ownership determines responsibility for the other types of prevention controls. If it concerns a portion of the system under your control, then you are responsible for protecting the data, ensuring auditability, and keeping the patches up to date.

8.7   Detection, Auditing, and Denial of Service

We have discussed preventative measures, but detecting attacks while they happen touches on a different set of controls. All of these controls involve monitoring. Resources can be monitored for abnormal usage patterns. Messages can be monitored for a wide variety of different characteristics, ranging from port scans looking for an open port to repeated login attempts to velocity of page fetching requests. All of these controls are provided by available tools and are the responsibility of the platform provider, the IT staff, and the security architect. The solution architect is usually not directly involved in these controls.

The R in STRIDE stands for repudiation. Both for business reasons (e.g., "I did not order that") and forensic reasons (e.g., "What damage did the attacker do?") auditing activities are important. Some of the items to be recorded include account creation, modification, override of access control mechanisms, use of privileged functions, creation or deletion of security attributes, connections from both internal and external sources, and changes to software or configuration.

Once an audit trail has been created, it must be protected. It does no good to record information if an attacker can modify that information to hide the trail. Audit records must be encrypted, stored independently of the systems that are being audited, and have protected access.

Do not confuse audit trails with logs. Audit trails persist for months or years, have legal standing, and are designed for security purposes. Logs persist for times measured in days (or less) and are designed to support operational and development needs.

Audit records are the responsibility of all of the stakeholders we mentioned. Stakeholders identify the significant events that can occur within their sphere of control and are responsible for determining that these events are added to the audit trail in a protected fashion.

The one element of STRIDE we have yet to discuss is the D—denial of service. Denial-of-service protection is the responsibility of the platform provider and the security architect. A variety of technologies and tools exist to limit the effect of denial-of-service attacks. For example, boundary control devices can filter certain types of packets and limit the ports accessed to protect interior systems. Rate-limiting or traffic-shaping switches are also used to protect against denial-of-service attacks.

8.8 Development

Controls exist in NIST 800-53 that specify aspects of the development process. To once again mention infrastructure-as-code, scripts and other inputs into DevOps tools must be developed and should be subject to the same scrutiny as application code development. On the other hand, security testing must be integrated with the deployment pipeline. Developers must demonstrate that they have explicitly addressed security requirements and have performed processes such as threat modelling and deriving quality metrics.

Five design principles for security are

1. Provide clients with the least privilege necessary to complete their task. If temporary access is needed it should be rescinded right after use.

2. Mechanisms should be as small and simple as possible. As we stated in Chapter 5, small modules with narrow interfaces are faster to test. The module will execute each test more quickly because it is smaller and the number of interface parameters to test will be smaller because the interface is narrow.

3. Every access to every object must be checked not only during normal use but also during initialization, shutdown, and restart.

4. Minimize the number of mechanisms common to more than one user and depended on by all users. Every shared mechanism is a potential information path.

5. Utilize fail-safe defaults. Argue why a particular process or client needs to have access, not why that process or client should not have access.

These design principles apply to both the application design and the deployment pipeline itself. Security is more than a matter of a good design; it is also a matter of good coding practices. Multiple lists of secure coding practices exist, and these lists have been built into static analysis tools. One of the security gates that a system should pass during the deployment pipeline is testing for coding practices. Another is testing for various runtime attack methods, such as cross-site scripting.

8.9   Auditors

With this background, what does an auditor look for? The answer is "all of the above." An auditor should want to consider everything from development practices on code and scripts to which controls are used to protect against what kinds of attacks.

As a concrete example, consider what the auditors should be asking about identity management—but note that they go through a similar sequence for all of the security elements we have discussed. First, they should consider the organization's policies with respect to provisioning and de-provisioning accounts. Are the roles within the organization clearly identified? What privileges are associated with a normal account or with specialized roles? How do the organization and their platform provider interact? Who has responsibility for the identity management system?

These questions involve the security architect and the platform provider. The concern is with policy, and the goal is to ensure that appropriate policies are in place at an organization level and that interfaces between the organization and the platform provider are well defined.

Platform providers can acquire independent certification that they are compliant to one or more of the domain-specific standards. If this is the case, they will not need to participate in this audit process.

Next, the auditors involve the solution architects and ask the same questions with respect to specific systems. Again, the goal is to examine the systems within the organization from a policy perspective. The auditors also ask questions about the development process. Is there security awareness on the part of the developers? Are there security tests in the deployment pipeline? Are reviews carried out? Are the design considerations enumerated earlier utilized and verified? Are the same practices carried out in developing scripts and using DevOps tools? and so forth.

The auditors are then interested in seeing how the policies are implemented. How is identity management implemented? How are passwords saved? How are new passwords confirmed as to strength? How are credentials for the platform managed from the organization? How is the system tested with respect to security? and so forth. Having security test cases in code and integrated in the pipeline or having security policy implementation automated in well-tested scripts is good evidence to auditors.

Finally, the auditors will ask for sample evidence. Create a new account for me, show me the privileges I get, show me the records that demonstrate how long it takes to deactivate an account once an employee leaves the organization, and show me how this links back into your change management system.

In many cases, multiple controls exist to solve the same problem. The organization being audited must demonstrate that their particular combination of organizational and technical controls will satisfy the requirements. There is no "one size fits all" type of response. If one control is defectively implemented or has no evidence, another control may satisfy the requirement being reviewed.

8.10 Application Design Considerations

The use of the cloud and microservice architecture leads to some special design considerations for security.

- A few additional security considerations must be taken for the application host, namely, the VMs in the cloud. We use AWS Cloud as an example.

  - Any cloud-wide AWS administration account (just like the root account) should not be used after initial registration and setup. Different identities (users or roles) with least privileges (to resources) should be set up using AWS Identity and Access Management (IAM) for different purposes.
  - No EC2 key pairs should be shared among different users.
  - Use server-side encryption to secure items in storage such as AWS S3.
  - No VMs should have access to the Internet except through a gateway with only the required ports. A virtual private network with appropriate subnets should be used.
  - Use AWS CloudTrail logs to monitor and audit access history.
  - Ship logs from EC2 instances to outside processing and storage components.

- Components should be able to be isolated and deployed independently without affecting other components. This is for security and other reasons we discussed earlier in the book.
- Components should be coded to be defensive and not to trust their invoker. This is true not only for security reasons but also for reliability reasons.
- Components are provided with configurations (sometimes through dynamically querying an external service) appropriate to the environment in which they are executing. The components should be coded to test all configurations at initialization and use these configurations when invoking other components or resources.
- Configurations should be saved in version-controlled persistent storage so that

  - setting and using the configurations can be tracked for auditing purposes, and
  - the values of the configurations are available in case a component fails.

- Invocation among services should be authenticated, with performance penalties of authentication being one of the considerations.
- Communication to the external world should be encrypted, and communications among internal services should consider encryption. The considerations include data sensitivity, perimeter security, and performance overhead.
- Use a well-patched base image to create other customized images for individual microservices so the attack profiles can be reduced. Consider a separate team responsible for creating the secure base image, and only allow each development team limited customization for their own services.

8.11 Deployment Pipeline Design Considerations

The deployment pipeline itself can also be hosted in the cloud, especially the testing environment, which can benefit from cloud elasticity, repetitive clean setup, and better consistency among different environments. The cloud hosting security considerations will be the same as we mentioned in the previous section. Other special security considerations may include the following:

- Lock down your pipeline environment most of the time and track all changes to the pipeline.
- Integrate continuous security testing throughout the pipeline, which includes IDE/pre-commit analysis, build and integration servers, and end-to-end testing environment.
- Integrate security monitoring in the production environment. An example we mentioned earlier is Netflix's Conformity and Security Monkeys.

- Tear down testing environments every time the respective tests are finished, or at least regularly. Not only does this reduce security risks in a long-running instance, but it also gives an opportunity to update security patches before relaunch.
- Automate the pipeline as much as possible through infrastructure-as-code, and promote code reuse, especially for improving environment consistency between various testing and production environments. This includes automating security operations through security vendors' APIs.
- Consider encrypting sensitive logs and test data, both at rest and in transit.
- No direct change is permitted to any of the environments without going through the pipeline (and its change tracking). For diagnosis, try to use monitoring data, shipped logs, and a replicated environment as much as possible without directly accessing and modifying an environment.
- Test your infrastructure code (not just application code) for security vulnerabilities.
- Be able to generate regular conformance and auditing output though automation.

8.12 Summary

Proving that your system is secure is important for any organization that wants to be certified as appropriately handling sensitive data. The proof usually is presented to an auditing organization that is trusted to perform a thorough audit.

Security requirements for particular domains have been codified into lists of controls that systems should implement. These controls are intended to protect against various threats. STRIDE—spoofing, tampering, repudiation, information disclosure, denial of service, and elevation of privilege—is one threat model. A commonly used list of controls is published by NIST. This list covers both organizational controls and technical controls. The technical controls can be categorized as those dealing with identity management, those dealing with access control, those dealing with detection of attacks, those dealing with maintaining an audit trail, those dealing with the development process, and those dealing with denial of service.

Each of these categories generates various security requirements, and they all come together when an organization is audited. An organization must know what their security requirements are, must provide evidence that controls have been implemented to satisfy these requirements, and must provide evidence that the implementation is correct.

Traditional Devs and Ops also form two areas of security concerns. Developers are concerned about application security design, while operators are concerned about infrastructure and operations environment security. Application security also depends on operations security. DevOps is moving some operations security responsibilities to developers and tools through infrastructure-as-code, developer-driven automation, and DevOps tools. This requires developers and application designers to be more aware of operation-environment security concerns.

Like any other crosscutting concerns, security verification and validation need to be considered from the beginning and performed at different stages throughout the DevOps pipeline automatically. It is nontrivial to perform proper and semi-automated security analysis and testing at the unit, integration, and system levels. Security analysis is often an expert-driven human-intensive activity. Now security analysis extends to deployment time and also requires full automation inside the continuous delivery and the deployment pipeline.

Security in DevOps is not only about application and operation security, it is also about the security of the pipeline itself, such as build/test server security, microservice component security, environment security, and security during dynamic provisioning. Treating infrastructure-as-code provides a mind set for ensuring that DevOps processes are secure.

8.13 For Further Reading

For general architecture-level security concerns, see Chapter 9 of [Bass 13].

For cloud-specific security issues, you can find an extensive catalogue of patterns at http://www.opensecurityarchitecture.org/cms/library/patternlandscape/251-pattern-cloud-computing

You can find more about the STRIDE threat model at http://msdn.microsoft.com/en/library/ee823878(v=cs.20).aspx

For ways of mitigating insider attacks, the Software Engineering Institute has a technical report [SEI 12].

NIST 800-53 is a catalogue of security controls for U.S. federal information systems. You can find it and many related publications at [NIST 13].

For some good analysis of recent security attacks, see Wikipedia's entry at http://en.wikipedia.org/wiki/Stuxnet and Verizon's report at http://www.verizonenterprise.com/DBIR/2013/download.xml

For microservice-specific security considerations, see the security chapter in [Newman 15].

You can find quite a few blog entries discussing the relationship between DevOps and security by searching for "Security and DevOps."

Wikipedia discusses security controls and their types at http://en.wikipedia.org/wiki/Security_controls

A discussion of the BrowserStack attack can be found at [ITSecurity 14].

Security Monkey is described at http://techblog.netflix.com/2014/06/announcing-security-monkey-aws-security.html

9

Other Ilities

As a child my family's menu consisted of two choices: take it or leave it.
—Buddy Hackett

9.1 Introduction

In Part Two of the book, we discussed the major functionalities of the continuous deployment pipeline, such as build, test, and deployment. There are other DevOps operations that resemble a process-like pipeline such as error detection, diagnosis, and recovery. In this chapter, we use the word DevOps pipeline to represent all aspects of DevOps.

If you are a software architect, you probably know the word "ility" is used to describe quality concerns other than those that focus on the basic functionalities and their correctness. In terms of DevOps, ilities correspond to questions such as: How well are these functionalities in your pipeline performing? Can you precisely repeat your DevOps operations when needed? How much time has passed between a business concept and its final release? How can different tools in your pipeline interoperate? We started discussing some major concerns such as monitoring and security in Part Three. In this chapter, we cover additional concerns. In Table 9.1, you can find a list of the ilities and their primary quality concerns that we discuss.

We focus on the ilities of the DevOps pipeline itself rather than the application the pipeline produces and operates on. There are certainly strong connections between the pipeline and the application. For example, the performance and recoverability of an upgrade operation may have significant impacts on the performance and recoverability of the application being upgraded—but we do not explore these connections here. We consider the ility issues of the DevOps pipeline from two different perspectives: product and process.

TABLE 9.1   DevOps Pipeline Ilities and Quality Concerns

Ilities	Quality Concerns
Repeatability	The degree to which repeating the same operation is possible
Performance	The time and resources required to execute a DevOps operation
Reliability	The degree to which the DevOps pipeline and individual pieces of software within it maintain their services for defined periods of time
Recoverability	The degree to which a failed DevOps operation can be brought back to a desired state with minimal impacts to the application being operated on
Interoperability	The degree to which different DevOps tools can usefully exchange information via interfaces in a particular context
Testability	The ease with which the DevOps operation software can be made to demonstrate its faults through testing
Modifiability	The amount of effort required to change the DevOps software, processes, or the operation environment of an application

First, the DevOps pipeline itself is a piece of software *product*, its end users are developers and operators. As with any piece of software, its design can be governed by good software architecture practices with early and explicit focus on quality concerns from its stakeholders. As advocated earlier, we consider it important to treat operators as first-class stakeholders, so as to uncover more functional and ility requirements for the DevOps pipeline.

Second, the DevOps pipeline has characteristics of a *process*. Some ilities covered here are more related to process quality and performance than product quality and performance. We can approach the improvement of such process-oriented systems at two different levels. At one level, a DevOps process may resemble a human-intensive process similar to a software development process. We can apply some of the lessons learned in improving software development processes to DevOps processes, including agility, life-cycle models, quality controls, and maturity models. In fact, the DevOps movement arguably started as an agile attempt to apply Dev tools and practices to the Ops realm. At another level, a DevOps process may fit with a workflow or business process management system where a predefined DevOps workflow is executed inside a workflow engine. The quality concerns of the workflow can be addressed by asserting pre/post-conditions of different tasks, better resource allocation, exception handling, and management of long-running transactions. In Chapter 14, we discuss treating operations as processes in more detail.

In the following, we discuss each of the ilities from Table 9.1. As in other software, the design of DevOps processes involves tradeoffs among the relevant quality concerns.

9.2 Repeatability

Repeatability is the degree to which a process can be repeated for a different application or branch. It can be measured by counting the number of failures and successes of that process. If a process that was previously successful now fails, this failure is an indication that the process is not repeatable in some different context.

Some processes, such as deploying a microservice into production, are defined by individual teams, whereas other processes, such as allocating features across microservices, are done across teams. Still other processes, such as using particular tools, may be enforced across organizations. A portion of the rollout of DevOps processes concerns deciding which processes are intra-team, which are inter-team, and which are across a whole organization. See Chapter 10 for a further discussion of this topic. Two activities are key to achieving repeatability: definition and enforcement of processes and maintaining version control over all artifacts. We discuss these activities next.

Measuring repeatability depends on being able to identify that two executions of an operation are executing the same process. One means for doing this is to examine traces of the process to ensure they have performed the same steps in the same order. In other words, we are equating repeatability and traceability. If the steps of a process cannot be identified, then knowing whether the outcome of a step is a repeat of a prior execution of that step is not possible.

Defining and Enforcing Process at the Appropriate Level

Software development and IT operations have always been human-centric, involving some creative problem-solving activities. Even with the trend toward full automation in the DevOps space, there are still human-intensive activities such as release planning and control, deriving complex monitoring rules, and problem diagnosis. This means there will be important tradeoffs between defining and enforcing repeatable actions to improve quality and allowing for leeway to enable desired creative activities.

Processes provide guidance, and, presumably, their development is the result of a rational process where various tradeoffs have been considered. Rigid enforcement of a process, however, reduces the flexibility of both Dev and Ops. Process enforcement is a matter both of automation and of social processes. Automating a process will enforce certain actions and certain gates. Social processes such as wearing a hat that says "I Broke the Build" also educate and encourage team members to conform to particular processes.

We look at developers and operators separately.

Modern developers perform their tasks using a range of different feature-rich tools such as code editors, compilers, debugging tools, static analysis tools, testing tools, and source code revision control systems. Integrated development environments (IDEs) may integrate some of these tools. Each individual tool makes its own decisions about defining and enforcing processes or allowing for leeway. However, the process flow between developer activities using the tools is less regulated. For example, a developer may choose to do minimal testing before committing large pieces of code into a repository. Not only is this large piece of code highly likely to break during building, fail the integration testing, and temporarily stop the continuous delivery pipeline for the whole team, the debugging and merging effort may also be disproportionally high.

In order to achieve repeatability, processes must enforce selected practices. The choice of which practices to enforce is a portion of the tradeoffs that go into designing a DevOps process. For example, a team may define pre-commit/ push hooks or tests as mandatory, to enable checks on a piece of code before it is integrated to an important branch. The pre-commit tests could include procedures ranging from coding-style checks to running a set of test cases. However, if these checks take too long and the developers have to wait, their productivity may decrease. The tradeoff is between the appropriate levels of enforced testing— the increased reliability that comes from extensive local testing and the risk of a build failing and affecting the pipeline.

The goal is to have some defined and repeatable best practices around the development workflow at an appropriate level. These best practices concern not only individual activities, but also the quantity and quality of the flow between individual activities in the team. In the past, this was largely promoted through education and management practices informed by life-cycle models, agile methods, and capability maturity models (CMMs). In DevOps, these best practices are increasingly enforced through repeatable automation although, again, there is a tradeoff between enforcement and rigidity.

For operators, the saying "Automate yourself out of the job!" has been a slogan of the community. IT operators have sophisticated automation tools to potentially repeat every aspect of their work. In the early days, configuration management tools such as CFEngine helped to manage the configuration updates of large clusters of servers. Even before the virtualization era, pioneers like LoudCloud and Opsware provided solutions around automated server and network provisioning. Virtualization technologies make repeatable operations much easier. Vendors like VMware and Amazon cloud have provided application programming interfaces (APIs) and tools to help achieve repeatability. Operators often have their own favorite scripts and Cron jobs to solve the special problems and pipeline different tools and platforms together.

These approaches have been useful, but they are not necessarily enforcing repeatable practices at an appropriate level. First, the flow between different automated tasks may be less regulated and repeatable. An operator may decide to perform an ad hoc sequence of tasks even when each task is embodied in scripts and is repeatable. This issue is particularly important when we consider the full pipeline and its repeatability. Second, operators also have to battle issues and outages in real time to reduce downtime. There is tremendous pressure to do something quickly rather than defining what you will be doing in repeatable scripts first, testing it, version controlling it, and then running it. Clearly defining when ad hoc nonrepeatable operations are allowed and how to remedy the situation after the event is a necessary step in balancing repeatability with real-time problem solving. Finally, defining an operation through scripts and automation tools does not inherently achieve repeatability, because scripts do change and different versions of the scripts may run at different times under different contexts. Making sure an operation is indeed repeatable when needed is nontrivial. This leads to the next section on version control.

Version Control Everything

As we have described, DevOps processes have at least two levels. Some steps are performed through the use of a single tool, and some steps involve multiple tools. Both of these levels should be under the control of a version control system to ensure repeatability. We begin by discussing the reasons why those steps under the control of a single tool (script) should be controlled by a versioning system. These steps are the scripts that operators use.

1. Scripts change over time. The change might be due to some improvements or the introduction of a new variant to do a slightly different job. It is easy to lose track of which particular version of which script was run on which systems and when. Any script or code that changes the infrastructure or environment should be version controlled just as application code is controlled by a versioning system. This is an example of treating infrastructure-as-code. In this way, not only are all the past versions of the scripts/code available, but also information about the changes is available, including the reasons behind the changes, the persons who made the changes, and the time of the changes.

2. A script often takes some parameters to run, and these parameters operate on a particular environment and make changes to that particular environment. Tracing or repeating a run or understanding a run requires more than the precise version of the script that was run. It also requires retaining the values of the parameters as well as a trace of the execution.

Tracing or repeating a run can be accomplished in different ways. The first approach is to log all the steps of a particular run, which includes what a particular step is doing to what states. This approach relies heavily on the quality and granularity of the logs your scripts produce and those produced by other people's tools and scripts (over which you do not have full control). Sometimes you have to deal with insufficient information in logs to attempt a reconstruction of a past run. A second approach is to capture the state changes of a particular run regardless of how and whether each step is logged. Some states (such as file-based configurations and artifacts) are amenable to version control since you can simply put these files into a version control system and any changes to them (by scripts or by humans) are tracked. Some other non-file-based states require additional work for periodic state capturing. For example, the states of the virtual instances running in the cloud and their relationships should be periodically captured and stored for future reference, especially if a DevOps operation has changed them. There are already tools, like Netflix Edda, that were developed to capture state changes of Amazon cloud resources and enable queries, including correlation with recent operations.

These tracing techniques reduce to a standard dependability technique of checkpointing plus logging. Checkpoint the state of the environment, and then log any requests for changes that occurred after the checkpoint was created. If the log becomes too long, then a new checkpoint can be created and the log restarted. The state of the environment and the parameters used can be determined by examining the log and the checkpoint.

This last point of responsibility for creating a checkpoint and a log of changes ties all of the steps together into a repeatable higher-level process. Several possibilities exist.

- *Deployment tools*. Maintaining traceability of the higher-level process could be accomplished by a deployment tool since it is the last stage of placing an instance in production.
- *Configuration management database (CMDB)*. As we advocate in Chapter 2 and as we see in the case study in Chapter 12, the configuration parameters are stored in a database. This database can also record accesses, so that tools and scripts that access configuration information will be known later.
- *Tagging data items*. Each script manipulates some entity. Tagging the entity with the identification information of each script that manipulated it will lead to the final deployed version having traceability information.

In all this, it is important to link particular (parts) of logs and state snapshots to a particular run of a versioned script so that your operation is completely repeatable and understandable at a later time.

9.3   Performance

A DevOps pipeline is like a piece of software where the performance is characterized by the amount of useful work it accomplishes and the time and resources used to accomplish that work. Like performance in traditional software, this can be measured by the response time to a given piece of work such as a build task or a deployment task, the throughput of these tasks at different stages of the pipeline, and their utilization of the underlying resources including both computing and human resources.

Measuring the Important Things

Before you can improve the performance of your pipeline, you should first measure it. In Chapter 10, we discuss some high-level business performance indicators of a DevOps pipeline. More detailed measurements are required in order to improve the performance of a pipeline.

At a high level, the performance of interest is the time between a business concept and its successful deployment. As the business concept is being realized and deployed, it travels through the subprocesses of the pipeline, sometimes iteratively. It is important to measure the time it spent inside each subprocess. This includes both the time the task spent waiting in a queue and the time taken for the actual execution of the task. For example, the integration test resources may be blocked by a commit on a different branch, and your commit is placed in a queue for some time until the resources are free again.

Also measure the different types of errors that occur and the reasons behind them. For example, a build error is a key source of problems slowing down the delivery pipeline. A recent empirical study from Google shows that the top build errors are related to dependency issues representing 52.68% (C++) or 64.71% (Java) of all build errors. Understanding these errors can guide your efforts for improvement.

A third type of measurement focuses on compliance. As mentioned earlier, for various reasons it is not always best to enforce best practices proactively and mechanically. Instead, monitoring compliance provides an indication of problems. Not all deviations are problems, some may be justified. On the other hand, multiple compliance deviations can indicate a need to improve a process. For best practices, this is optional; for regulatory rules, it may be mandatory. For instance, the financial industry is often required to ensure that a code review is done before any release into production, by a developer who was not involved in the actual development of a feature or patch. While this rule should be enforced by the tools in use, it is also good to monitor the compliance at release time, to make sure the enforcement mechanism has not been bypassed in some fashion or other.

Another performance measurement can focus on the time that elapsed between when a problem happened and when it was detected and subsequently repaired. Delays in detection and repair may point to improvement opportunities.

In general, our advice is: Measure the performance of those things that could slow down the pipeline and prioritize improvements based on the relative cost and benefit of each one.

Improving Resource Utilization

The provisioning of computing resources to the development team can be expensive and cumbersome. A developer needs to have access to a high-performing development environment. The provisioning of an in-house and physical development environment takes both significant time and money. A potentially extensive set of build and test servers also need to be provisioned. The test-ing and staging environments need to resemble the production environment as closely as possible, which can require expensive replication. Waste can happen anywhere in this scenario as developer machines, build/test servers, and testing/ staging environments are often provisioned for peak times and thus are underuti-lized during off-peak times.

Waste can be reduced using several different strategies.

- *Moving all the above environments to the cloud, thereby switching off machines that are currently underutilized and only paying for what you use.* This not only improves resource utilization but also helps with repeatability. Tearing down an environment when it is not in use and starting it up again when needed automatically forces a repeatable process to be defined. This results in consistent and clean environments and well-tested scripts. It further alleviates the problems caused by inconsistent environments—the "it worked on my machine" problem. With the flexible scaling of the cloud and a pipeline setting, more resources can be allocated and utilized through parallelization. These extra resources might be used to remove a bottleneck or generally increase the speed of various pipeline tasks.
- *Using containers rather than virtual machines (VMs).* Containers can be more quickly deployed than VMs. The use of containers to support a deployment pipeline is only in its infancy, and this class of applications is certain to grow.

The downside of completely moving your pipeline into the cloud is that you lose full control of and visibility into your environment if the environment is hosted on a third-party cloud. There is also some small but high-consequence risk of an outage of your entire development and testing environment.

9.4 Reliability

Software fails. Reliability refers to the capability of the overall DevOps pipeline and its individual pieces to maintain service. A DevOps pipeline has to deal with a large number of different types of tools. Some tools are local to the develop-ment environment, such as code editors and IDEs. Some services are provided through dedicated servers such as continuous build/integration. The deployment process has to deal with infrastructure services either through specific mecha-nisms of the OS/middleware or, in the cloud environment, through infrastruc-ture APIs and VMs. Some of these services have to be accessed remotely over a network. The DevOps pipeline can be seen as a distributed system of systems dealing with various distributed services. And these services and their reliability are often out of your direct control. To improve the reliability of the pipeline, you can apply a number of solutions.

Understanding the Reliability Characteristics of Different Services

Empirically understanding the reliability of various services and software in your pipeline is a critical first step in improving the reliability of the total pipeline. The increase in frequency of software release and deployment means many of these services and software are now accessed tens and hundreds of times a day. You should stress test these services and build reliability and timing profiles of the services. It is important to note that the reliability of these services cannot necessarily be improved, due to both the control and ownership of the service and the sheer complexity of the services.

Once you understand the reliability of individual services, you can use several techniques to improve the reliability without modifying or controlling the original services.

- Use a wrapper around the original service to improve reliability. The wrapper can employ standard fault-tolerant mechanisms. For example, you can use the timing profile to implement a fail-fast mechanism so that you do not wait for any service response that is slower than the 95th percentile. You can hedge your requests by issuing slightly more requests than you need to anticipate some failed or slow requests. Although this may incur additional cost, it can dramatically improve the reliability of your pipeline at critical points. You can also use the wrapper to intercept some requests so that you can redirect or reprioritize these requests to checkpoint critical states in order to enable more efficient undo upon failure.
- Use local mirrors of the remote services. This is often done in practice for dealing with remote code/software repositories and dependency resolutions. A DevOps pipeline often needs to access third-party libraries and software packages for provisioning new instances. Downloading all packages over the Internet can be unreliable at times and result in version conflicts when a new version is downloaded and used accidentally. A local mirror can both improve the reliability of the repository services and enforce versioning expectations.

Detecting and Repairing Errors Early

Just as with regular software development and debugging, a lot of the time spent on a DevOps pipeline is not the time spent on successful builds, testing, and deployments. Instead, when things go wrong, you spend a significant amount of time analyzing and fixing problems. For example, the time spent in determining build errors or deployment errors and the time spent rolling back can be a significant negative contributor to the performance of your pipeline.

One solution is to run more tests at early stages of the pipeline. But testing takes a significant amount of time, especially when multiple target platforms and large suites of integration/systems testing suites are involved. And some subtle errors only manifest themselves over time and in the large-scale production environment.

Another solution is to judiciously check some high-frequency errors earlier through better tooling. For example, as a result of the Google empirical study mentioned earlier, significant research is being done to have better dependency resolution servers enabling both backward and forward dependency resolution and thus to detect dependency-related issues earlier (i.e., before a build error is triggered).

Many early errors are subtle but they do leave traces in various places such as logs and monitoring. You can build mechanisms to examine logs and assert expected states earlier rather than react to failure alarms. Some other errors can only be detected by comparing with historical trends over time or past successful runs. We introduce some recent research results in Chapter 14 that use logs and assertions to detect errors earlier than would otherwise be the case. Once you detect these errors early, you can improve the reliability by recovering from them, which leads to our next section on recoverability.

9.5 Recoverability

Like many quality attributes, recoverability of your DevOps operation should not be an afterthought but a built-in quality from the start. The goal of recoverability is to enable easy recovery after a failure, whether the cause is an internal or external system, or human operators. There are a number of ways you can achieve this.

1. Include extensive exception handlings in your operation logic. This includes more defensive programming techniques in checking various pre- and post-conditions of a particular step, and using exception handling to repair or gracefully exit to a desired state, such as a consistent state, before the step was taken.

2. Build in support for external monitoring or recovery systems. As many operations are long-running, it is not always easy to synchronously check the outcome of an operation step and be certain the desired states will be maintained even after initial success. Imagine your task is to launch an application instance. It takes several minutes for a typical successful launch, with the instance going through several intermediary states

indicating the successful provisioning of the VM, the middleware stacks, the application, and its correct configuration. You will only know some of the intermediary results minutes later through periodic checking. Meanwhile, external monitoring and health checking services could have examined some of these conditions and, if need be, recovered from certain errors such as a failed VM. The external monitoring and recovery services should work in conjunction with the scripts specifying operations processes.

3. Design your software with operators as first-class stakeholders. Many complex recovery tasks have to be done by human operators after diagnosis of the cause. It is important for your operation software to produce relevant information either through logs or state-capturing facilities to make it easier for operators to make informed recovery decisions.

4. Make each individual step of long-running operations able to recover itself so that there are only a few situations in which the whole operation needs to be rolled back.

9.6 Interoperability

Interoperability refers to the degree to which different tools can usefully exchange information via interfaces in a particular context. The DevOps pipeline usually consists of many different tools from different commercial vendors and open source projects. This is the expected norm for such pipelines, where individual tasks are best served with highly specialized software and the interoperation of different tools is achieved through best effort rather than top-down planning. There are a number of ways one can achieve better interoperability among different pieces of the software.

Paying Attention to Interoperation of Interfaces

Although a team can build an in-house version of a tool or customize an existing tool for their tasks, most of the time they have to enable interoperation between existing tools, where they have limited control. It is important to select tools that have stable APIs, flexible scripting facilities, and an active plug-in ecosystem that contains many plug-ins for interoperating with other tools.

For example, the popular source control system Git can support the interoperation with static analysis, testing, build, and notification/messaging systems through event-based hooks: The invocation of other systems using appropriate Git outputs can be carried out before or after a Git event such as commit or push.

Understanding Existing Data Models

Good interoperability relies on the data models implied in each of the tools in the pipeline. It is important to determine the syntax and semantics of the major data models that need to be exchanged among the interoperating tools. This is not always easy.

For example, continuous integration (CI) practices are relatively mature, and there are a large number of tools supporting CI. The data models in these tools have an explicit concept around *build*. However, when we extend the pipeline to continuous deployment (CD), we need to track which build was deployed where and when. Also, not all builds will be deployed or a particular deployment may need to link back to information coming from multiple builds. The implied data model in CD is more about artifacts and mappings to infrastructures and environments. The gap between these two data models is causing some problems in using CI tools for CD purposes. These issues are particularly important when feedback is needed from deployment to build for debugging and monitoring purposes. If the interoperation is simply about a trigger from CI to CD tools, critical information will be lost. Some tools, such as Go continuous delivery software, are addressing the issue by having richer data models to capture the needs of CI/CD interoperation. If you are working with existing tools, you may need to have additional data models in your coordination scripts to track the mappings.

9.7   Testability

Testability concerns the effort required for the software to demonstrate its faults through testing. For application software, developers practice unit testing, integration testing, and so forth. However, a DevOps pipeline poses additional challenges. The challenges come from the difficulty of testing infrastructure outcomes. Recall that infrastructure-as-code is about using code (rather than manual commands) for setting up (virtual) machines and networks, installing packages, and configuring the environment for the application of interest. However, the testability of infrastructure-related code is difficult as the real execution of the code involves long-running tasks such as spinning up VMs, downloading and installing pieces of software, and performing all tasks reliably on a large number of nodes. It is not enough to know your command has been received and started—you also need to know if the expected outcomes were achieved, minutes or even hours later.

Consider Chef as an example. Chef is a popular tool to configure a large number of systems for both infrastructure provisioning and application deployment. You write Chef cookbooks to express what you would like Chef to do to nodes (physical machines, VMs, LXC containers, etc.), such as installing/updating packages and applying configuration changes. The Chef system will try to apply the cookbooks on all the nodes. How do you test your Chef cookbook code to make sure that it will do what you expect, and that the code quality is good?

Just like any other type of code, you can do unit testing on your cookbook. ChefSpec is a tool for running unit tests of Chef cookbooks. The meaning of unit-testing infrastructure code (such as a Chef cookbook) is slightly different from traditional unit testing. Remember that the code is about installing/updating packages and configurations in real nodes through convergence. It will be slow and costly to unit test if you actually launch a large number of test instances and wait for the installation/update to finish with them. This violates the key goals of unit testing—being fast and running locally so that developers get quick feedback. Thus, ChefSpec actually tests whether the inputs to Chef are what you expect, especially when the logic is complex. ChefSpec runs in the memory of a development machine and never actually executes or does the convergence. This type of unit testing can still tease out some problems early on.

Once you have passed all the unit tests, you can run integration testing, which is really testing the outcome of a Chef run in a test environment. Tools for this purpose include Test Kitchen and Serverspec. Test Kitchen is responsible for managing the integration tests, such as actually launching test machines (e.g., EC2 instances or LXC containers) and converging a given Chef run on these machines. Test Kitchen then runs the actual tests to make sure the machines are in the states you expect. The tests themselves are written in Serverspec using the RSpec language, which uses a human-readable form that links back to business scenarios, to make specifying integration test cases easier.

If you follow the test-driven development practices and write your test suite first, you are likely to produce code with improved testability.

Unit and integration testing give you confidence about your code quality and the expected behavior. However, running large-scale system tests mimicking the real production environment is still difficult to achieve.

When moving to integration and system testing, you may notice that the test cases you write often resemble monitoring rules you set up. This is not surprising as monitoring is about runtime assertions and keeping an eye on a successful provisioning. In the spirit of reuse and "once-and-only-once," you can consider the reuse of test cases in your monitoring setup or express them as monitoring rules. In turn, if there are monitoring rules that are relevant to your expected outcome for a deployment, use these monitoring rules as test cases.

As mentioned in earlier chapters, testing in the production environment is often used for testing large-scale complex applications operating in complex environments where certain problems can only be discovered in the production environment. Canary testing—running a new version or configuration on a small subset of the servers in the production environment—can minimize the risk of such testing. The same idea can also be applied to infrastructure-as-code testing where the infrastructure-affecting code is executed in a subset of the production environment with impact on a small part of the overall application and close monitoring of the behavior.

9.8   Modifiability

Modifiability is a measure of the ability to make changes in existing software. When applied to a deployment pipeline, it means the ability to change either the interactions with one of the stages in the pipeline or the conditions for moving from one stage to the next. Designing for modifiability means, in some sense, anticipating the types of changes that might be required. We divide our discussion into modifications dealing with a single tool in the pipeline and those dealing with interaction among the tools in the pipeline.

Modifications Within a Single Tool

One fundamental technique for achieving modifiability within software is to encapsulate related activities into modules and make the individual modules as loosely coupled as possible. The idea behind keeping related activities within a single module is that changes in one activity in the module will require changes in other activities within the module, but changes, hopefully, do not extend beyond that single module.

This general advice also works for scripts for the tools in the pipeline. What encapsulation means and what it means for two modules to be loosely coupled may be different, however. Tools such as Chef or Puppet are declarative rather than procedural. Fundamentally, a cookbook describes the desired arrangement of a collection of entities that is the result of executing the cookbook rather than explaining how to achieve that arrangement.

The advice for encapsulation-related activities when applied to cookbooks is: Keep the cookbooks small and focused on a single task. Changes to that task can then be accomplished by modifying a single cookbook where the interactions among the statements are clear; in a larger cookbook, there may be unexpected interactions.

There may still be interactions among cookbooks, and these can be difficult to control. One technique is to use the sequencing mechanisms provided in Chef or Puppet to control the order of the execution of the cookbooks. Use of the sequencing mechanism will provide much more insight and control over the interactions among the cookbooks than allowing Chef or Puppet to decide on the order of execution.

A second fundamental technique for achieving modifiability within software is the parameterization of variables rather than building the variables into the code. This creates a configuration parameter for the pipeline tool. We discussed the management of configuration parameters in Chapter 5. A configuration parameter provides a place to specify values for activities that may vary among users or context but these parameters also must be managed. Placing the configuration parameters in a CMDB provides a central location where the parameters can be controlled, modified, and accessed.

Modifications in the Interactions Among the Tools

In the case study in Chapter 12, we see an instance of the fact that deployment pipelines can vary among different development teams. The constituents of the pipeline can also vary over time. The types of changes that can occur to a pipeline as opposed to individual tools include:

- *Replacement of one version of a tool with another.* Version dependencies can exist across tools just as version dependencies can exist within a software application. It is hard to predict what will change in a new version. We discussed how to isolate one section of a system from changes in another section in Chapter 6.
- *Replacement of one tool with another.* Typically, replacement of a tool will require rewriting the connecting script. It is very difficult to automatically move from using one tool to another. Sometimes the tool vendor will have a migration tool to assist in the change but this is rare in the DevOps world.
- *Changing parameters that must be sent from one tool to another.* Using a CMDB reduces the scope of this problem. One tool writes information to that database, and the other reads it.

9.9   Summary

Just as there are quality concerns about any piece of application software, there are similar quality concerns about the DevOps pipeline. The DevOps pipeline has to deal with different types of software ranging from desktop IDEs to code repositories, build/testing servers, cloud infrastructure APIs, and potentially complex environments for testing/staging/production. Given the increasing frequency of software delivery and deployment, new challenges arise for achieving the ilities discussed in this chapter. The take-away message is that ilities and quality concerns should be considered early and built in, rather than adding them in as an afterthought. This is not easy when you are dealing with existing tools in a system of systems.

Table 9.2 summarizes the techniques we have described to achieve particular qualities, but nothing comes for free. Every technique for achieving a desired result for one of the ilities that we mentioned involves tradeoffs with other ilities. Understanding those tradeoffs is important to achieving a pipeline that satisfies your needs.

TABLE 9.2 Summary of Techniques to Achieve Particular Qualities

Ilities	Techniques to Achieve this Quality
Repeatability	Maintain traces of activities. Version control everything. Use a CMDB to maintain parameters. Enforce where necessary.
Performance	Measure to determine bottlenecks in processes. Tear down an environment when it is not used. Perform as many operations as possible in the cloud, where resources can be freed if not used.
Reliability	Identify failure rates of different services. Mirror services with high failure rates. Detect failures as soon as possible through tools whose job it is to monitor components for execution times outside of the norm.
Recoverability	Build in exception handling in scripts. Provide information for monitoring services. Ensure that appropriate diagnostics are generated to enable faster debugging.
Interoperability	Select tools with stable interfaces and flexible scripting facilities. Ensure data models of various phases of the pipeline are consistent.
Testability	Use unit and integration test scripts for specialized tools. Coordinate test cases with monitoring rules.
Modifiability	Modularize scripts based on expected changes to the tools. Encapsulate operations actions into small modules that are loosely coupled with each other.

9.10 For Further Reading

For ilities in software architecture, [Bass 13] contains dedicated chapters for many of them.

For common build errors, you can read the Google study published in [Seo 14].

For more about testability and test-driven development for infrastructure code, you can find good materials in [Nelson-Smith 13].

10

Business Considerations

If you want to make God really laugh, show him your Business Plan.
—Barry Gibbons

10.1 Introduction

This chapter discusses the management perspective on DevOps. As such, it is oriented toward organizations with defined processes. If you are in a startup, your management structure is going to be sparse, with low levels of bureaucracy. As your organization grows, the structure changes in all but the rarest of cases.

Introducing a substantial new technology in an established enterprise is typically both a bottom-up and a top-down process. Only the simplest technological changes, those that impact only a single team, can be introduced without buy-in from management, and no technological change can be introduced without buy-in from the technologists—in this case, Devs and Ops. The proponents for DevOps are asking for major changes in organizational structure and in how the organization interacts with external stakeholders. As such, for management to be on board, it needs to believe that the benefits outweigh the costs. We begin, therefore, with the business case for DevOps, before discussing measurements and compliance to the DevOps practices. We close this chapter by touching on other areas within an organization where Dev and Ops have interactions.

10.2 Business Case

A business case must convince management that there is a real problem being attacked, that the approach is reasonable, that the benefits outweigh the costs, and that stakeholders will not be unduly upset. Management also wants to see an

TABLE 10.1 Sections of the Business Case for the Introduction of DevOps

Section Title	Content
Problem	Why is introducing DevOps practices going to be good for the organization?
Costs	What are the expected costs of the introduction?
Stakeholder impact	What is the impact on stakeholders, both internal and external?
Risks and mitigation	What are the organizational and technical risks associated with introducing DevOps practices? How are these risks to be mitigated?
Rollout plan	What is the plan for rolling out the DevOps practices?
Success criteria	How will we know if the introduction of DevOps practices is successful?

enumeration of risks and their mitigation, an initial rollout plan, and success criteria for the project. Table 10.1 shows the sections of a typical business case for introducing DevOps. The remainder of this section discusses these points.

The Problem and Benefits from Solving the Problem

The overall case for using agile is to reduce the time between a business concept and its deployment to users. To make this more concrete for DevOps, which is arguably inspired by agile, refer to Chapter 1. DevOps is about reducing the time between committing a change to a system and the change being placed into normal production, while ensuring high quality. Ensuring high quality implies that there could be multiple iterations of problem detection and repair before the final high-quality system is promoted to normal production. Reducing the time between problem detection and its repair is also important.

The two important measures are, therefore, the time from commit to initial production and the time from problem detection to repair. For these, the current state of the organization should be benchmarked. What is the current (distribution of/median/average) time from business concept to code commit and then to deployment, and what is the current time between problem detection and repair? The business case should also set targets for these values that are to be achieved by the introduction of DevOps practices.

Setting targets is a difficult exercise. First, there are a limited number of quantitative reports on the effectiveness of DevOps practices. Second, as we identified in Chapter 1, there are five different categories of DevOps practices and each practice has some impact on achieving the target values. We return to the categories of DevOps practices in the section on rollout plans. Finally, every organization is different—so although having industry benchmarks would be helpful, such benchmarks still would need to be adapted for local circumstances.

The difference between the current values and the target values represents the benefit of DevOps. The values do not necessarily need to be financial. The benefit of reducing the time between a business concept and its deployment, for example, may be expressed in terms of time. The financial value accruing from reducing the time is even more uncertain than the estimate of the reduction in time. The case that should be made is that significant stakeholders would benefit from this reduction.

Organizational change requires champions. Ideally, these champions exist at both the technical level and the managerial level. Again ideally, the champions should include representatives of both primary affected groups—Dev and Ops. These champions should be the individuals who are responsible for preparing the business case.

Costs

The costs associated with DevOps are partially continuing and partially one-time costs. The continuing costs are associated with tools and people. Introducing DevOps requires the acquisition of a tool collection. Once these tools are acquired, whether open source or commercial, they need to be managed. Someone needs to be responsible for acquiring and building the new releases and making them available, whether at the team or organizational level—see also the discussion in Chapter 12. This responsibility can be assigned to an existing team, but that does not make the costs less real. These costs must be identified. Furthermore, there is training involved in the use of the tools and their idiosyncrasies. New employees must learn how to use the tools and the processes associated with them. Where the new tools replace existing tools, the change in license costs and maintenance efforts should be taken into account. In general, the continuing costs can be compared with respective existing costs to determine whether there is a reduction or an increase in these costs.

A one-time cost is the expense of the introduction of DevOps practices. The initial execution of these practices is inherently less efficient than subsequent uses. Tools need to be introduced, and people need to be trained. These tasks can be accomplished either internally or externally. Your organization could hire consultants that guide you through the introduction of DevOps practices, or your organization could decide to introduce DevOps totally with internal personnel. Our case study in Chapter 12 gives an example of consultants guiding the adoption, whereas another case study in Chapter 13 gives an example of executing the adoption with internal personnel. The business case should make a recommendation and, in either case, should provide a rationale for the choice.

Another one-time cost is the modification of existing systems to support DevOps practices. These existing systems could be software tools, existing processes, or existing products. The business plan should explore two aspects: How extensive are the modifications required to these existing systems? What is the impact on future development plans of diverting resources to modify existing systems?

Stakeholder Impact

Stakeholders can be impacted by the shift to DevOps. If not, why do it? The stakeholders can be divided into internal and external.

Internal Stakeholders

Two categories of internal stakeholders that are affected by the introduction of DevOps are, obviously, Dev and Ops. In addition, a new category of stakeholder—those individuals performing the DevOps role—will be created. In general, the Dev group gains additional responsibilities and control, the Ops group loses responsibilities and control, and the DevOps role will be new. How many responsibilities and how much control is shifted depend on which DevOps processes are adopted. We discuss additional and shifting responsibilities in terms of the five categories of DevOps processes we identified in Chapter 1.

1. Treat Ops as first-class stakeholders. In this case, Dev has additional responsibilities of eliciting requirements from Ops, and Ops has additional responsibilities of providing requirements. In addition, Dev and Ops both have additional responsibilities of ensuring that the requirements are satisfied.
2. Involve Dev more directly in incident handling. In this case, Dev assumes responsibilities for more intimate association with handling incidents that include a single system. Ops and Dev assume responsibility for defining a process to identify which incidents are referred first to Dev and which are referred first to Ops.
3. Enforce a consistent process for placing software changes into production. In this case, both Dev and Ops are involved in defining the process. Most likely, the DevOps role is responsible for ensuring that the process is enforced.
4. Develop infrastructure code with the same set of practices as application code. Since infrastructure code is primarily developed by Ops or by the DevOps role, the responsibilities for defining and enforcing the practices should be accomplished by them.
5. Implement a continuous deployment pipeline. The Dev group has responsibility for allocating resources, for release planning, and for making deployment decisions insofar as these items affect systems developed by Dev. The Ops group loses those responsibilities when they are associated with a single system or deployment. The DevOps role has overall responsibility for the DevOps tools. This includes not only installing and maintaining the appropriate versions of the tools, but also training the other teams to use the tools.

Disaster recovery is a shared responsibility. The Dev group has responsibility for the extent to which replication is built into the architecture for the system. The DevOps role has responsibility for the portion of disaster recovery that is managed through deployment decisions, such as in the case study in Chapter 11.

Collecting and reporting overall availability measures is a shared responsibility between the DevOps role and the Ops team. The Ops team has responsibility for triggering a shift to a backup site if a disaster occurs.

Coping with changes in the DevOps tools may cause some heartburn within the Dev team. If the DevOps role is continually improving the processes for using the tools then the changes may overwhelm the Dev team. Improving the processes is a portion of the charter of the DevOps role, but the DevOps team needs to be sensitive to the limits of other teams in absorbing continual change.

External Stakeholders

Using a formal release process, such as described in Chapter 1, provides the business and management stakeholders with a high degree of visibility into the progress toward releasing particular features. Determining progress in releasing a feature can get difficult when features require multiple development teams to all have released their portion, but an individual team decided when to release its portion.

However, the main goal of the DevOps practices is to reduce the time between committing a change to a system and the change being placed into normal production (while ensuring high quality). Business and management stakeholders need to understand that they are making a tradeoff when adopting DevOps deployment practices: They are giving up the visibility afforded by a formal release process in order to achieve faster cycle times. While quality and speed may be high for each of the teams, their independence comes at the cost of lowered coordination in terms of releases.

Risks and Their Mitigation

The risks associated with the introduction of DevOps practices are both organizational and technical.

Organizational Risks

Much of the discussion about DevOps in blog posts and other forums is about breaking down barriers between Dev and Ops. Barriers exist because these two organizational units have different missions, different cultures, and different incentives. Aligning these different organizational units requires that each unit gains at least a high-level understanding of the other unit's mission, culture, and incentive. Furthermore, different reporting chains provide one barrier, and physical distance yet another one. Social science research has identified that a physical distance of more than 30 meters creates a barrier to coordination between people.

The creation of a new role of DevOps engineer also causes stress within an organization. The role must be staffed, and a reporting line must be developed for the role. Staffing and reporting a new role can cause tension among those not involved in the new role.

In addition, placing scripts and configurations under version management and controlling how new versions of systems are deployed may represent a change from current practice. As such, the affected personnel may resist this change.

Mitigating these risks involves dealing with the aspects we mentioned—different missions, cultures, incentives, reporting chains, as well as physical distance between the affected personnel and changes in existing practices.

Managing such changes is a subject of both academic research and the expertise of multiple consultants. In the business plan for DevOps, you should identify, within your organization, similar efforts to the introduction of DevOps and how these efforts were managed and with what degree of success. One suggested solution to mitigate these risks is to adjust the key performance indicators (KPIs) of each group to reflect overall rather than individual success in deployment. That is, current Dev KPIs emphasize the coding of new features, and current Ops KPIs emphasize the stability of the system. Instead, you want to reward both units for new features successfully placed into production, without affecting the stability of the system.

Technical Risk

From a management perspective, there are two fundamental technical questions the business plan should answer: What changes are required to existing production architectures of applications? How is the integrity of the production database going to be maintained? If production architectures are going to be modified to support continuous deployment, then the affected architectures should be identified as a risk. Also, an organization's production database represents one of its most valuable assets. Threats to the integrity of the production database should also be identified as a risk.

Changes Required to Existing Production Applications

Two types of changes to existing production application architectures may be required to support continuous deployment—see Part Two for details of the concepts.

- *State management.* Components should be stateless if at all possible. Stateless components are more resilient to failure because replacing a failed component is not difficult. Continuous deployment practices also build on replacing of components and services, which is often done frequently. Those components that contain state need to be identified and then modified to remove the state maintenance from them. Removing state from a component can be done by storing state in a database, by having clients maintain state, or by using a state coordination service such as ZooKeeper.
- *Feature toggles.* If a blue/green deployment model is being used, then feature toggles are not required. If a rolling upgrade deployment model is being used, then feature toggles should be used to control new features, and a feature toggle manager should be introduced to control the feature toggles.

Maintaining the Integrity of the Production Database
The integrity of the production database can be compromised in one of two fashions.

- Data from a test can be mistakenly included in the production database. Ensuring that the staging environment is kept distinct from the production environment, and hence the production database, can be accomplished through the use of automated scripts, credentials, and firewall rules.
- A deployment into production compromises the database. Recovery from erroneous data in the database is no different than it is without the use of DevOps practices. The business plan should include a discussion of the current rollback/roll forward plans to correct erroneous data.

Rollout Plan

Any rollout plan depends on where your organization currently is and what your final target is. As with DevOps tools, you could implement a "big bang" delivery where everything is done at once, or an incremental delivery where practices are introduced, allowing some time to both get the bugs out and enable people to understand and get accustomed to the new practices. The big bang delivers results more quickly, but is likely to introduce more resistance and be subject to more errors. With changes to existing software products (e.g., adopting a microservice architecture to facilitate DevOps practices), incremental delivery is usually desirable. In the case study in Chapter 13, we discuss how such incremental changes are implemented. The case study in Chapter 12 suggests setting up an onboarding team, whose sole job is to help other Dev teams move their applications onto the new DevOps tool set. As such, this mandates an incremental approach—there are only so many projects the onboarding team can handle at any given time.

Maturity models have become quite popular as a means of determining both where your organization is on a particular scale and what your organization would need to accomplish to become more "mature" on that scale. The DevOps maturity model cited in Section 10.6 defines five different categories that represent the key aspects to consider when implementing continuous delivery. These categories are: culture and organization, design and architecture, build and deploy, test and verification, and information and reporting.

For the purposes of the rollout plan section of the business plan, for each of these categories identify where you want the organization to be after a period of, for example, two weeks, one month, two months, and six months. Identify the steps that you need to take to get started in each activity, as well as the specific goals for each of the periods you choose.

For example, in the design and architecture category, you can identify which applications have which percentage of components made stateless in each period. In the build and deploy category, you can identify which tools are used in production in which of the stages of the deployment pipeline, and who uses those tools initially and after each period of time.

In Chapter 1, we identified five different aspects of DevOps. They can be used as a guide to rolling out a set of DevOps practices.

- Have Dev treat Ops as a first-class stakeholder when developing requirements for a system. On the one hand, this is the easiest practice to implement. Every organization has a process for developing requirements for a system, whether these requirements are specified as user stories or in some more formal form. Stakeholders should be involved in some fashion in developing the requirements, so implementing this practice is a matter of involving Ops like any other stakeholder. On the other hand, viewing Ops as a first-class stakeholder represents a cultural shift for some organizations. Cultural shifts are among the most difficult changes that an organization can make. One technique is to have an influential member of the Dev community take the lead. Organizations have hierarchies of influence that are independent of the management structure. Having an influential member of the Dev community be involved in the rollout and in gathering requirements from Ops has a ripple effect on the rest of the Dev community.

- Involve Dev more directly in incident handling. This topic is more difficult than treating Ops as first-class stakeholders. It not only involves a cultural shift but it also involves changes in duties and processes. For the applications being used as pilots, the first step is to define the incidents that are being handled by the development group. These incidents should be specific to the pilot applications. Generalizing across applications to characterize incidents can wait until you have gained some experience with characterizing incidents. Once a set of incidents have been defined, then a procedure for funnelling those incidents to Dev must be defined. This procedure depends on the type of incident and how knowledge of the incident arrives at the organization. If it is a bug report from outside, then it can be directed to both Ops and Dev and the point of contact for Dev can decide the next step. If it is an internal report such as a monitoring tool–based alert, then the monitor can assign the point of contact based on rules. See Chapter 11 for an example. Each source of an incident requires its own method of informing either Dev or Ops of the incident. Finally, a point of contact within the Dev group has to be found. In this case, personality is more important than influence. The individual who acts as a point of contact should be quick at solving problems because their first task is to remedy what caused the incident report. The individual should also be assertive (if not abrasive) because one of their next tasks is to recommend changes to the Dev processes in order to prevent this class of incident from reoccurring.

- Enforce a consistent process for placing software changes into production. For this case, start at the end. That is, define a consistent set of gates for deploying a system into the production environment. These gates include checking that the architecture is such that deploying a new version does not disrupt the operations of the currently operating version. Next, you can define a set of gates for modifying a system to be used in deployment. This set of gates should be applied to any change to the system, whether patching an existing virtual machine (VM) (if you choose to allow that) or baking a new image. This set of gates is applied to both Dev and Ops. Rollback is an important consideration when placing software into production, and so a rollback process should be a portion of the consistent process. Once the gates have been defined and are working well, then it is possible to consider the steps leading up to the modification of the system and additional automation. The first step, however, is to begin with defining the gates.

- Develop infrastructure code with the same set of practices as application code. In this case, our recommendation is to begin with early stages of the software development cycle rather than the last stage as we recommended for placing changes into production. Configuration management and version control are well-established practices for the development of application code. Ensure that these practices are followed during the development of infrastructure code. Automated testing of infrastructure code can be accomplished through the use of independent environments, as well as through specialized test frameworks for the specific code type.
- Implement a continuous delivery pipeline. Our case study in Chapter 12 describes a continuous delivery pipeline implemented by Sourced Group. One fundamental decision to make when implementing a continuous delivery pipeline is the extent to which different development teams need to coordinate to generate a release. The more coordination required, the less independence each team gets. We discussed this in Chapters 4 and 6.

Success Criteria

The success criteria are based on both the rollout plan and the rationale for adopting DevOps. The rollout plan provides metrics for the categories in each of the periods identified. Even if these metrics are met, progress should also be made in achieving the overarching goals of a DevOps adoption: reducing the time between committing a change to a system and the change being placed into normal production, while ensuring high quality. This has an impact on the higher-level goals of getting business concepts to end users and depends on more concrete ways of reducing the time between error detection and repair.

An important element from the perspective of a business case is to have measurable success criteria. Focus your efforts on metrics that you can collect, both before the introduction of DevOps and after. You do not want to be in the position of arguing that a project is successful without having sufficient data to back you up.

10.3 Measurements and Compliance to DevOps Practices

In Chapter 7, we stated that the measurement should be designed with specific goals. In this section, we discuss the kinds of measurements that are of interest to the business with respect to DevOps and its adoption. Three categories to measure are: how well the DevOps practices are succeeding, what are the cases of noncompliance to DevOps practices, and what is the level of stakeholder satisfaction with the DevOps practices.

Measuring the Success of DevOps Practices

The goals of the DevOps practices and the stages of the pipeline dictate the types of measurements that should be taken. In particular, the two main measurements for the success of DevOps are the times from commit to production and from error to fix.

Reducing the time between commit and deployment. Figure 10.1 repeats the deployment pipeline from Chapter 5. The time between a commit and its successful deployment is the sum of the time waiting in the queue at each stage of the deployment pipeline and the time spent processing at each server in the pipeline. At the continuous integration server, measurements should be taken of the number of branches active over time, the time between the creation of a branch and its merge into the trunk, and the time it takes to run tests. Since best practice discourages the usage of branches or, at least, demands their merge back into the trunk as quickly as possible, measuring the number of branches and their lifetime enables you to assess the degree to which best practice is followed. Extensive testing time is another source of delays, although this is traded off against the number of errors that slip through the test suites.

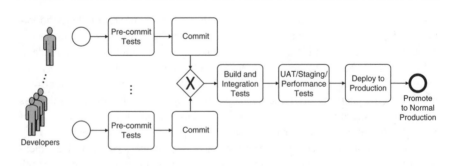

FIGURE 10.1   A deployment pipeline (Repeated from Fig. 5.1) [Notation: BPMN]

Measurements that are taken in the staging environment document the time spent in this phase. How long does it take to perform the tests? What is the dwell time of an image on the staging server? If a human gatekeeper is involved, how long does it take to get approval for deploying the changes?

Not all commits result in a successful deployment. Some commits fail tests and generate rework and reentry into the pipeline. Damon Edwards advocates measuring rework separately. Since breaking the build keeps every team member from successfully promoting code through the pipeline, monitoring broken builds and their repair is also important. In particular, such repairs should be the first priority, and measurements can determine if this guideline is followed.

Finally, you should be able to determine the number and types of errors and the actual time spent on fixing them when placing an image from the staging environment into service. That is, measure the errors that occur during the deployment process, itself. These errors are distinct from the errors in the system being deployed, which are discussed in the next section. These measures could be taken by the deployment tool and the production environment.

The aggregate of these measures gives you a good picture of the performance of the deployment pipeline. You want to understand where the longest delays in the pipeline are and focus your energies on reducing these delays.

Reducing the time between the discovery of an error and its repair. Errors in this context mean errors in the production version of a service. There are actually two different facets to this goal. First, does the automation of the various stages of the pipeline increase or decrease the number and severity of errors that escape into production? Secondly, has the time between discovery and repair of a problem changed as a result of introducing DevOps practices? Your ticket system records production errors and their consequences, and these records can be mined to determine answers to these two questions.

Measuring Compliance to DevOps Practices

It is naïve to think that people always follow prescribed practices. People might not follow a practice out of ignorance, out of obstinacy, because the practice introduces overhead, or just because they do not wish to change. We identify two practices where compliance might be an issue.

1. *Launching VMs.* If everyone is following the deployment practices, then the tools used can maintain a history and the pedigree of an instance can be discovered. An example of noncompliance with the practices is when an operator launches a VM from the console during some incident. In order to discover VMs that did not go through the documented processes for placing modifications into production, it is necessary to scan running VMs. Every running VM should have been created from a fully tested image that has passed all the gates.

2. *Removing feature toggle code.* Feature toggle code should be removed
    from the source code when the feature has been committed into production
    and has remained stable. The feature toggle manager knows when a feature
    has been committed into production. Stability can be assumed after some
    period of time has passed. At this point, an entry can be created in the issue
    tracking database that identifies the removal of the feature toggle code as
    an activity to be performed. The removal of the feature toggle code can
    then be tracked and prioritized as any other entry in the issue tracking
    database.

Measuring Stakeholder Satisfaction

One method for measuring stakeholder satisfaction is through asking stakeholders to fill out short questionnaires. Another method is to identify disruptive events
under the assumption that disruption leads to dissatisfaction.

- *Short questionnaires.* Internal stakeholders can be asked to rate their
  satisfaction on a scale of, say, 1 to 5. Different classes of stakeholders have
  different concerns, and so the questions can be tailored to particular types of
  stakeholders. Stakeholders should be instructed that their ratings are from
  their perspective. For example, Dev and Ops personnel could comment on
  the usefulness of monitoring information. Ops personnel can comment on the
  configuration management policy for changes to scripts. Business stakeholders
  can comment on overall cycle time for placing ideas into production.
- *Crises.* One of the goals of any process improvement effort is to remove
  the necessity for heroic efforts on the part of those who actually carry out a
  process. Heroic efforts in the DevOps context can be sparked by outages or
  by inadequate lead time for events.
  - *Outages.* When an outage occurs, there is usually no time for performing
    a deep analysis of the cause. The initial focus is on mitigating the impact
    of the outage. Once the system has been restored to production, however,
    there should be a postmortem. Those outages whose underlying cause is
    in the interaction between Dev and Ops, in the inadequacy of the DevOps
    practices, or in the noncompliance to these practices should become
    a means for measuring user satisfaction with the rollout of DevOps.
    Ideally, the number of such items decreases as the use of these practices
    increases.
  - *Inadequate lead time for events.* Events such as a security audit, a rollout
    of a change to an existing system, or an installation of a patch have the
    potential to be disruptive. As with outages, disruptions caused by these
    events should become a means for measuring user satisfaction with the
    DevOps practices.

10.4 Points of Interaction Between Dev and Ops

Several points of interaction occur between Dev and Ops that we have not yet discussed in detail. The two points this section is concerned with are licensing and incident handling.

Licenses

A software license is a legal agreement governing the use or redistribution of software. Our interest is in those licenses for which your organization pays or should have paid a fee and the resulting implications on DevOps practices. We begin by describing how licenses work.

A license can be viewed as a token providing access to the licensed software package. Licenses can be enterprise-wide or intended for a specific number of applications or users. Licenses are issued for a particular version of the licensed software package. They can have a specific expiration date, or not.

Licenses are dynamically verified by the licensed software package. At some point in its initialization, the licensed software package checks to see if it has been provided with a valid license. The license can be located in a known position, provided by the application, or, most commonly, provided by a license server. A license server is a location on a network where licenses are stored and can be accessed.

We identify three situations where both Dev and Ops are involved in issues associated with licenses.

1. *Expiration.* If the licenses for an application have expired, the application can no longer run. Typically, the responsibility for renewing licenses lies with Ops, and there should be procedures in place to detect upcoming license expirations and determine which ones should be renewed. Any lapse in this procedure, however, can result in the failure of an application and will be reported to Dev. The application should have a specific failure message that identifies which version of which software system was unable to get a license, so that you do not spend additional time determining what caused the application to fail.

2. *License unavailable.* Some licenses are "floating licenses." That is, a maximum number of application instances can simultaneously use the licensed software package. If a new VM is created that utilizes the licensed package in excess of the maximum, it will fail. Again, it should fail with an explicit error message. At this point, it is a problem for Ops. They should be able to determine which running VMs are currently using which licenses, and whether these VMs are still needed.

3. *Software audit.* In rare circumstances, a software vendor may request an audit of an organization to ensure that all copies of their software are appropriately licensed. Some organizations perform their own software audits to ensure they are in compliance with all of their license requirements. Ops can perform the audit, but they need to be able to enumerate all of the executing VMs at any point in time and to determine which licensed packages are included in those VMs and whether those packages were appropriately licensed at that time. All of these requirements are satisfied if Dev maintains traceability for running software, so that the components included in a running VM and their history can be determined. License servers typically keep a history of the starting and stopping of VMs using their licenses. Failures may make the history inaccurate, and so one of the consequences of detecting a failed VM should be to update the license history.

Incident Handling

One of the virtues of Dev "throwing a release over the wall" to Ops for moving an application into production is that roles and responsibilities for incidents are clear: Ops handles any incidents that occur involving that application; if it is a problem they cannot handle, then Dev gets involved through an escalation procedure. The situation becomes much more complicated once Dev is in control of the deployment process.

Once an incident occurs, there are three possible cases.

1. The incident is clearly related to an application. In this case, the Dev group is the initial point of contact for managing the incident. We discussed the role of reliability engineer in Chapter 1. This role would be responsible for any activities that result from the incident.
2. The incident is related to a hardware or infrastructure failure. In this case, Ops is responsible for diagnosing and repairing the failure. The incident could be raised with Dev, who refer it to Ops, but whether this is an option is up to your organization to decide.
3. The cause of the incident is not clear. Suppose, for example, the network slows noticeably. This could be due to a hardware/infrastructure cause, or it could be due to an application incorrectly flooding the network. Other examples can be more subtle, such as those involving "long-tail" effects we discussed in Chapter 2. The first challenge is to diagnose the cause of the problem. Once the diagnosis has been made, the responsibility for rectifying the problem brings us back to the prior two cases. Fundamentally, your organization needs to have a clear escalation policy that answers these questions: Who is responsible for the initial examination of a problem? How long before the problem is escalated? To whom is the problem escalated?

10.5 Summary

Implementing DevOps practices requires management buy-in, which, in turn, requires champions who can convince management that DevOps practices are of benefit. The normal method for convincing management to adopt new technological practices is through the creation of a business case. A business case for DevOps covers costs, benefits, risks and their mitigation, a rollout schedule, and success criteria.

Once a DevOps adoption process is under way, it is important to measure the success of the adoption, the compliance with the associated practices, and how well stakeholders are responding to the changes to their environment.

In addition, Dev and Ops must interact within an organization in dealing with licenses and with incident response.

10.6 For Further Reading

You can find more information about business considerations at

- The blog "DevOps Considerations" at http://techopsexec.com/2013/09/10/devops-considerations/
- The book *Communications Networks in R&D Laboratories* [Allen 70]
- Wikipedia's entry on change management: http://en.wikipedia.org/wiki/Change_management#Managing_the_change_process

Just like software development maturity models, you can find more information on maturity models for DevOps at [InfoQ 13].

For understanding more about measuring rework, Damon Edwards' article is helpful [InfoQ 14].

PART FOUR

CASE STUDIES

In this part, we describe three case studies intended to solidify what we covered in many of the previous chapters. All of our case studies are from organizations actively involved in implementing DevOps practices, and each has been chosen to exemplify a particular aspect of DevOps.

One option that many organizations choose in order to achieve business continuity is to maintain multiple datacenters. Such an option requires synchronizing the datacenters not only with the data they maintain but also with the software and hardware installed in each datacenter. Chris Williams of Rafter walks us through how to achieve the synchronization of two datacenters in Chapter 11.

Many enterprises would like to adopt DevOps practices but do not have the expertise to do it directly. John Painter and Daniel Hand explain to us how Sourced Group, a consulting company, guides enterprises through the implementation in Chapter 12.

In Chapter 4, we advocated the use of microservices as a means of improving the velocity of deployment. Most organizations have legacy systems that must be re-architected in order to move them to microservice architecture. Sidney Shek of Atlassian walks us through the implementation of one such microservice in Chapter 13.

11

Supporting Multiple Datacenters

With Chris Williams

*Rafter is making course materials
(and higher education as a whole) more affordable for students.*
—http://www.rafter.com/about-rafter/

11.1 Introduction

For many years, students have been frustrated by the high cost of new textbooks and their low value as used textbooks. Rafter (originally BookRenter.com) saw this as a business opportunity and created a business in 2008 renting textbooks to students. The premise is simple: A student determines the textbooks needed for the new semester and orders these textbooks from the BookRenter website. Rafter ships the chosen books to the student. At the end of the semester, the student returns the books and the books are available for other students for the next semester.

As you may have deduced, this business is seasonal. If the BookRenter.com website is down at the beginning of the semester, customers are lost. Business continuity during the high-activity portions of the year is sufficiently important to Rafter that they implemented various measures, the foremost of which is running two datacenters in parallel for redundancy.

With two datacenters, Rafter has the capability not only of moving service from one datacenter to another, in the case of an outage of the primary datacenter, but also maintains a testing site that replicates the production environment. Keeping two datacenters synchronized poses the challenge of not only keeping the data synchronized but also keeping the environment replicated and making sure that applications are architected appropriately. In this chapter, we explore how Rafter accomplishes these different forms of synchronization.

Two fundamental use cases exist for moving servicing requests from one datacenter to the other—controlled and uncontrolled. A controlled move means that the primary datacenter is still available and there is time for a variety of preparatory measures before switching to the secondary datacenter. This type of move is used to test the measures involved in switching datacenters as well as to allow for maintenance of the primary datacenter. An uncontrolled move occurs as a result of a disaster—whether natural or manmade. We return to these use cases after we describe the solutions that Rafter has put in place.

11.2 Current State

Rafter currently runs two datacenters with exactly the same hardware. They run their own datacenters because, at the time the multiple datacenter decision was made, Rafter could not get the necessary input/output performance from a public cloud. This decision is currently being reevaluated. While Rafter has the option to switch to the public cloud, many organizations are required to operate their own datacenters for regulatory reasons. These two datacenters are on opposite sides of the North American continent but the users do not see a difference in response time. Each datacenter contains about 300 virtual machines (VMs) using VMware. A typical VM has 16GB of RAM and four virtual CPU cores. The front-end tier throughput averages about 30,000 to 50,000 requests per second. The workload is approximately evenly split between reads and writes, with about 80% of the requests coming from application programming interfaces (APIs) and the remainder from web browsers. Approximately another 150 VMs are used for analytical and staging/testing purposes. These run in a combination of onsite private cloud (Eucalyptus) and public cloud (Amazon Web Services). Because the service level agreements (SLAs) on these servers are more relaxed than the servers in Rafter's datacenters, real-time disaster recovery is not necessary.

Rafter has about 35 Ruby on Rails applications, about 50 back-end applications in Ruby, and a couple of applications in other languages (Clojure, R). Rafter uses a standard three-tier architecture—web tier, business logic tier, and database tier. We describe the business logic tier and then the supporting database tier.

11.3 Business Logic and Web Tiers

We discuss two aspects associated with the business logic and web tiers. The first aspect is the logic of the applications, and the second aspect is the infrastructure that Rafter uses to support the applications.

Application Logic

If an application needs to store state that persists across multiple requests, then it must use either datastores that can switch (e.g., Rafter's SQL database) or a resource that is externally available from both datacenters (e.g., AWS S3). This restriction even applies to a single datacenter in a load-balanced environment. As discussed in Chapter 4, storing application state on a local server is not a good practice because a subsequent request that needs this data might get sent to another server that does not contain the data. Rafter follows the practice of keeping the application state in the database tier, which is external or replicated.

Additionally, no application configuration changes are necessary to support datacenter switching, as all external resources are accessed through Domain Name System (DNS) hostnames that do not change during a switch.

Every time Rafter deploys a new version of an application to production, it is deployed to both datacenters at the same time. This ensures that both of the datacenters are running the same version of the applications. The deployment system uses an infrastructure library to figure out which servers an application is deployed to, so there is no need to maintain separate lists of servers in the deployment system. This is how Rafter achieves the traceability that we discussed in Chapter 5.

One issue in deploying a new version to the secondary datacenter is that a physical server and, consequently, application VMs might be offline and unavailable for deployment. This problem is resolved by storing the information about the latest version of every application in Chef Server. Once the operations team finishes their maintenance and starts the VM up again, Chef will detect that the application on the server is out of date and deploy the latest version of the application. This ensures that application code stays in sync across VMs, even in the situation where VMs may not always be available for every code deployment.

Infrastructure

The infrastructure support exists as a library. The library is packaged as a gem in RubyGems, a package manager for the Ruby language that provides a standard format for distributing Ruby programs and libraries. The library is used inside many of the infrastructure-related applications and provides a framework for both adding new applications and discovering information about the infrastructure. We discuss these aspects and maintaining synchronization next.

Adding an Application

Every application in the Rafter platform has a small JSON (JavaScript Object Notation) file that serves as a blueprint containing instructions on how to properly install the application on the infrastructure. Examples of attributes in these JSON files would be:

- Name of the application
- Type

- Git repository
- Hostname
- Cronjobs
- Daemons
- Log rotations
- Firewall rules
- Database grants
- Secure sockets layer (SSL) certificates
- Load balancer virtual IPs

The infrastructure library, which can run inside Chef, reads these JSON files and determines how to set up the application. The library contains many defaults for the platform (which can be overridden if desired), so the JSON files tend not to be too large.

For example, consider a simple Ruby on Rails application named "cat" that lives in a repository on GitHub. The JSON for this app might look like:

```
{
  "id" : "cat",
  "repo_url" : "git@github.com:org/cat.git",
  "type" : "rails"
}
```

On the Chef Server, the "cat" application is assigned to a VM (or set of VMs) either via a role or node attribute. Chef then runs on this VM and uses the library to query the latest JSON for the cat application and apply the appropriate setup steps, such as:

1. Check out the "cat" application from GitHub.
2. Deploy the "cat" application to the local VM.
3. Set up nginx and unicorn (Ruby on Rails app server) with the proper virtual host for the application at cat.rafter.com, and set up the proper SSL certificate.
4. Set up default log rotations for the app.

This is just a simple example, but the library can handle more complex application setups, like installing cronjobs and daemons, creating database accounts, managing database grants, controlling which developers have access to the application on the VM, handling development and staging environments, and so forth. It can also create separate tiers for an application on different sets of VMs. For example, an application can be set up to only serve web traffic on one set of front-end VMs, and only run cronjobs and back-end daemons on another set of VMs so the two instances of the application do not compete for resources.

Discovering the Infrastructure

Chef stores information about the entire infrastructure in Chef Server. The Chef Server exposes a set of APIs for both querying this data and storing additional data about the infrastructure (via JSON-based documents called data bags). The Rafter library utilizes the Chef Server as a database for information about the infrastructure.

Here are some examples of the use of the infrastructure library. Note that some of the variables are reused in examples following their definition.

- Get a list of all applications on the entire infrastructure by calling:

```
DevOps::Application.all
```

- Get detailed information about a particular application (everything from where its GitHub repository lives to the database it uses):

```
myapp = DevOps::Application.load("myapp")
myapp.repo_url
      >git@github.com:org/repo.git
myapp.application_database
      >myapp_production
```

- Find the first VM an application is deployed to:

```
node = myapp.nodes.first
node.name
>web01
```

- Get detailed information about the VM, such as the datacenter hosting the VM:

```
node.datacenter.name
>dc1
```

- Get the state of the datacenter:

```
node.datacenter.active?
>true
```

Different applications use this library for accomplishing different tasks:

- When Chef is running on VMs to apply a configuration, the library is used extensively. Everything from which cronjobs to set up for an application, which daemons to set up, which firewall rules to add, and so forth, is determined by the library. For example, here is part of a Chef cookbook that adds a firewall rule to the VM, based on the state of the datacenter the VM is in:

```
if node.datacenter.active?
      iptables_rule "block_api" do
                enable false
      end
```

```
else
    iptables_rule "block_api"
end
```

- The deployment system uses this library to discover to which VMs it should deploy a particular application. It may also need to make special considerations if a VM resides in a particular datacenter. For example, two such deployment constraint are
  - Do not run database migrations from the inactive datacenter on deploy, since this is too slow,
  - Skip deployment to any VM in an offline datacenter.
- The testing and staging systems use the infrastructure library to get information about all applications that can be deployed to testing and staging VMs and to determine inter-application dependencies.

Keeping the Infrastructure in Sync

The secondary datacenter is set up exactly as the primary datacenter. It contains the same number of VMs as the primary datacenter, and all application VMs are intended to be configured identically. So any time a new VM is created in the primary datacenter, it is also created in the secondary datacenter at the same time. Chef keeps all of the VMs configured the same way across both datacenters. There are, of course, some minor configuration differences between the two datacenters due to naming (different IP space and domain), but otherwise they are identical. Whenever a configuration change is pushed to Chef, it gets applied to VMs in both datacenters.

11.4 Database Tier

While replication of stateless VMs in the upper tiers is relatively straightforward— exact duplication is the goal—this is somewhat more complex for the database tier. Three different databases are used in this tier, each with a specialized purpose.

Transactional Data

The majority of the data for Rafter is stored in a transactional, ACID-compliant, SQL-backed database called Clustrix. Clustrix is a clustered database appliance and a drop-in replacement for MySQL. There are three Clustrix nodes in each datacenter, although they behave as a single database. About half a terabyte of data is stored in this database, and there are usually several gigabytes a day of changes.

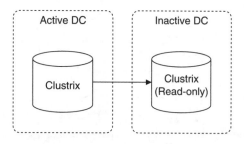

FIGURE 11.1 Clustrix database management systems (DBMSs) in master-master replication mode [Notation: Architecture]

The Clustrix databases in each datacenter are configured in a master-master replication scheme. However, the databases in the secondary datacenter have a READONLY flag set on them, so no applications can accidentally write data to them—see Figure 11.1. Rafter's goal is to keep the replication delay between the two datacenters as small as possible. Most of the time it is under 1 second—but this is a metric that demands close monitoring, since application changes can introduce new queries or data constraints that increase delay.

This form of replication has the same sort of pain points as standard MySQL replication. The replication is single-threaded and asynchronous, so both the complexity and rate of incoming write queries can cause the secondary database to get behind the active database. Luckily, there are lots of tools for dealing with both of these issues, and database vendors are coming up with new solutions every year (e.g., hybrid replication, multithreaded slaves, slave prefetching, etc.). One way Rafter uses to tackle complex queries is by rewriting the query so it runs faster or is broken into smaller chunks (e.g., LIMIT 10000). Another way is to switch to row-based replication (RBR), so the slave does not have to run complex queries and can simply update any changed rows. Tackling sheer write volume can be more difficult though. One particular application was responsible for half of the total write volume. This data was not necessary for any real-time application data, so instead of writing the data to Clustrix, Rafter changed the application to write out flat files. These files are then picked up by a specialized application on an hourly basis and imported into the data warehouse, which does not have the same SLAs that the production infrastructure has. Although not currently used, Clustrix also allows setting up multiple replication streams for different databases, so that is another tool available for dealing with high write volume.

Infrastructure Support

Redis is a key-value cache and store. Rafter uses it in their infrastructure for both job queuing systems (Resque and Sidekiq), caching, and as a fast key-value store

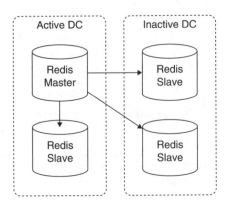

FIGURE 11.2   Redis DBMSs [Notation: Architecture]

database. In each datacenter, there are two separate Redis clusters—set up as shown in Figure 11.2. One Redis node serves as the "master" where all applications send their reads and writes. It can then fail over to any of the slaves in the event of a failure. As the Redis usage increased, the Redis slaves could not keep up with the master due to the rate of writes being sent. Rafter started to notice the delay because the master server's memory was slowly growing, yet the data being stored inside Redis was not growing. Rafter diagnosed this to find Redis was buffering all pending commands for the slaves in memory, but because the replication to the slaves could not keep up, this number kept growing. Other organizations had also diagnosed this problem. The underlying problem was that Rafter was generating more Redis traffic across the datacenters than the available bandwidth would allow. The solution utilized was to run Redis replication inside of an SSH (Secure Shell) tunnel with compression enabled. The compression in the tunnel allows for substantially less bandwidth to transmit the data across the WAN (wide area network) at about a 20% CPU utilization increase. This change enabled the replication to the slaves to keep up with the master.

Session Data

Rafter uses Couchbase's implementation of Memcached for storing session data and caching throughout their platform. This is an example of one database in the platform where the data is *not* synchronized between the datacenters. See Figure 11.3 for a representation of Couchbase in the datacenters. Both Couchbase clusters are completely separate, so when the secondary datacenter is activated, the cache will be stale. This does not cause a problem, since it is either temporary (session data) or it is cached data that the applications automatically repopulate from other data sources on a cache miss.

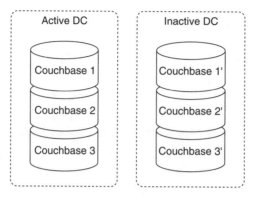

FIGURE 11.3   Couchbase (Memcached) [Notation: Architecture]

11.5   Other Infrastructure Tools

Several other tools are used in the Rafter infrastructure. These include gem repository servers and Elasticsearch. The management of DNS is also an important element of failing over from one datacenter to another. See Chapter 2 for a discussion of DNS management and TTL (time to live). We discuss Rafter's use of DNS servers below.

Gem Repository Servers

Ruby applications use "gems" as a way of packaging external libraries. Typically, Rafter packages shared code between their applications into such gems. Particular gems and their versions are bound as dependencies inside applications. Rafter built a gem repository cluster in both datacenters as a place to publish private gems. Figure 11.4 gives a representation of the gem repository servers. Rafter began with an open source gem server called Geminabox, which provides a simple user interface (UI) for developers to upload a new version of a gem to the server. However, it does not provide support for high availability and simply uses the local file system as its repository to store gems. In order to build high availability around this, Rafter first created multiple gem servers in each datacenter and put them behind a load balancer. However, this did not automatically synchronize the data between all of the gem servers. Rafter then built a script that runs on each gem server. This script synchronizes the underlying gem repository with its two neighbors (one in the local datacenter and one in the other datacenter). Under the hood, they utilized Unison, an open source bidirectional file synchronization tool similar to rsync, which synchronizes the gem repository files every minute. They also built a monitoring script to query each of the gem servers and alert for any inconsistencies.

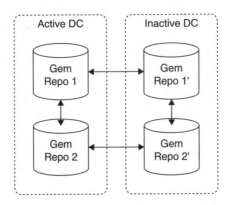

FIGURE 11.4   Gem repository servers [Notation: Architecture]

Elasticsearch

Rafter has a single six-node Elasticsearch (a search and analytics engine) cluster that spans both datacenters. Elasticsearch's shard (a horizontal partitioning of data) allocation feature can ensure that all shards are fully replicated to the secondary datacenter. Elasticsearch can also be taught datacenter awareness, so it prefers nodes in the same datacenter for queries. When Rafter first deployed Elasticsearch, they had connectivity problems between the datacenters since Elasticsearch's cluster features were developed for stable, low-latency links between all of its cluster nodes. Rafter resolved these issues by tuning several TCP kernel parameters and Elasticsearch's own timeout settings, so as to avoid having nodes in the other datacenter constantly leave and join the cluster due to timeouts. There are not a lot of users running Elasticsearch clusters over a WAN link yet, so this is somewhat new territory—but besides the easily solvable points above, Rafter has not encountered any significant issues thus far.

Domain Name Systems

Rafter maintains two DNS servers in each datacenter that provide local DNS service. One DNS server behaves as the master for the other three. All DNS servers are standard BIND DNS servers running the Webmin management interface. Webmin provides a simple web-based UI for updating and deleting DNS records and more advanced settings, like promoting a DNS slave to master or changing a slave's designated master. Rafter built a Ruby library that interacts with this UI so that DNS changes can be automated. Rafter set a 60-second TTL on most DNS records and a 1-second TTL on DNS records that point to database virtual IPs. The choice of times is a tradeoff between speed of change and Internet traffic created by querying the DNS at short intervals.

11.6 Datacenter Switch

A datacenter can be in one of three different states—active, inactive, or offline. Active means there are no restrictions on servers that reside in this datacenter. Inactive means that cronjobs, daemons, and back-end applications are stopped and disabled. Offline means a datacenter is inactive and will not receive any new code deploys. Offline mode is typically used for maintenance. Rafter makes use of the first two states when performing a datacenter switch. A controlled switch happens for maintenance or testing purposes. The primary datacenter remains active during a controlled switch. During an uncontrolled switch, the primary datacenter is inactive. We present the steps that Rafter uses in both of these cases below.

When Rafter first started performing datacenter switching, some of these steps were done manually and there was no process tying them all together. They simply wrote down all the steps in a Word document and executed them one by one. Once they were confident in the process, they began automating it. Rafter started by building a Ruby library that uses a domain-specific language (DSL) for defining steps in the switching process. After discussing the steps for controlled and uncontrolled switches, we explain their automation.

Controlled Switch Steps

A controlled switch consists of 18 steps, from initial checks temporarily disabling monitoring alerts to switching all tiers over to the other datacenter. For the purposes of these steps, assume the following key:

- DC1: Datacenter to switch from
- DC2: Datacenter to switch to

1. Verify the Clustrix databases have a low replication delay. First check that the replication delay is less than 60 seconds. This check is done because it happened once that Rafter took all of their sites down for a datacenter switch, only to find out that their database replication was 30 minutes behind due to a large query. They had to wait for the database to catch up before continuing the switch, which incurred additional downtime.
2. Disable alerts on the monitoring system (Scout). Scout is a monitoring system similar to Nagios that is used by Rafter for monitoring servers (CPU, disk, network, URL healthchecks, etc.). Rafter disables alerts temporarily in order to prevent getting pages and e-mails during the switch.
3. Put up a "Website going down soon" banner. Rafter puts a small banner on their website telling customers the website will be going down for maintenance in 10 minutes and warning them to finish up their purchases. The deployment system does this automatically by placing a special file in a directory on each application server.

4. Mark DC1 as "inactive" in the Chef Server. Since the Chef Server is used as a deployment database, a new JSON document is pushed to the Chef Server, marking DC1 datacenter as "inactive." Any clients using the infrastructure library will be able to see this change. At this point in the process, both DC1 and DC2 are now in the inactive state.

5. Start Chef Client on all VMs in DC1. Chef provides a command called "knife ssh" that allows one to run commands in parallel across a set of VMs matching a particular search. The command: knife ssh "roles:dc1" "sudo chef-client" starts Chef client on all VMs in DC1.

    Because Chef uses the infrastructure library, it will detect that the VM it is running on is now in an inactive datacenter—so the Chef client takes the appropriate steps to reconfigure the VM. This has the effect of removing any application-specific cronjobs and stopping/disabling any back-end daemons.

6. Send a "TERM" signal to any running cronjobs or back-end scripts in DC1. A significant number of applications run in the back end via cron, and they are stopped by sending a TERM signal. This step is accomplished with a command similar to the following:

    ```
    knife ssh "roles:dc1" "ps hww -C ruby -o pid,user,cmd
    | grep app_user | awk '{print \\$1}' | xargs -i kill
    -TERM {}"
    ```

7. Send a "-9" signal to any stubborn scripts that refuse to stop in DC1. Sometimes a TERM signal is not enough to make the script stop. For example, an application may mistakenly catch all exceptions (including the TERM signal). By now, most of these problem scripts in Rafter's applications have been fixed, but this step covers the case where some new application appears that is not a good citizen.

8. Put up a maintenance page on several web properties that have external customers. Rafter puts up a maintenance page with a message like "We're currently performing scheduled maintenance, we'll be back in 15 minutes." The deployment system can do this automatically by placing a special file in a directory on each application server. This is done in both datacenters.

9. Promote a new Redis master server in DC2. Redis, by default, does not have any automated switch technique, so Rafter had to build their own system for doing this. It operates as follows (see Figure 11.5):

    a. Configure all applications to connect to hostname "redis-master01." This resolves to a local IP alias in the datacenter.

    b. Release the IP alias from the current Redis master, which has the effect of severing any open Redis connections. Then write the current time as a heartbeat key into the master Redis server, and check that this key has the same value on the slave in DC2 to be promoted. This ensures the slave's replication has caught up to the master.

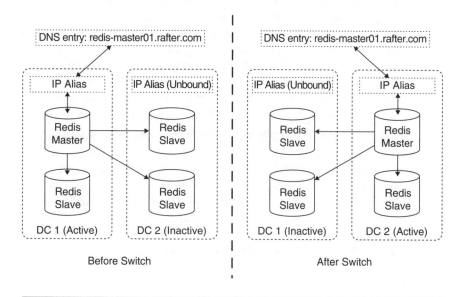

FIGURE 11.5 Redis promotion [Notation: Architecture]

   c. Promote the chosen a Redis slave to master, demote the previous master, and reconfigure all slaves to use the new master server.

   d. Bind the IP alias to the new Redis master server. Send a gratituous ARP (Address Resolution Protocol) message to ensure all ARP caches are flushed.

   e. Update the redis-master01 DNS record to resolve to the new IP alias. Relying on DNS has been one area of concern with this solution, since clients can cache it. However, Rafter had no such problems. The conjecture is that this is because client connections to the old master are interrupted when the IP alias is released, which forces the Redis client library to reconnect—only then it connects to the new master. Set a 1-second TTL on the DNS record.

10. Promote a new clustrix master in DC2. Because the Clustrix databases in each datacenter are configured in a master-master scheme, there is no need to reconfigure the replication on a switch. As for Redis, pointing to the currently active Clustrix database is achieved through DNS. These are the steps in detail:

   a. Add a READONLY flag to the Clustrix database in DC1.

   b. Ensure that both databases are completely in sync by checking the binary log positions on each database. Check that DC2 has received all of DC1's binary logs and vice versa.

    c. Remove the READONLY flag from the Clustrix DC2 database.

    d. Update the Clustrix master DNS record to point to the virtual IP address for Clustrix in DC2. Simply updating the DNS record is not sufficient, as connections from applications will continue to stay open to the DC1 database. To close these connections, loop through all of them on the DC1 Clustrix using "show processlist," and killing all open sessions using the "kill" command. This forces applications to open a new connection to the database, and they end up connecting to the database in DC2 now.

11. Mark DC2 as "active" in Chef Server. This follows the same process as Step 4. At this point in time, DC1 is now inactive and DC2 is now active.

12. Start Chef Client on all VMs in DC2. Similar to Step 5, the "knife ssh" command is used to start the Chef client on all servers in DC2. Now that DC2 is in an active state, Chef will perform all necessary configuration changes in order to convert the VMs to an active state. This essentially means installing cronjobs for all back-end applications, installing and starting up application daemons, and reconfiguring application-specific firewall rules.

13. Remove maintenance pages and banners on all customer-facing web applications. This is done using the deployment system.

14. Update Akamai CDN (content delivery network). Akamai sits in front of Rafter's main shopping cart application as a proxy providing CDN services. Using a provided SOAP API, Akamai is updated to send traffic to DC2. Over the course of about 5 minutes, Akamai will start sending traffic to the new datacenter.

15. Update public DNS for all applications. For applications that do not use Akamai, the public DNS records are updated to point to IP addresses in DC2 using AWS Route 53. Because of the 1-minute TTL for the public DNS, within a few minutes of these changes most customers start hitting applications in DC2. The RubyGem infrastructure library assists in this task. The pseudo-code for this looks something like this:

```
DevOps::Applications.all do |app|
  update_public_dns(app.fqdn, app.external_ip)
end
```

16. Update local DNS for all applications. The local DNS servers are updated, so URLs of internal services point to IP addresses in DC2. Again, the library assists:

```
DevOps::Applications.all do |app|
  update_local_dns(app.fqdn, app.internal_ip)
end
```

17. Update escalation priorities in Rafter's monitoring system (Scout). In the monitoring system, the priority of alerts generated from servers in DC1 is changed to "normal." This means that operators continue to receive alerts via e-mail from servers in this datacenter, but not pages. Update the

escalation priority for servers in DC2 to "urgent". This means that critical alerts for servers in DC2 can open alerts on Pagerduty, which in turn sends out pages. Rafter has found that monitoring servers in the inactive datacenter is still important, since one does not want to find out about potential server problems on the day of a switch. However, e-mail-based alerts instead of pages are sufficient. This step is accomplished via Ruby code that interacts with Scout's website via the "Ruby mechanize" library.

18. Reenable alerts on Rafter's monitoring system (Scout). After updating the priorities, it is still necessary to reenable the alerts.

Uncontrolled Switch

The need for an uncontrolled switch arises when the currently active datacenter is completely unavailable (e.g., through a power outage at the datacenter). There are fewer steps for this type of switch, since it is not possible to do a clean shutdown of the active datacenter. In this situation, there is significant potential for data inconsistency. Most likely, some data cleanup will be needed after the initially active datacenter comes back online. Even with only a 1-second database replication delay, it is likely the inactive datacenter will be missing some data at the time of the outage.

As before, we use the following key:

- DC1: Datacenter to switch from
- DC2: Datacenter to switch to

The nine steps taken to implement the uncontrolled switch are

1. Mark DC2 as "active" and DC1 as "inactive" in Chef Server. Publish a new JSON document to Chef Server to that effect. All applications using the infrastructure library can now find out what the correct state of the datacenters is.

2. Promote a local DNS server in DC2 to master and reconfigure slaves, if necessary. If DC1 contains the current master, then no local DNS updates can be processed. Thus, one of the DNS slaves in DC2 must be promoted to master and the other server should become a slave of the new master. This is done with a Ruby "mechanize" script using the Webmin web-based UI.

3. Promote a new Clustrix master in DC2. A subset of the steps performed for a controlled switch need to be done here, namely:

   a. Remove the READONLY flag on the database in DC2.
   b. Update the Clustrix master DNS record to point to DC2.

4. Promote a new Redis master in DC2. A subset of the steps performed for a controlled switch need to be done here, namely:

   a. Promote a Redis slave in DC2 to master, and reconfigure the other Redis slave in DC2 to be a slave of the new master.

  b. Bind the IP alias to the new master.

  c. Update the redis-master01 DNS record.

5. Update local DNS for all applications. This is the same step as in the controlled switch.

6. Update public DNS for all applications. This is the same step as in the controlled switch.

7. Update Akamai CDN. This is the same step as in the controlled switch.

8. Start Chef clients on all servers in DC2. This is the same step as in the controlled switch.

9. Update escalation priorities in Rafter's monitoring system. This is the same step as in the controlled switch.

Defining and Automating Switch Steps

Switch steps fall into two use cases: they launch either an external shell command (e.g., "knife ssh" commands) or Ruby code (such as checking database delay). Here is an example of Step 1 in the controlled switch:

```
step "Check: Ensure replication delay is low on Clustrix" do
  prereqs :clustrix_databases, :datacenters
  ruby_block do
    result = nil
    puts "Checking Slave Delay in each datacenter"
    @datacenters.each do |datacenter|
      client =  Mysql2::Client.new(:host =>
@clustrix_databases[:vips][datacenter], :username =>
"root", :password => @clustrix_databases[:password])
      row = client.query("show slave status").first
      puts "Slave delay in #{datacenter}:
#{row["Seconds_Behind_Master"]}"
      if row["Seconds_Behind_Master"] > 60
        result = failed("Slave delay must be less than
60.")
      end
      client.close
    end
    result ? result : success
  end
end
```

  In the preceding step, the infrastructure library automatically runs the Ruby code in the ruby_block (from line 3) during the datacenter switch. The block will return either failure or success using the provided success/failed helper methods. Every step in the datacenter process has a corresponding step defined in the DSL.

The DSL also contains the concept of "prereqs" since most steps needed a common set of data inputs (e.g., the datacenters being swapped, database information, and gathering credentials). Instead of gathering the same data over and over again, each step defines which prerequisite data it needs. The prerequisites are defined in another DSL. At the beginning of the datacenter swap scripts, before any steps are executed, code is inserted to query the information needed to fulfil the prerequisites. For example, here is what the clustrix_databases prereq looks like:

```
prereq "clustrix_databases" do
  if ENV['CLX_PASS']
    db_info = {:password => ENV['CLX_PASS']}
  else
    puts "Please enter the root password for the database:"
    db_info = {:password => STDIN.noecho(&:gets).chomp!}
  end
  db_info[:vips] = DevOps::Clusters.load("clustrix")[:vips]
  db_info
end
```

Next, the DSL was expanded to logically group steps together into lists to match the two types of datacenter switch. For example, here is the list of steps for a controlled switch:

```
list "Controlled Switch" do
  step "Check: Ensure replication delay is low"
  step "Disable Scout Notifications"
  step "Put up 'Site Going Down Soon' message"
  step "Set current datacenter to inactive"
  step "Run chef in DC to swap from"
  step "Run killer with -TERM"
  step "Run killer with -9"
  step "Put up 'Maintenance' pages"
  step "Swap redis"
  step "Swap DB"
  step "Set new DC to active"
  step "Run chef in DC to swap to"
  step "Remove 'Maintenance' pages"
  step "Swap Akamai"
  step "Swap Route 53 DNS"
  step "Swap Datacenter DNS"
  step "Update Scout Notification Groups"
  step "Enable Scout Notifications"
end
```

For each step used in the list, the library finds a step implementation with the corresponding name.

Based on this framework for defining steps and grouping these steps in a specific order, Rafter built a console-based application for running these lists interactively. Upon startup, it displays all the lists that have been defined by their names. For example:

```
Pick a set of Steps to perform: <enter defaults to #1>
1. Controlled Switch
2. Uncontrolled Switch
Choose: 1
```

In the console, the operator chooses a list to run. The UI then displays the names of all steps in the list and asks for confirmation. It also allows skipping over steps or starting from a different step if so desired.

```
The following steps will be run:
1. Check: Ensure replication delay is low
2. Disable Scout Notifications
[...]
Press Enter if satisfied with order, or type in alternative
order of steps, comma delimited, ranges allowed:<enter>
```

Next, the console application runs any prereqs code for the selected steps and then begins running each step, displaying any output of the step in the console. The degree to which the "auto pilot" is used is up to the operator. Either the operator can run each step requiring an "enter" in order to proceed to the next step, or the list can run automatically by going to the next step once the previous step finishes. In the case of a step failing, the operator can choose to skip to the next step or retry the step again.

The console application can be run from either a developer's machine or a utility server that has network access to servers in both datacenters and Internet access in order to access Chef Server. All commands are run using the operator's own provided credentials (sudo password, SSH keys, Chef key, etc.), so even if unauthorized users gained access to the console application, they would not have the required level of access to run the steps.

11.7 Testing

As with all other processes and software, the infrastructure and switch control must be tested.

Datacenter Switching Application

Unit tests are written in RSpec for each step from the previous section, the underlying DSL library, and the console application. This provides a good sanity check for obvious bugs in the code or logic. However, not everything can be fully tested since connections to resources like databases and external commands are stubbed out in the tests. In order to help find bugs that the unit tests might not be able to catch, the entire console application can be run in a dry-run/debug mode by default. This will execute every step in the process but skip over parts of steps that perform potentially unsafe tasks like changing state. A helper method "debug?" is used in the steps for checking if the step is running in the debug mode. This allows a safe run through an entire datacenter switch in a dry-run mode ahead of time.

Infrastructure Testing

A lot of the "heavy lifting" being done during the datacenter switch is actually outside of the entire datacenter switching application and is performed by the infrastructure library and Chef when reconfiguring a server. The infrastructure library and Chef cookbooks are constantly changing, and so they require more rigorous testing. In order to verify that a change does not break existing functionality, unit tests using RSpec are run. In addition to unit tests, Rafter also built a suite of integration tests. These tests first boot up a brand new server on the staging server platform, and then use Serverspec to verify that Chef and the infrastructure library configured the server properly.

Continuous Deployment Pipeline

All changes to Rafter's infrastructure and datacenter switching applications go through a continuous deployment pipeline using TeamCity. Any new changes are committed to a branch named "test." TeamCity then runs syntax checking, lint (coding style checker), and unit tests on this test branch. If everything passes, it then boots up a VM and runs the suite of integration tests against it. Finally, if no tests have failed, TeamCity automatically merges the changes into a "staging" branch and then automatically publishes all infrastructure changes to the staging environment. After everything is working well in staging, the changes are manually merged into a production branch, tests are run again on the production branch, and then the new version is automatically published to the production environment if no tests fail.

11.8 Summary

Having two datacenters with the ability to fail over smoothly from one to another involves the applications, the database systems, and the infrastructure management system. In this chapter we described how Rafter achieves this ability.

At the application level, applications had to be designed using the following principles:

1.   Applications should store state only in approved datastores.
2.   The data storage needs of an application must be considered at the design phase. Application changes and new features can cause significant delays in replication, which, in turn, harm the ability to fail over quickly. Usually some concessions can be made; for example, if the data is not business critical it may not need to be replicated to both datacenters. Alternatively, an application can store data differently, so that the data volume gets reduced (e.g., by storing aggregate data instead of every record).
3.   Back-end applications must be designed to stop gracefully. Most of Rafter's back-end applications are safe to be killed at any point, but some applications may cause inconsistencies if killed at the wrong moment. For example, imagine an application that charges a customer and then records the charge in the database. If the application is killed after charging the customer, but before recording the charge in the database, the customer could be charged again later. In order to prevent this, applications that are sensitive to being killed are built to intercept the TERM signal (using Ruby's trap callback), finish up only their current iteration, and then exit gracefully.

At the infrastructure level, Ruby on Rails and Chef are important tools, but they had to be made datacenter aware through the construction of an infrastructure library that manages both the infrastructure and the deployment of various applications to the appropriate datacenter.

At the database level, a key ingredient is a database system that understands distribution and can be configured to support distributed data. Rafter had to make special provisions to enable the systems to perform appropriately.

Even with the appropriate architecture at each level, managing the switch from one datacenter to another involves a sequence of steps that can be automated but that must be performed in a particular sequence.

11.9 For Further Reading

We mentioned many technologies in this chapter. You can find more details at the following links:

- Chef: http://docs.opscode.com/chef_overview.html
- Ruby on Rails: http://rubyonrails.org/
- Ruby Gems: https://rubygems.org/
- GitHub: https://github.com/

- Clustrix: http://www.clustrix.com/
- Redis: http://redis.io/
- Couchbase: http://www.couchbase.com/
- Memcached: http://memcached.org/
- Elasticsearch: http://www.elasticsearch.org/
- Unison: http://www.cis.upenn.edu/~bcpierce/unison/
- Scout: https://scoutapp.com/
- RSpec: http://rspec.info/
- Serverspec: http://serverspec.org/
- TeamCity: http://www.jetbrains.com/teamcity/
- Resque: https://github.com/resque/resque
- Sidekiq: http://sidekiq.org/
- Akami: http://www.akamai.com/

Virtual IP addresses (VIPs) are discussed on the Wikipedia site http://en.wikipedia.org/wiki/Virtual_IP_address

The replication problem in Redis is discussed in [3Scale 12].

12

Implementing a Continuous Deployment Pipeline for Enterprises

With John Painter and Daniel Hand

> *Sourced Group is an enterprise consulting organization,*
> *working on bringing the benefits of Cloud-based*
> *solution architecture and automation to the enterprise.*
> —http://www.sourcedgroup.com.au/

12.1 Introduction

Over the past few years, enterprises have been increasingly utilizing cloud computing services from providers such as Amazon Web Services (AWS). With the move to cloud computing, enterprises are generally looking to achieve two primary outcomes: cost efficiency gains and increased agility and velocity of their products or business outcomes. One of the core characteristics of cloud computing platforms is the widespread availability of programmatic interfaces and automation frameworks. These interfaces were initially used to manage base infrastructure (such as servers and storage), but have quickly evolved to include the deployment and management of the application itself, and are now used by an overarching continuous deployment system, such as a continuous deployment pipeline (CDP). As described in Part Two, the CDP monitors an application's source control status. When changes to the source code have been committed, they are retrieved by the CDP, the application is built and packaged, and then a number of tests in various environments and with various goals are run. Once the application is "production-ready," the CDP calls specific programmatic interfaces to deploy an updated copy of that application. Automated control of the infrastructure and application deployment allows teams to focus on the application code—not application deployment—and leads to achieving the agility and velocity targets for development projects in an enterprise.

This case study introduces the CDP reference architecture developed and refined by Sourced Group while working with leading Australian enterprises within the financial services, media, telecommunications, and aviation sectors. Sourced Group is an enterprise consulting organization founded in 2010 by a set of individuals with financial services backgrounds. Currently, Sourced Group's team comprises engineers who fall into one of two core skill areas—data management (databases and data warehousing) or solutions architecture and automation.

In this chapter, we discuss different facets of implementing a CDP within an enterprise: the organizational context, the CDP itself, and how security is managed. Then we introduce advanced concepts and new services provided by AWS, before concluding the chapter.

12.2 Organizational Context

For CDP projects, Sourced Group is typically engaged with an enterprise via midterm strategic consulting engagements to design and deliver a CDP framework into an organization. Any such implementation must fit within the customer's organization and its culture. Since Sourced Group's engagement is for a limited period, one activity is to identify and train personnel who will be responsible for the CDP after the engagement is completed. Figure 12.1 presents the organizational structure that Sourced Group typically aims for. Two groups should be formed: a *CD onboarding group*, which is responsible for interfacing with developers to get their applications onto the CDP, and a *CD engineering team*, which designs and manages the pipeline and its components. The CD engineering team and the tools it maintains together form a CDP center of excellence (COE). In smaller organizations, CD onboarding and CD engineering may be a single team. It is common for developers themselves to become part of the CDP onboarding team. These groups remain responsible for the CDP after Sourced Group's engagement is complete.

Education and knowledge transfer are key to the success of adopting any new technology. To this end, Sourced Group organizes an onboarding team to consist of virtual or seconded members of the CD engineering team early in an engagement. The onboarding group helps DevOps teams develop or migrate their existing applications onto the CDP. In addition to smoothing the transition of the deployment process, the onboarding team provides real-time feedback to the CD engineering team from the digital portfolio managers and their application teams. Feedback typically consists of a mixture of platform requirements and consumer feedback.

A typical Sourced Group's customer has multiple development teams, each with their own projects, skill set, and utilization of the cloud (if any) for their applications. This organizational diversity complicates the task of introducing a CDP. It is common for an enterprise organization to successfully conduct one or more small application pilot projects on a cloud platform, with varying degrees of human involvement and automation in their deployment techniques. These pilot projects are a good starting point for the introduction of the CDP. See Chapter 10 for a general discussion of rolling out DevOps practices.

The effort required to design and implement a new CDP and train an organization around it depends on a number of factors, including the existence of one or more existing platforms, availability of personnel, skills and prior experience, and the support and commitment from the wider business. Another important factor is the degree to which the customer's environment is regulated or constrained by one or a number of governing bodies, for example, the Australian Prudential Regulatory Authority (APRA) or the Payment Card Industry (PCI).

In addition to the onboarding team, observe the role of security operations (SecOps) as shown in Figure 12.1. Since SecOps already has interactions with the development teams and since security is such an essential consideration for

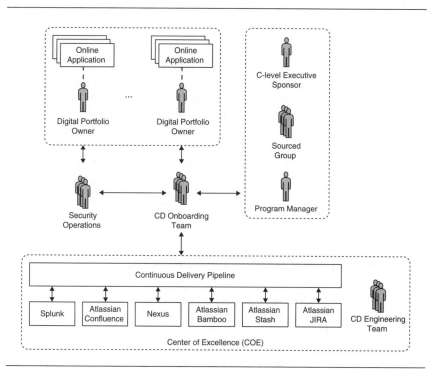

FIGURE 12.1   Project team structure [Notation: Architecture]

any enterprise, the SecOps team becomes a natural adjunct to the introduction of a CDP. As a result, SecOps is always a key stakeholder throughout each engagement. As we discussed in Chapter 8, SecOps has a challenging role to fulfill and needs to balance the desire for speed and agility against business risk.

Security is a core concern for the CDP, both the security of the CDP itself and the applications it deploys. The use of a common CDP not only maintains the current security mechanisms but in most cases significantly improves on them, in part because the CDP is able to enforce policy and procedure against all components that it deploys. Another improvement is the reduction of the number of privileged users and systems. Although SecOps teams typically start out by questioning the CDP, with time and experience, they tend to become enthusiastic advocates. This is partially because their concerns are automatically incorporated into the builds, as we discuss in the section on the stages of the application life cycle.

Executive sponsorship and cross-portfolio project management are also critical during each engagement. Enterprise-level deployment of any technology needs senior executive sponsorship and an experienced program manager to navigate internal challenges, organize resources, mediate between teams, assist with stakeholder management, and generally ensure smooth delivery. We discuss these issues more generally in Chapter 10, as well.

At the start of a CDP implementation engagement, it is common for each application DevOps team to have its own CDP. These CDPs tend to be discrete and disparate. In order to achieve centralized security, compliance, and economies of scale, ownership of common tools and technologies is assigned to the CD engineering team. This team has enterprise-wide responsibility for the support of the involved tools. The typical tools introduced by Sourced are Splunk, Atlassian Confluence, Sonatype Nexus, Atlassian Bamboo, Atlassian Stash, and Atlassian JIRA. The tool teams, which are part of the CDP COE and hence the CD engineering team, are populated from members of existing DevOps teams. Ideally, the members want to specialize in the respective technology, and either already have developed or want to develop the skills necessary to support an enterprise-wide platform.

12.3 The Continuous Deployment Pipeline

The CDP provides a standardized method for an enterprise to manage the life cycle of an application. Larger enterprises, particularly those in the financial sector, have strong risk management frameworks and are generally willing to trade small amounts of agility in exchange for assurance and risk reduction. Standardization of the application life cycle reduces risk by isolating change into feature branches, testing that change, and providing a moderated path into production.

This section, which is by far the most detailed in the chapter, discusses the CDP with respect to tooling and the standardized application life cycle, as well as management of state and persistence.

CDP Tooling

Figure 12.2 gives an overview of the tools that form the CDP and their interactions. Information from Atlassian JIRA (the ticketing system) is fed both to Atlassian Stash (the source code revision system) and to Atlassian Bamboo (the continuous deployment system). Stash provides application and configuration source code for Bamboo to build images, which Bamboo then deploys onto AWS. Since Bamboo does not natively interact with AWS, it utilizes the commercial plug-in "Tasks for AWS."

Two essential elements of any CDP are a source repository and the continuous integration/deployment (CI/CD) tool. A wide range of open source, hosted, and commercial source repositories exist in the market, but enterprises generally have regulatory concerns or IP protection requirements that dictate the use of behind-the-firewall solutions such as Atlassian Stash or GitHub Enterprise. Sourced Group uses Atlassian Bamboo as the CD tool of choice, which forms the backbone of the CDP. Atlassian Bamboo offers several key features that are important to an enterprise CDP, such as tight integration with ticketing and audit trails systems, but its unique branch management is critical to the objectives of the CDP as we discuss next.

A core feature of the CDP is its enforcement of a standardized application life cycle, along with the assurance benefits that leads to. That life cycle is defined as a (software) plan that is executed in conjunction with the source control system. In order to provide assurance, it is essential that the same life cycle (or plan) is used on a feature or testing branch and on the mainline or integration branch. Atlassian Bamboo achieves this by supporting branch awareness in plans,

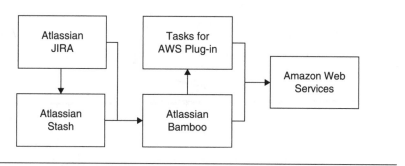

FIGURE 12.2 The complete CDP tool set [Notation: Architecture]

allowing the execution of copies of the plan against an arbitrary number of source branches. The branches are automatically detected and cleaned, further reducing human effort. Figure 12.3 shows the use of the virtual plans for branches.

This is in contrast to many CD systems that manage each branch as a different plan. As demonstrated in Figure 12.4, managing each branch as a different plan creates a point of administration and inevitably leads to drift between the plans, which in turn results in the loss of standardization and assurance.

While not critical to the success of the CDP, it is common to use a ticket management solution such as Atlassian JIRA. This greatly improves cross-referencing of code changes against issues or feature requests that have been logged by the business. The integration can go as far as the automated generation of release notes based on the tickets that were closed in the latest application build.

The CDP reference architecture can be adapted to multiple public and private cloud environments. For the purposes of this chapter, AWS is the target platform. The remainder of this case study assumes a foundational understanding of a

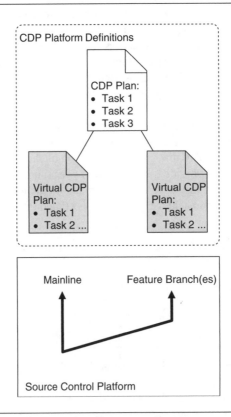

FIGURE 12.3 Virtual CDP plan for each branch [Notation: Architecture]

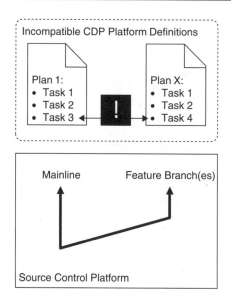

FIGURE 12.4 Many CD tools need discrete plans for each branch, leading to drift. [Notation: Architecture]

number of AWS services and products. Readers should refer to Chapter 2 for general cloud concepts and AWS's detailed documentation for specific information.

Environment Definition Using AWS CloudFormation

The CDP depends heavily on Amazon's CloudFormation (CF). CF provides the ability to define a complete virtual environment, including resources and security components, as a declarative configuration file written in JSON. Environments can be replicated consistently and benefit from the same level of unit testing commonplace with application code. If a particular resource request fails, possibly due to a misconfiguration, the whole stack is simply torn down. This is done to spare the customer the cost of keeping a faulty stack.

Developing and maintaining Amazon CF templates for a small number of applications is reasonably easy. However, as the number of applications increases, it becomes increasingly inefficient to maintain an individual template for each application. Furthermore, the CDP makes use of a separate CF script for most of its steps and for each tier in the application.

AWS frequently releases updates and best practices that users want to take advantage of. However, introducing change to the templates can be time-consuming and complex, as different code bases must be managed. Sourced Group addresses this challenge by managing a common set of generic operation templates, which are dynamically merged with an application-specific template at bake or deployment time—as shown in Figure 12.5. This ensures that changes and updates are effectively permeated throughout all environments under the control of the CDP. Another benefit of providing a centrally managed set of templates is that it significantly reduces the time and effort required by teams to add a new application to the CDP. This is particularly important when a team has little or no prior experience in deploying to AWS as it removes much of the heavy lifting.

Figure 12.5 shows the CF merging process. A template for the application at hand is merged with independent operations templates to create a single template that is used in the baking process. The operations templates include the perimeter security group (responsible for preventing external access to the organization's virtual private cloud (VPC)) and the network security group (responsible for security within the network inside the VPC perimeter). These and other templates are merged in a priority fashion, so that an application template cannot override settings specified by one of the operations templates.

Operations templates are stored in one Git repository, and application templates are stored in another. This provides greater levels of control and separation. Atlassian Bamboo merges the various templates into a single CF template.

The merge of separate CF templates also enables the implementation of controls outlined in the enterprise security policy. In particular, the requirements on different components based on the security policy can be specified, and the

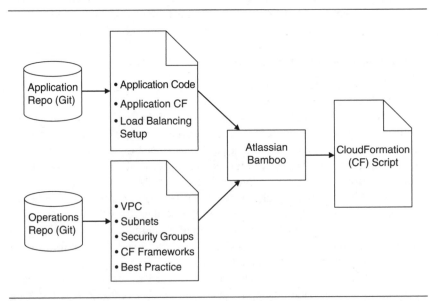

FIGURE 12.5 Merging operations templates and application configuration into a single CF script [Notation: Architecture]

fulfillment of those requirements can be implemented centrally, as so-called "units of consumption." For example, if the enterprise has a requirement that all S3 (Simple Storage Service) buckets are logged and version control enabled, and if the application's CF template uses S3 buckets, then, in the merged CF template, the standard S3 buckets are replaced with a version that has been built on top of the standard offering but fulfills those requirements. This extended version is built by the CD engineering team in cooperation with SecOps. Therefore, by consuming the S3 "unit" they are, by definition, compliant.

Overview of the Standardized Application Life Cycle and Its Usage

The primary technical outcome of the CDP is the standardization of the application life cycle. The application life cycle can be broken down into five main stages, as shown in Figure 12.6:

1. *Building and testing.* Performing functional code testing and producing application artifacts. Both topics are not in the focus of this chapter—see Chapter 5 instead.
2. *Baking.* Bootstrapping the application artifacts and configuration onto a temporary target operating system, then "baking" the image by taking a snapshot from which new VMs can be created. In AWS, this is called an Amazon Machine Image (AMI).
3. *Deployment.* Deploying a new, independent "stack" of the application, comprising newly launched VMs as copies of the AMI through an AWS autoscaling group (ASG), as well as supporting infrastructure and configuration such as load balancing, scaling, monitoring, networking, and—potentially—databases.
4. *Release.* Releasing the new stack by changing the domain name system (DNS) entry that points to the existing stack to now point to the new stack. Prior to release, the new stack needs to be modified to match the capacity and scale of the existing stack, so as to ensure continuation of service when rolling out. This stage optionally includes patching or modification of persistent data.
5. *Teardown.* Once all traffic has been moved to the new stack, the previous stack is torn down as it is no longer required. It is prudent to perform safety

FIGURE 12.6 The stages an application goes through in the CDP [Notation: Porter's Value Chain]

checks on the stack prior to teardown to ensure that all traffic has been moved away from the environment. It would be embarrassing to tear down an environment that is still serving production requests.

In the next section, we discuss each stage in detail—here we describe the overall workings and the usage of them. The standardized application life cycle is implemented as a plan in the CD system (Atlassian Bamboo). Bamboo monitors the source control system and runs the plan against each commit on any of the branches. The coupling of a standardized application life cycle and source control system provides a high degree of assurance to both the application developers and the business. If the life cycle successfully runs in a lower-order branch, such as a feature branch or a testing branch, then you have some assurance that the change will be successful in a higher-order branch such as production.

When tasked with making a change, say, adding a new feature, an application developer branches the source code, makes the change, and commits to the branch. This triggers the standard application life cycle target via the CDP. The CDP will build discrete and independent environments for that feature branch, allowing for individual testing and experimentation, without interrupting other feature development. In this environment, the functional artifact is validated—preferably with a high degree of automated testing. The nonblocking, independent environment approach is one of the foundations of the platform. Large and experimental features can run in parallel with small changes, while still being held to the same standards. Developers are given clear guidelines on what constitutes a complete, releasable feature, and the business gets a real-time view of the progress of a sprint or individual features.

When a feature is releasable, or production-ready, the developer makes a Git "pull request" to get the respective feature branch merged into the higher-order branch. A lead developer is then responsible for reviewing the build results for that feature branch, visiting the validation environment and accepting it into the sprint branch—see also Figure 12.7. Once the sprint is complete, the team lead submits the entire block of changes to the testing team. Smaller teams, or teams with less governance and risk management requirements, may choose to simplify this model, so that feature branches are released directly into the user acceptance test (UAT) or staging environment.

You may have noticed that the CDP as introduced in Chapter 5 has a fairly different shape from the CDP discussed here. In particular, the earlier CDP was concerned with pre-commit tests, commits, building/packaging/unit testing, integration testing, UAT/staging, and, finally, production. This is mostly in line with the set of branches discussed here. The CDP here is enacted for each branch: Feature branches check local tests; a sprint branch tests the integration between the different branches, with other systems and third-party services; the stacks created from the UAT branch are used for acceptance and performance tests; and the production branch actually corresponds to the live application.

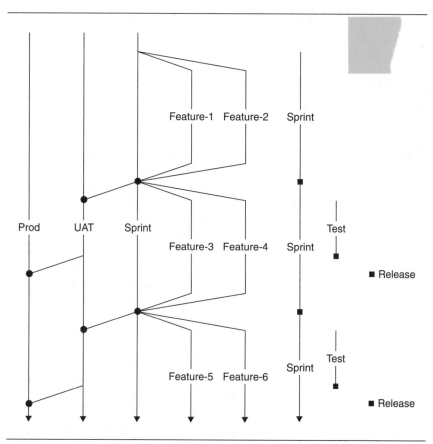

FIGURE 12.7 Developing, testing, and integrating features independently [Notation: left: version control branches; right: timing of stages with development sprints, independent testing, and releases]

The use of higher-order branches other than production is specific to each organization, but DevOps generally advocates fewer branches over more—see the discussion in Chapter 5. Enterprises often have large, potentially geographically dispersed teams with the majority of teams adopting a "sprint" methodology to software development. Due to regulatory and risk requirements it is often necessary to have all changes assessed through a separate testing team prior to release. The CDP caters to that by provisioning discrete nonblocking environments for each branch. This allows development to continue while an independent team completes testing. Using this method, developments are not blocked for long periods of time, awaiting testing and signoff—while the time between feature submission and release may still be long, the overall velocity of the project is not impacted.

Figure 12.7 shows the flow of features into UAT and production. Independent branches can be developed, tested, and deployed independently.

Stages of the Standardized Application Life Cycle

The stages of the standardized application life cycle we discuss here are: bake, deploy, release, and tear down.

Bake

The baking stage creates a self-contained image (AMI) of the application on a disposable server. The server is "baked" into an AMI, which can then be copied to any global region of AWS. In Chapter 5 we discussed the levels of baking that can be implemented. The CDP creates heavily baked images as well as one AWS ASG per AMI, for deploying that AMI without the involvement of any other processes or systems. The AMI is immutable and directly associated with a commit in the Git repository, leading to a high degree of visibility and confidence as to the contents of the AMI. Hence, Git forms a single point of truth, not just for the source code but for all known copies of the application, as they were baked from that source code at a given commit and thus at a given point in time. The image requires no further bootstrapping—instances of it can be launched and are ready to go. Note that VMs are called instances in AWS (i.e., instances of an AMI), but we use both terms interchangeably in this chapter.

While this process leads to a larger number of AMIs an organization has to manage, it has a number of benefits. These include simplification of the deployment and ongoing operational support of the application, reduced VM boot times on scale events, reduced failures during the boot process, and increased consistency.

Figure 12.8 illustrates each of the steps in the baking process. Each tier of the application requires a separate image. If a business application consists of the

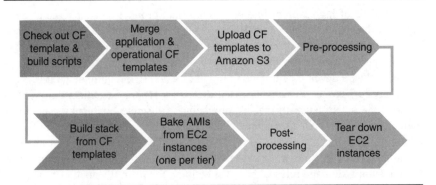

FIGURE 12.8   The CDP baking process [Notation: Porter's Value Chain]

usual three tiers (i.e., a web tier, an application tier, and a database tier), the CDP bakes three distinct AMIs, one for each tier. In brief, the steps for baking are

1. Check out Amazon CF template and build scripts from Atlassian Stash.
2. Merge application and operational Amazon CF templates, as discussed around Figure 12.5. The resulting CF templates prepare the environment for baking.
3. Upload Amazon CF templates to Amazon S3.
4. Run pre-processing, which collects all available build artifacts from DynamoDB (see the section on managing the pipeline state).
5. Create the environment for baking from the combined CF template. This will create a builder instance for each tier, which respectively forms the base for each image to be baked. This step also loads the necessary software and configuration into the builder instances, through the use of a bootstrapping system like CF's cfn-init as detailed in the next paragraph.
6. Bake a copy of each builder instance into an AMI.
7. Run post-processing, which collects the new AMI IDs, places them into the artifact repository (see the section on managing pipeline state), and tags them with appropriate identifying information, such as commit ID.
8. Destroy and clean up the builder instances.

The baking process uses CF to launch an instance of a vanilla or predefined enterprise standard operating environment AMI, such as Amazon Linux, Red Hat Enterprise Linux, or Microsoft Windows Server. The instance independently bootstraps the application using the AWS CF bootstrapping system, cfn-init. The installation of packages, files, and service management is handled via the cfn-init agent. cfn-init is declarative and implements atomic behavior, so either it signals that all declared items completed successfully or it signals a failure and aborts. This provides a high level of assurance that the configuration is correct and the application is correctly installed. If the success signal is not received after a specified timeout, the instance is destroyed and the build is marked as broken—recall the discussion around breaking the build from Chapter 5. In case of success, Amazon's EC2 API is called via the Bamboo "Tasks for AWS" plug-in to bake an AMI from the running instance. After that, the instance is no longer needed and is terminated.

Deploy

By heavily baking images in the previous stage, the deployment stage of the life cycle becomes fairly simple. For each tier, the baked AMI is handed to a newly created AWS ASG through its launch configuration (LC). The CDP then specifies a minimum number of instances in the ASG, which in turn launches that number of instances of the AMI straight away. Elastic Load Balancing (ELB) is configured for each ASG, distributing the incoming requests over the available VMs. Node registration is not required, since the ASG and load balancer maintain this information. And instances need no further configuration, as that was bootstrapped during the baking stage.

The operations repository defines the base standard for ASGs through its CF templates. Therefore, all ASGs are set up with the best practice CloudWatch alarms, triggers, and autoscaling policies. Application teams do not need to be autoscaling experts to consume the service, and many implementation errors can be avoided via this standardization.

The ASG instances are provided with an identity and access management (IAM) role to allow secure access to other AWS services, such as S3. Because the role is part of the independent stack and defined in the application repository, any changes to the role are tracked and audited via the source control and deployment systems. This creates secure IAM credentials, avoiding the need to pass credentials to the instance as plain text strings or configuration files. The IAM profile is also directly associated with that stack, so if a breach were to occur the stack can be updated to refresh the IAM credentials.

Release

One of the most vital parts of the CDP is the release stage. Unlike the previous stages, the release stage impacts current production systems. In this section, we focus on release into production. The CDP can be executed for any branch, and most stacks this way will be created for testing. While release still is a step that may be relevant for testing (i.e., to point UAT testers to the latest build), release in the production environment is where it gets interesting: How do you redirect a constant flow of requests from users to a new version of the application?

Although the release process itself is automated, the CDP can pause at this step and wait for a gatekeeper to manually approve the step in the pipeline. The use of a manual trigger at this point also allows indefinite time for further testing and validation prior to release, where the newly created stack is already available. Alternatively, if there is a high degree of confidence in the automatic test sets, then the CDP can execute this step as soon as all prerequisites are met.

Figure 12.9 shows how the adjustment of a DNS entry can be used to redirect traffic from an old stack to a new one. We here make use of the AWS DNS service called Route 53.

In Stage 0 of the release, only the old version (v1.0) is running. Stage 1 is the point in the process where we have two application stacks: the current production stack, which we refer to as the "red" or active stack, and the newly built, "black" or inactive stack. The release is achieved in Stage 2, where the live traffic has been redirected from the red stack to the black stack. As shown in the figure, the stateless parts of the stack are kept completely separate between the two versions—but the persistent database is retained from one build to the next. Therefore, the testing shown in Stage 1 has to remain nondestructive, since it is conducted on the live production database. More details on how persistence is handled is deferred until the section on managing persistence.

Figure 12.10 illustrates the DNS structure in more detail. Using Route 53, a DNS entry of type ALIAS is created for each stack—that is, the ALIAS points to the load balancer of the top tier in the stack. Testers are sent to a specific build

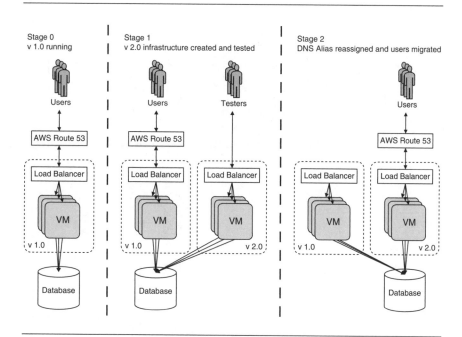

FIGURE 12.9   Application release stages [Notation: Architecture]

(as in Stage 1 in the figures) using this ALIAS. The users of the system typically go through a user-friendly host name (CNAME) as a point of entry. This CNAME is resolved to a "floating DNS record," another CNAME that always points to the active stack. Release is achieved by switching the floating DNS record from the old ALIAS to the new one. We discussed DNS in general in Chapter 2 and its role in deployment in Chapter 6. One specific aspect here is the layering of three DNS records on top of one another. A second point to note here is that ALIASes and CNAMEs are used, which refer from one host name to another, instead of simple "A" records, which refer from one host name to one or more IP addresses. For the CNAMEs, it is clear why this is necessary. The ALIASes, however, are used because AWS ELB provides an autogenerated (non-user-friendly) DNS host name. This is done so that AWS can scale the resources for load balancing transparently.

Updating the floating record is done using a separate CF script for release. Unlike previous stages, where a discrete CF stack was created, during release an existing CF stack is updated. This leverages the native update feature of CF, which requires setting the "update stack if already exists" flag in the AWS Bamboo plug-in. With this feature enabled, Bamboo will first attempt to find a stack with the desired name and update it; if no such stack is found, Bamboo creates it. With the DNS change controlled via CF, a release or rollback becomes an auditable CF stack update. Listing 12.1 shows a sample CF DNS record that will support the update. The CDP feeds the current build number in via the "BuildNumber" parameter.

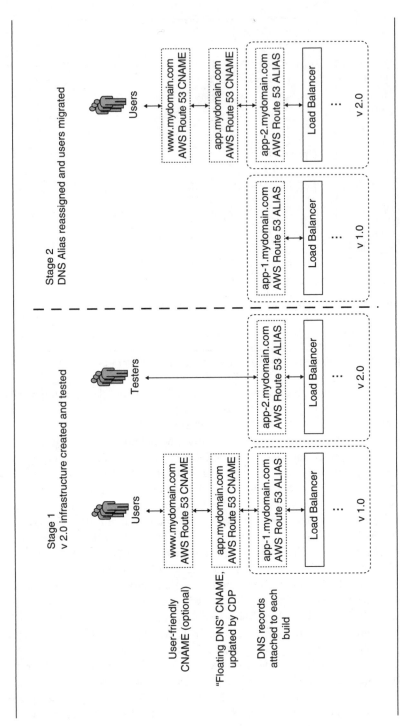

FIGURE 12.10   DNS structure and changes during release (stages from Figure 12.9) [Notation: Architecture]

LISTING 12.1 Example of a release CloudFormation

```
"Resources" : {
  "Route53DNSRecord" : {
   "Type" : "AWS::Route53::RecordSet",
   "Properties" : {
    "HostedZoneName" : mydomain.com.,
    "Comment" : "Application DNS Record",
    "Name" : "myapplication.",
    "Type" : "CNAME",
    "TTL" : "10",
    "ResourceRecords" : "myapplication-",{"Ref:
       "BuildNumber"},".mydomain.com"
   }
  }
 }
```

By its very nature, the release is the riskiest stage of the CDP, as it has a direct impact on the production application. We use a number of techniques to reduce this risk and allow smooth autonomous deployments, the most critical ones being traffic matching and rollback.

Traffic Matching

Once an application stack is confirmed to be ready for production release, a number of steps still need to be taken to ensure a smooth transition between stacks. When moving traffic from the current production stack to the new stack, we are moving traffic from a busy, "warm" environment to a "cold," unscaled environment. If not managed correctly, this can have a detrimental impact on performance and may result in an application outage. Therefore, it is important that we prewarm (scale up) the new environment prior to rolling live traffic over to it. By utilizing AWS APIs we can programmatically check the number of healthy instances currently associated with the current production load balancer(s). Obtaining this information allows us to scale the new environment to match the same number of instances currently required in production. This is achieved by adjusting the *desired* instance number of the relevant ASG. It is equally important to ensure the newly added instances reach the "InService" state on the load balancer prior to rolling the traffic over. Depending on the ASG settings, the new environment may begin to scale back down due to low traffic. Therefore, either this task is undertaken immediately prior to rolling the traffic over, or it is necessary to set the *minimum* number of instances to the same value as *desired*, and change that back after rolling the traffic over.

If the application being deployed utilizes an instance-based file or memory cache system, it can be advantageous to prewarm the cache prior to traffic rolling. This will ensure the first users of the application are not hindered by a cache (re-)creation process.

Rollback

If the release fails for some reason, it may become necessary to roll back, that is, switch back to the old version of the application. Utilizing Route 53 and CF for release simplifies the rollback process. After releasing a new stack into production, we keep the previous stack up and running until all post-release testing is complete. During this time, if an issue is detected with the new release, rolling back to the old environment is a simple and automated process, basically the inverse of release. Rollback can be manually initiated via Bamboo, which then updates the floating DNS record to point back to the old stack, again through CF. During this process, it is again essential that the CDP instigates traffic/load matching—the previous production stack will have likely scaled down during the time when it did not actively receive load. The traffic matching step can be skipped for critical rollbacks, where a period of lower availability and performance may be preferred to the condition that made the rollback necessary.

Teardown

Once production traffic has been redirected to the new stack and the rollback opportunity has passed (as decided through risk assessment or another business process), the old stack is no longer needed. But before the old stack can be torn down, a few steps need to be taken.

First, in order to avoid tearing down a stack that is currently in production, the CDP is configured to verify the stack is not receiving any traffic prior to teardown. There are a variety of checks, including polling the ELB for indications of traffic and measuring the CPU utilization for each associated VM. If any of these indicators return an unexpected value, the CDP stops the teardown activity and warns the operator. Once the operator verifies the stack is not in use, she can rerun the task. This step is vital to protect against inadvertent early teardown, for example, if the old stack is still processing any batch or queue-based tasks even after the traffic has been rolled away from that stack.

Second, if the application stack includes S3 buckets, the CDP must first remove all objects from these buckets prior to teardown. CF will only permit the teardown of empty S3 buckets to ensure that data is not inadvertently destroyed.

Finally, because each stack is completely discrete, the CDP can delete the old stack, which in turn terminates all the associated resources.

One of the main benefits of the CDP is the simplification of creating new development application stacks for various testing environments. This simplicity often results in the rapid consumption of AWS resources, with new development stacks now being created for a number of branches and environments. To ensure AWS costs are kept at acceptable levels, it is essential that development stacks be torn down when no longer required. In most enterprises this is achieved through a combination of team responsibility and a set of automatically enforced rules. Development teams become responsible for ensuring their environments are cleaned up and torn down after use. On development branches, teardown is the final stage of the CDP and is manually triggered. Any stack that has not been torn down will still appear as "in progress," and this becomes visible in Bamboo as an active environment. A set of automated tasks can help to ensure unused stacks are removed:

- Shutdown of all non-production environments during non-working hours.
- Compulsory teardown of all non-production stacks over weekends and holiday periods.

By tagging all CF resources, we can ensure that these processes apply only to non-production stacks.

Managing Complex Applications and Pipeline State

Complex applications can consist of tens or even hundreds of components. Even if DevOps best practices are followed and close dependencies between large numbers of components are avoided, many application stacks would still consist of a handful of components. Say, for instance, an application consists of a web tier, a business logic tier, and MySQL and S3 on the data storage level. Then it is typically necessary to create the datastores before creating the upper tiers, so that the upper tiers can be configured to use the datastores. Therefore, the CDP agents—where each component of the application gets its own agent—can be scheduled to be part of distinct *phases*. This is shown in Figure 12.11: The CDP agents for the datastores are scheduled in Phase 1, the CDP agents for the web and business logic tiers in Phase 2. This scheduling has to be defined per application, by assigning phase numbers to each component. While the agents generally proceed independently, there is one exception: Release is happening synchronously, over all agents in the same phase. This is required so that live traffic can be redirected consistently, namely, at any point in time the stack from one single build is used for handling the live traffic.

Another aspect is that not each component actually requires each stage in the CDP to be executed. The datastores used in the example are AWS products, and

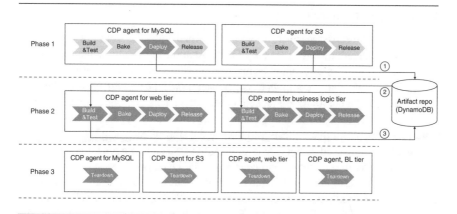

FIGURE 12.11   Pipeline state [Notation: Porter's Value Chain + Architecture]

as such can be deployed directly without the need for any of the other stages. In Figure 12.11, this is depicted by the light-gray color of the other stages in both datastore agents in Phase 1. Phase 3 contains the teardown stage for all components. This is implicit in the definition: Teardown is done synchronously across all components. Note also that this customization of the CDP for a given application does not have an impact on the CDP implementation or the best practices—all of it is done in the application-specific CF templates, which are merged with the enterprise-wide operations CF templates. Thus, changes to the CDP or the operations CF templates can be implemented with relative ease and can be tested against and finally applied to hundreds of applications instantaneously.

The final component of the CDP is a pipeline state repository. It provides a highly available, consistent, and dependable storage service to store CF outputs and other artifacts that may be consumed by later stages of the pipeline or the application itself. The CDP uses Amazon's DynamoDB as an artifact repository to manage pipeline state, as shown on the right-hand side of Figure 12.11. DynamoDB provides a fully managed NoSQL datastore that is highly available, distributed, secure, and offers consistent low-latency performance.

The encircled numbers next to the artifact repository in Figure 12.11 outline the sequence of data creation and consumption for the example of the build and test stages of two components. When a CDP agent for a component reaches the end of a stage, its post-processing system collects all relevant outputs and places those in DynamoDB. The CDP agent moves to the next stage and retrieves *all* known artifacts for the build from DynamoDB, giving it access to the combined information from all previous build stages, phases, and agents. By decoupling data handling (DynamoDB) and control (CDP), the CDP becomes more scalable: The number and complexity of the individual phases, components, and stages become irrelevant. An individual stage consumes data from DynamoDB, performs its task, and stores the newly formed information back to DynamoDB, ready for consumption by the next stage.

Managing Persistence

The preceding discussions were mostly concerned with the transient or stateless components that are managed via the CDP. Most applications also contain a number of persistent resources that cannot be managed via the same life cycle as the transient stacks. To specify that a component is persistent, *on a particular branch*, the relevant records in DynamoDB are tagged as persistent. This tagging is applied by setting a variable in the build plan that modifies the relevant entries in DynamoDB. The pre-processing script that collects variables at the start of each stage first assesses if a component is marked as persistent—if so, the persistent component is reused and shielded from both re-creation and teardown. The DynamoDB record contains, for example, the URL of a MySQL database or an S3 bucket. All subsequent builds will receive the persisted records, such as the S3 bucket URL, until the variable is unset.

Refer to Figure 12.11: Say the S3 bucket is marked as persistent; then the CDP agent for S3 neither performs the creation in Phase 1 nor the teardown in

Phase 3. Instead, the artifact repository retains the URL to the existing S3 bucket, and all other components are configured to use that.

Since the persistence flag is a per-branch setting, most components outside the production branch will not make use of it. Consider the branches shown in Figure 12.7. By setting the persistence flag on the production branch, the live production database is protected from replacement and teardown. However, the lower branches such as UAT do not set this flag. Therefore, the automated test suites can rely on a clean, consistent database to start with—even if the last build was broken and left the database in an inconsistent shape.

How to upgrade the persistent datastores (e.g., their schema or database engine) is another complex matter—which is outside of the scope of this chapter.

12.4 Baking Security into the Foundations of the CD Pipeline

Security is addressed at a foundational level within the CDP, both in terms of operation of the pipeline itself as well as the resources associated with the applications it manages.

Chapter 8 discusses security in some detail. In this section, our focus is the separation of duties with Amazon CF, as well as authentication and authorization using AWS IAM.

Implementing Separation of Duties with Amazon CloudFormation

As previously mentioned when discussing CF, enforcing separation of duties between network transport, network security, operations, and applications groups is achieved using a combination of Amazon CF templates and a destructive (i.e., overriding) merging process based on priorities.

The *network transport group* is responsible for inter-datacenter connectivity, for example, ensuring corporate datacenter to AWS transport connectivity. This includes configuration of AWS Direct Connect, Border Gateway Protocol (BGP), and IPsec/VPN, as well as redundant link setups with automatic failover. The *network security group* is responsible for perimeter networking and security. These two groups maintain CF templates that define the environment in which the CDP manages resources. For example, the network transport group's CF templates relate to VPCs, peering connections, and routing tables. In contrast, the network security group's templates are concerned with VPC subnets, security groups, and access control lists (ACLs).

Operations maintains CF templates that implement best practices around host and resource logging, effective use of Amazon availability zones, resource tagging, and so forth. Similarly, each application group develops and maintains an application-specific CF template. These templates focus on application health checks, autoscaling rules, triggers, and thresholds.

When deploying a particular application, the CDP starts from the application template, first overlaying the operational template, which effectively masks or overrides any unprivileged configuration settings specified by the application developers. The merge is destructive with a bias toward operations, thereby enforcing best practices and standards. For example, say an application owner specified that all application components should reside in a single availability zone to minimize latency, but the corporate policy requires high system availability—then, the operational CF template would override the configuration and place resources in multiple availability zones.

Identity and Access Management

There are a number of areas where identity and access management need to be considered within a CDP. The first area is that of host system administration. When hosts are managed outside of a CDP, it is common and generally necessary that administrators can log in remotely or issue remote commands. For example, if an application server stops providing a service, an administrator may log on to the host, investigate the problem, and potentially restart the failed service. When an environment is deployed efficiently and reliably, logging on to hosts becomes unnecessary—and can actually lead to increased issue resolution times. Removing administrator access reduces the overall attack surface and removes the need to manage Secure Shell (SSH) public and private keys.

Amazon IAM roles, profiles, and policies can be used extensively to restrict access to and permissions of EC2 instances, users, and AWS services such as AWS S3. For a detailed explanation of each of these services, consult the relevant product documentation, which is referred to in Section 12.7. Operational and security checklists are in part available as AWS white papers.

Where possible, EC2 instances that require privileged access to AWS resources, such as objects located in an S3 bucket and Amazon Simple Queue Service (SQS), have an IAM role associated with them. This allows access permissions to be managed centrally and revoked instantly if required. IAM roles are the preferred means to restrict access to sensitive AWS resources whenever possible. All compatible resources deployed via the CDP are issued with an IAM role or policy by default.

For applications that do not provide support for IAM roles but require IAM credentials (such as access keys and secret keys), the CDP can embed IAM credentials into each VM that requires them. As an additional security measure, the credentials are rotated upon each deployment of the stack. That is, during the bake stage, a new set of credentials is created and baked into AMIs that need it; during teardown, those credentials are invalidated. This restricts the impact of a security breach to a single stack and prevents the same credentials being used to gain access to resources belonging to another application or environment. In addition, the credentials are rotated at least every three months.

12.5 Advanced Concepts

In this chapter we have sketched the basic design of the Sourced Group CDP framework. As enterprises mature, there are several advanced areas that can be explored

Minimizing Drift Between Production and Non-production Environments

A common issue in the enterprise is that long-running non-production environments continually drift away from production. Sourced Group solves this problem by refreshing all aspects of the non-production environments against recent production snapshots for each and every build, as depicted in Figure 12.12.

Non-production environments utilize nightly snapshots of persistent datastores from production. Resources are created on-demand from the snapshots. This allows development/testing/integration against persistent datastores that are only a few hours behind production.

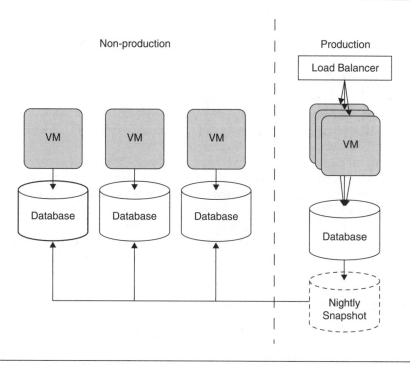

FIGURE 12.12 Using production database snapshots for non-production builds
[Notation: Architecture]

Working Around Provider Limitations

Some of the common cloud platforms impose hard limits on some elements of their services. It's often the case that limitations reflect the service at a point in its product development. Whether limitations are short-lived or more permanent, a CDP needs to take such factors into account. One such limitation is AWS's current limit on the number of security groups per VPC—see the documentation mentioned in Section 12.7. The default limit is 100 security groups, with a fuzzy hard limit of 200 for most practical enterprise deployments. This limit influences the deployment of resources within a single VPC and clearly impacts a CDP. In response to those challenges, an "autoscaled VPC model" was implemented for one customer. In this model, VPCs were dynamically created or deleted in response to availability and eventual exhaustion of security groups. The result is an "autoscaled" number of application-delivery VPCs that scale out as per security group requirements. The high-level process flow is:

1. Receive stack build command from user.
2. Calculate how many security groups the stack requires.
3. Check if the required number of security groups can be fit into an existing application delivery VPC:
4. If yes, provision application.
5. If no, call the VPC build job to build a new application delivery VPC.
6. Required IP/subnet details are retrieved from a prepopulated configuration table in DynamoDB.
7. Deploy application stack. Register the stack against the requisite VPC ID in DynamoDB.

A janitor process continually polls DynamoDB data for all running VPCs and active applications. If no running applications use a given VPC, it terminates the VPC container and relevant components.

This advanced process depends on the ability to dynamically provision IP address spaces and features such as VPC peering. In an interconnected enterprise environment, it is essential that backhaul datacenter connections can be managed exclusively via an API, with solutions such as AWS Direct Connect that can create virtual interfaces. Some prepopulation of cross-connected elements may be required (such as virtual local area networks (VLANs)). These are inserted into DynamoDB, and a capacity management process is put in place to prevent exhaustion.

Vendor Lock-in

Sourced Group's CDP is heavily tied into AWS, particularly CF, and therefore brings with it migration challenges to other platforms like VMware, OpenStack, or Cloud Foundry. Today, this is due to a lack of cross-platform standards at the Infrastructure as a Service (IaaS) layer. While advances in Platform as a Service

(PaaS) compatibility between providers will increase mobility in the future, it is reasonable to assume that, if you require control at the IaaS layer, there will always be a certain amount of initial heavy lifting required to support multiple public cloud providers.

Outlook on New AWS Native Services

A number of new products were released at the AWS global conference in November 2014, which focused on the configuration, deployment, and management of the application life cycle—a clear indication that continuous deployment techniques and processes have now reached the point of maturity and standardization that they can be offered as a generalized Software as a Service (SaaS) offering.

One of the recently introduced AWS services with a strong potential to simplify parts of the CDP is AWS CodeDeploy. CodeDeploy is a service that automates code deployments to Amazon EC2 instances. CodeDeploy replaces many of the bootstrapping activities that were included in the bake process; it essentially offers a more advanced version of cfn-init. Sourced Group's technique of merging CF templates allows for a rather straightforward integration with AWS CodeDeploy, resulting in reduced complexity in the CDP.

12.6 Summary

Sourced Group has been assisting enterprises in installing a CDP for several years. Sourced's pipeline is built around a five-stage view of the life cycle: build and test, bake, deploy, release, and tear down. Each of these stages relies on a set of tools that are utilized to automate the process. This standardized life cycle is then applied to all of the branches within the application source control system, providing developers and the business with a high degree of assurance as they merge features into production. The use of discrete application stacks and automated release management greatly reduces the risk and time taken to release software.

Security is a major concern within the enterprise, and SecOps supports a key to success for any platform. The CDP offers a single point of entry into the AWS environment, where enforceable CF templates from operations provide the governance and compliance capabilities that SecOps requires.

Education and culture are core to widespread adoption of the CDP. While the CDP engineering team supports the pipeline itself, the CDP onboarding team provides support for new development teams. This support covers onboarding as well as conveying knowledge, both on continuous deployment techniques in general and on the specific CDP implementation.

12.7 For Further Reading

For further reading or extended information on any of the tools listed here, please see the following links:

- Atlassian: https://www.atlassian.com/
  - Bamboo: https://www.atlassian.com/software/bamboo
  - Bamboo branch management: https://confluence.atlassian.com/display/BAMBOO/Using+plan+branches
  - Bamboo "Tasks for AWS" plug-in: https://marketplace.atlassian.com/plugins/net.utoority.atlassian.bamboo.tasks-for-aws
  - Stash: https://www.atlassian.com/software/stash
  - Stash branch permissions: https://confluence.atlassian.com/display/STASH/Using+branch+permissions
  - Stash pull requests: https://confluence.atlassian.com/display/STASH/Using+pull+requests+in+Stash
  - JIRA: https://www.atlassian.com/software/jira
  - JIRA and Bamboo integration: https://confluence.atlassian.com/display/JIRA/Viewing+the+Bamboo+Builds+related+to+an+Issue

- Amazon Web Services: http://aws.amazon.com
  - CD/CI best practices: http://www.slideshare.net/AmazonWebServices/continuous-integration-and-deployment-best-practices-on-aws-adrian-white-aws-summit-sydney-2014
  - CloudFormation initialization: http://docs.aws.amazon.com/AWSCloudFormation/latest/UserGuide/aws-resource-init.html
  - CloudFormation helper scripts including cfn-init: http://docs.aws.amazon.com/AWSCloudFormation/latest/UserGuide/cfn-helper-scripts-reference.html
  - Identity and Access Management (IAM): http://aws.amazon.com/iam/
  - DynamoDB: http://aws.amazon.com/dynamodb/
  - Security documentation: http://aws.amazon.com/security/
  - White papers, including operational and security checklists: http://aws.amazon.com/whitepapers/
  - VPC limits, such as the number of security groups: http://docs.aws.amazon.com/AmazonVPC/latest/UserGuide/VPC_Appendix_Limits.html
  - CodeDeploy: http://aws.amazon.com/codedeploy/

- Splunk: http://www.splunk.com/
- Sonatype Nexus: http://www.sonatype.com/nexus

13

Migrating to Microservices

With Sidney Shek

> *Our products help teams of all sizes track and share everything,*
> *work smarter, and create better software together.*
> —https://www.atlassian.com/company

13.1 Introduction to Atlassian

Atlassian produces team productivity tools such as JIRA (for issue tracking and software development), Confluence wiki, HipChat messaging, and JIRA Service Desk, and development tools such as Bamboo continuous integration server and Bitbucket hosted repositories. The case study in the previous chapter describes how Sourced Group's pipeline makes use of some of these tools. Many of these tools are available for both on-premise server installation and through Atlassian's hosted cloud offering.

Atlassian Cloud currently services almost 20,000 customers from 130 countries. A "customer" represents a team or organization that has signed up to one or more applications and may have a handful to thousands of end users; there are currently approximately 60,000 application instances handling about 1TB of network traffic *per day*. To support this load, Atlassian has two production datacenters in the United States (approximately 60 racks serving customer requests, with 8,200 CPU cores and 5,300 physical disks). The case study in Chapter 11 describes an example of how to keep multiple datacenters synchronized. Instances of a customer's applications are currently hosted in OpenVZ containers. See Chapter 5 for a discussion of lightly baked versus heavily baked and the use of containers. Leveraging state-of-the-art containers has been successful and has helped Atlassian reduce cost by customer per an order of magnitude.

Going forward, Atlassian is transitioning from monolithic applications to a tenantless microservice-based architecture where end-user requests can be serviced by any front-end server, typically in the same geographic region as the user, with common business logic and data tiers shared across applications and customers. Atlassian's goals in this transition are to:

- Provide better performance for customers by locating data and services closer to end users.
- Improve the scalability of Atlassian Cloud to handle increasing numbers of customers at further reduced cost. The target is to support double the current customer base with the existing infrastructure in Atlassian datacenters.
- Support using public cloud providers where appropriate for better performance and cost.
- Support easier disaster recovery of data in the event of datacenter outages.
- Improve the speed at which features can be deployed to serve customers.

Atlassian plans to deploy many of these microservices in public cloud providers such as Amazon Web Services (AWS), with a virtual private network (VPN) infrastructure such as Amazon Direct Connect set up to allow bidirectional communications with Atlassian datacenters. Application instances will remain in Atlassian datacenters during the transition period.

One major challenge for Atlassian is that changes must not result in outages or poorer performance for end users, especially during the transition to microservices. As a result, many operational concerns are at the forefront of requirements for new microservices, such as:

- Ensuring data is migrated in to the appropriate format and location without risk of loss.
- Ensuring applications are modified as required to support new microservices without potential loss of functionality while the new microservices are rolled out.
- Ensuring new functionality in microservices can be rolled out with no downtime, and rolled back in case of any unexpected failure.
- Providing replacement support tools for support teams. For example, currently support personnel can log in to customer containers to debug and access data and logs as required. In an environment where services are shared, new tools must be provided to facilitate the same support use cases.
- Ensuring sufficient performance monitoring and alerting is in place. Poor performance and outages for microservices can impact a significant number of customers, so issues must be identified as early as possible to reduce resolution time.

13.2 Building a Platform for Deploying Microservices

Many infrastructure components such as the deployment platform, network connectivity to Atlassian datacenters, logging, and monitoring are common to all microservices. These are being consolidated into a single highly available Platform-as-a-Service (PaaS) for microservices to prevent unnecessary duplication and inconsistencies in technology and configuration choices. Currently, the PaaS runs on AWS infrastructure and builds upon AWS tools such as CloudFormation while providing additional functionality where necessary. For the most part, the underlying cloud service provider is abstracted away from microservice developers. The architecture diagram shown in Figure 13.1 displays the main components of Atlassian PaaS within AWS. These include Route 53 for DNS services, Elastic Load Balancing (ELB) for balancing incoming requests across services deployed to EC2 instances in multiple availability zones (AZs), and CloudWatch for metrics and alarms. Services can access various AWS resources such as Relational Database Service (RDS), DynamoDB, S3, and Simple Queue Service (SQS). Outgoing requests from services to the Internet and AWS resources outside of the VPC are directed through an ELB in front of Squid proxies deployed to multiple AZs for high availability. Also, log messages are sent to Elasticsearch/Kibana clusters deployed to EC2 instances in multiple AZs fronted by ELB.

Atlassian's microservice PaaS provides the following functionality:

- *Consistent container for running microservices.* Microservice instances are run on individual AWS EC2 instances with a baked AMI that is controlled by the PaaS team, not the microservice developers. This AMI contains necessary runtimes and PaaS infrastructure. Instance size can be controlled by microservice developers (e.g., compute-optimized instances can be specified for CPU-intensive microservices). To deploy a microservice onto the PaaS, developers only need to provide a service descriptor that includes service configuration and metadata (e.g., required resources, environment variables), and an artifact to be run (e.g., a binary JAR file for JVM services, or a Docker image).
- *Resource provisioning and management* such as creating and managing S3 buckets, DynamoDB tables, and Simple Notification Service (SNS) topics. The intent is to abstract resource implementations (e.g., AWS versus Google) away from microservice developers, and to support better management for specific resources; for example, AWS SNS topics currently cannot be updated with CloudFormation templates and must be re-created.
- *Autoscaling and load balancing between microservice instances.* Microservice developers only need to specify the minimum number of instances required in the service descriptor and criteria for autoscaling.

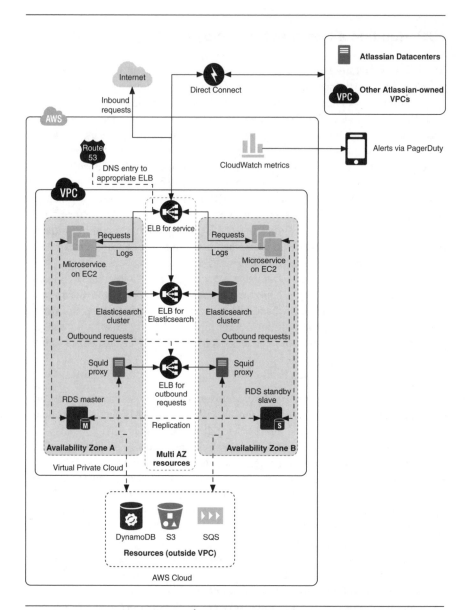

FIGURE 13.1   Components used in the Atlassian microservice PaaS [Notation: AWS Simple Icons]

Atlassian PaaS will create the necessary AWS load balancer/autoscaling configuration for each deployment. Currently, AWS ELB with autoscaling groups is used.

- *Log consolidation and searching.* Microservices need only output
  log entries to the console (standard output or standard error), ideally
  in JSON format. Log entries are automatically picked up and parsed
  by fluentd and delivered to an Elasticsearch cluster. Developers and
  support teams have access to consolidated logs via Kibana, which allows
  searching of logs and graphing of statistics (e.g., histogram of errors
  over time).
- *Metric collection, consolidation, reporting, and alerting.* Standard
  infrastructure-level metrics such as CPU load, as well as ELB latency and
  error rates, are supported via AWS CloudWatch and Stackdriver. Alerts
  through PagerDuty are triggered when thresholds are crossed for important
  metrics. Additional microservice-specific metrics are also collected via
  logging infrastructure for graphing via Kibana.
- *Secured network infrastructure* between microservices in AWS and
  existing applications in Atlassian datacenters. There is bidirectional and
  high-speed connectivity between applications in Atlassian datacenters
  and microservices deployed to AWS, including services such as Atlassian-
  internal DNS.
- *Zero-downtime deployments and support for rapid rollback.*
  Microservice stacks are seamlessly upgraded by creating a new stack
  (e.g., new AWS ELB, autoscaling group, EC2 instances), and then
  switching the DNS entries (currently in Route 53) to the new stack
  once microservice instances are in service. If the upgrade is deemed
  successful, the old stack is removed, otherwise rollback to the old stack
  can be performed by switching DNS entries again. This process is
  described in more detail in Chapter 2 and the case study in Chapter 12.
  DNS TTLs are set low (60 seconds) to facilitate rapid switchover. Also,
  these stacks represent only the microservices themselves; resources
  such as RDS tables or S3 are managed separately through the resource
  provisioning mechanism described previously.
- *Multiple environments to support different levels of development and
  testing.* Four separate environments are provided by the PaaS. The intent
  of these environments is to ensure that each application or microservice
  progresses through each stage; therefore they are being tested against
  software that will be run in the next environment. The environments are as
  follows:
  - *Domain development.* This environment is used for testing during
    development by microservice teams.
  - *Application development.* This environment supports testing with external
    dependencies such as applications (e.g., JIRA, Confluence) and other
    microservices. This environment is available to all application developers
    within Atlassian. Microservices in this environment are typically

connected to all Atlassian Cloud–based application development instances to support "dogfooding."
- *Staging*. This closely resembles production; for example, there are deployments in multiple AWS regions. Atlassian dogfooding instances (i.e., production-grade instances used internally by Atlassian) are hooked up to these environments. This environment is used primarily to test production configuration.
- *Production*. This environment supports customer Atlassian Cloud instances. There is a PaaS deployed in two separate AWS regions, providing high availability in the event of region failure.

13.3 BlobStore: A Microservice Example

The selection of microservices to develop has been driven by value to end users (e.g., improved user experience) and to Atlassian itself (e.g., disaster recovery support). To date, there are Atlassian-designed microservices for single sign-on, consolidated billing, user experience experimentation, document conversion, binary object storage, and application instance management, with many more microservices in the pipeline. As a canonical example, we discuss BlobStore, a microservice for storing binary data (or "blobs") from applications, such as attachments in JIRA issues, Confluence pages, or even software binaries. BlobStore is an early-stage microservice, the fourth within Atlassian, and the first to be run in production on the Atlassian PaaS.

The primary business driver for BlobStore is to enable simpler disaster recovery of customer data. Currently, a customer's attachment data is kept in storage nodes alongside the compute node running customer instances. At the time of writing, there were approximately 40TB of attachment data across the two datacenters, so supporting disaster recovery involves a time- and resource-intensive operation of transferring this data between the datacenters. In addition, there is also a challenging "packing" problem as copied data must fit into available gaps in the destination storage nodes. With BlobStore, application binary data will be stored in AWS S3 instead, utilizing S3 replication between AWS datacenters, so the custom inter-datacenter transfer is no longer required and failing over a customer instance to the second datacenter becomes significantly easier. Having customer data in a store such as S3 also makes it feasible to move customer instances between datacenters in order to provide colocation of end users with their data and allows better load balancing across datacenters.

From a technical standpoint, BlobStore also represents an obvious and relatively simple component that can be abstracted from all Atlassian applications, and was a logical early step toward shared microservices across applications.

Architecture

One of the main benefits of microservices is that since they are small, they can be developed using the most suitable technology stack for the problem at hand and be quite varied in the implementation approach. Indeed, this is the case within Atlassian, where microservices are currently a mix of Java, Scala, and Node.js. BlobStore is small Scala-based microservice, approximately 2,500 lines of code, developed and managed by a small team. It uses the lightweight Finagle RPC framework created by Twitter to expose a simple HTTP application program-ming interface (API) for blobs. The key components of BlobStore are shown in Figure 13.2. A collection of BlobStore servers are deployed to the Atlassian PaaS in AWS, storing blobs in S3 and key mappings in DynamoDB. There is a small BlobStore client plug-in installed in application instances to the abstract access to BlobStore away from application code (e.g., to add necessary HTTP headers to requests) and to ensure blobs are streamed without in-memory buffering on the client side.

BlobStore at its core is a "content-addressable" store. Consumers (e.g., JIRA or Confluence) send binary data (or blobs) to BlobStore with a "log-ical key," and the blobs are stored in AWS S3 keyed by a SHA-1 hash of the blob's content (known as a "content hash"). BlobStore maintains a mapping between the consumer's logical key and the content hash. This mapping is cur-rently stored in AWS DynamoDB, a low-maintenance, highly available, and scalable key-value store. Consumers can access blobs via RESTful resources based on the logical key or content hash. Blobs and mappings are replicated to be available in different AWS regions. BlobStore servers are run in active-passive configuration between the two AWS regions as this provides lowest latency from the Atlassian datacenters. A BlobStore DNS CNAME entry in the Atlassian datacenter's DNS servers directs traffic to the BlobStore services in the appropriate AWS region.

Safety and Performance Through Pure Functional Architecture and Programming

BlobStore has a pure functional architecture; the key principle is *that data is always immutable*. This means that no data (blobs or records representing changes to key mappings) are destroyed or modified; instead "facts" are only appended to the system in order to change the current representation of data. Data is essentially stored in a single-ancestor version control system. An underlying immutable datastore also makes it possible to expose immutable APIs—for a given request, the response will always be the same. Immutable APIs support caching, composability of requests for simpler business logic, and easier testing where responses can be easily mocked out with little knowledge of underlying

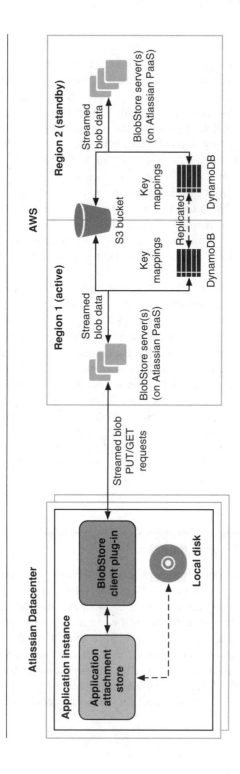

FIGURE 13.2 Architecture of BlobStore [Notation: AWS Simple Icons]

services. Using a functional architecture led to two key design decisions with many resulting benefits.

First, blobs are stored against a content hash in S3. This means that for a given piece of content, the location in S3 will always be the same. A piece of content may be uploaded multiple times to BlobStore, but the content will only need to be stored once in S3 using the content hash as the key. Using the SHA-1 algorithm ensures an infinitesimally small chance of collision. This not only allows data deduplication, but also simple data caching for a blob: A consumer can request a blob via either its logical key or the content hash; a request via a logical key is redirected to the persistent URL for the content's hash that can be cached as it remains the same for a given piece of content. This caching is important for minimizing the effect of network latency across the link to AWS; although there is a high-speed link to AWS from each datacenter, there will be inevitable network latency in accessing blobs that is greater than the latency to access files on disk. BlobStore is able to use either a cache local to the HTTP client, or a caching server such as Varnish in the Atlassian datacenter to reduce this latency. Deleting a blob is a quick and nondestructive operation as it is only necessary to delete the corresponding key mapping instead of the blob itself. This means the data itself is recoverable in case the deletion was accidental; and at some later point old data without mappings can be garbage-collected.

Secondly, key mappings are stored using an event sourcing model. Instead of storing mappings themselves, "events" on the mappings are stored (i.e., insertion or deletion events). To recover a specific key mapping at a given point in time, one would retrieve all events up to that point in time and replay them in order. In this model, no data is deleted, so mappings that may have been inadvertently deleted can be recovered; we can simply query the key mapping store for a mapping at a given point in time. Also, an audit trail of changes to mappings comes for "free." In addition, event sourcing provides basic transactionality even with a simple yet highly scalable key-value store such as DynamoDB. Specifically it does not require a traditional RDBMS, which is difficult to scale in a cross-region replicated environment. Another benefit is that schema evolution is relatively easy to implement. Using a NoSQL datastore means no "stop-the-world" activities are necessary to perform schema updates. Also new events or changes to attributes can be handled through data version–aware object marshallers that always present data in the latest schema version; no existing data needs to be updated or rewritten.

In addition to a functional architecture, BlobStore embraces functional programming concepts. The server is written in Scala in functional style, the basic concepts being that variables are immutable wherever possible and new types, including types representing logical functions or operations, are created as necessary instead of using primitive types that can be easily mixed up. This allows

Atlassian to test code via compile-time checks instead of relying on unit tests or runtime checks and provides the following benefits:

- Less reliance on explicit tests as the compiler can assist greatly with ensuring correctness of code through compile-time checks of types.
- Code is concise.
- Immutability and concurrency concepts such as futures allow you to more easily solve concurrency issues.
- Pure functional code is much easier to unit test as outputs are deterministic for given inputs. "Mocking" is rarely required, and we are able to use property-based testing (via ScalaCheck with Specs2) to automatically generate test data to help cover corner cases.

One of the biggest challenges in applying functional concepts to microservice development has been developing the appropriate skill set for developers. While functional programming and functional concepts have been around for quite some time, they are generally unfamiliar to most developers (although that situation is changing with languages such as Scala, Clojure, and Haskell gaining popularity). The BlobStore team was bootstrapped by developers with more functional programming experience, allowing other team members to learn quickly. Also, the culture of sharing knowledge within Atlassian is helping to build functional programming and architecture experience across the company.

Solving the "Ilities"

We have already hinted at how some of the design and implementation decisions for BlobStore address scalability and availability considerations. Table 13.1 discusses how some important desirable architectural characteristics are achieved.

TABLE 13.1 Addressing the Ilities for BlobStore

Scalability	The BlobStore server and client make heavy use of streaming. Data buffering is limited to the order of ~10kb so that blobs of up to gigabytes in size can be transferred safely and concurrently without risk of out-of-memory conditions. This allows the BlobStore server to support a high number of concurrent connections, and servers can be deployed to low-memory instances, or instances can be shared with more memory-intensive microservices.
	The BlobStore server is also stateless; no consumer state is retained between requests. New server instances can be started as load requires. Server performance is currently CPU limited, so new instances are started by the autoscaling group when a specified CPU level is maintained for 10 minutes. The autoscaling group also scales down the group during periods of low load.

Availability	Atlassian PaaS has separate production environments in different AWS regions, and there are independent deployments of BlobStore in each. Application instances connect to a BlobStore server deployment through a well-known DNS hostname and are normally directed to the active deployment by appropriate DNS entries. Upon failure of an AWS region, application instances can be redirected by changing DNS entries to the second BlobStore deployment.
	Both key mappings and blobs are replicated between AWS regions (AWS Data Pipelines for key mappings, and AWS in-built cross-datacenter replication for S3), so that if application instances are moved to the other Atlassian datacenter (for disaster recovery or load balancing), they will have access to their data.
	BlobStore uses highly available datastores (DynamoDB and S3) that support cross-availability zone replication.
Security	Each request is authenticated and authorized to ensure only a specific customer's application instance has access to that customer's data.
	In addition, there is per-customer encryption of blobs by BlobStore to ensure compartmentalization of data; in the event that a specific customer's instance is compromised, only that customer's data is accessible, and in the event that AWS access keys to the entire S3 bucket are leaked, no data is easily obtainable.
Extensibility	The BlobStore server architecture is designed to support easy replacement of underlying datastore and key mapping storage.
Maintainability	The use of functional programming techniques throughout BlobStore supports easier testing, and the heavy use of types ensures that it is easier to be confident that future code changes by existing or new team members will be correct.

13.4 Development Process

Most teams in Atlassian are small, up to about five developers, and use some form of agile or lean development methodology determined by the team itself. As an example, the BlobStore development team consists of five developers using Scrum with one-week sprints.

Teams typically also have some involvement from a quality assurance (QA) tester. Unlike traditional testers, the role of QA team members is to provide oversight of testing and guidance on testing approaches and tasks. For example, QA may be involved with setting up "developer on test" processes (where a second developer verifies test code and performs any necessary manual testing) and reviewing test cases for completeness, especially in the context of software developed outside of the team. QA also assists with exploratory testing and setting up testing events such as blitz tests for verification prior to deployment of major functionality changes and QA "demo" sessions, where entire solutions are demonstrated and "tested" end-to-end with a larger group of people.

One major challenge for Atlassian, and especially for microservice development teams, is maintaining a manageable level of interaction between teams. Microservices have a significant impact on how the core applications are developed, deployed, and supported. There are also deployment dependencies between teams, such as between the PaaS and BlobStore teams where certain PaaS features may be blocking deployment of new BlobStore versions. Traditionally, ongoing identification of these interactions has been somewhat informal through knowledge built up by architects and experienced personnel, and through knowledge sharing across the organization via blog posts and pages on internal Confluence instances and at all-hands demo presentations. This collaborative approach has worked well for sharing and developing solutions, but in more recent times more formality through "project managers" has been introduced to ensure dependencies between teams are identified more consistently and are tracked. Some examples of BlobStore team interactions include:

- Early engagement of architects from product teams ensures that relevant requirements are captured. These have been formally captured as JIRA issues and have been regularly reviewed. There is, in general, controlled interaction between product and microservice teams to minimize noise; architects and team leads represent the main conduit of information flow.
- Product and infrastructure teams have also raised new requirements on BlobStore as product backlogs have evolved. These have started as informal discussions before being tracked as features in JIRA.
- Close interaction between PaaS and BlobStore teams as new requirements and issues are identified and fixed as both are rolled out in parallel. The teams use a combination of informal chat room interactions and formal issue tracking in JIRA. Team coordination is also more formally managed by a project manager.
- Relevant product code changes are reviewed by both product and microservice teams.
- Microservice code changes are freely viewable by other teams—this has served as a great way of sharing knowledge and techniques between teams and identifying possible issues such as potential performance and security issues.

Developers and Support

Development teams in Atlassian are becoming more responsible for the deployment of their software to production. In the case of BlobStore, the development team is responsible for the rollout of the BlobStore server to production and the staged rollout of relevant functionality to customer application instances, including identifying suitable instances at each stage, developing necessary scripts and rollback procedures, "flipping the switch" on customer instances, and being alerted via PagerDuty upon error conditions. This greater level of responsibility encourages production code to be thoroughly tested and reviewed, and relevant tools exist for both in-band and out-of-band access to underlying data.

While Atlassian does embrace some DevOps concepts, it has in fact moved away from a full DevOps process model over the past couple of years to having a dedicated service operations group responsible for the availability of application instances and underlying platforms. This change was in response to the problem that shared responsibility for uptime between multiple groups was ineffective for fast incident resolution. An application or microservice is not deemed fully in production until it is handed over to service operations, and there are distinct definitions of responsibilities between development, infrastructure, and operations teams. Operations teams are the first point of call for incidents, providing 24/7 support for the underlying platform for applications and services. They follow runbooks provided by development teams for initial incident resolution and can escalate to service owners—typically including a member of the development team—for further investigation. They are also responsible for service metric reporting (e.g., service uptime, incident statistics, whether service level agreements (SLAs) have been met), and supporting infrastructure such as service catalogue, alert integration with JIRA, and reporting systems. There is collaboration between service operations and development teams before, during, and after handover. Prior to handover, development teams must provide necessary documentation and tooling for operations use cases; for example, with BlobStore, backup/restore procedures for attachment data have changed to involve AWS assets, and the necessary documentation and scripts need to be developed. During handover, service operations begin measuring service metrics and act as the first point of call. After handover, in addition to working together when necessary to resolve incidents, development teams are involved with any post-incident reviews. Service operations can provide developers with metrics that can assist with new user story identification and backlog prioritization (e.g., new features that can ease operations load, or prioritization of bug fixes).

There are also dedicated support teams (customer advocates) responsible for customer-facing requests. While many microservices may be "under the covers," inevitably there will be impact on end users, and as a result there needs to be interaction between microservice developers and support teams. For example, in specific cases, data imports or exports for end users may need to be out-of-band (e.g., if their application instance is unavailable for some reason). Transitioning from local file-based attachment storage to the BlobStore microservice means there is no longer easy access to application attachment data through standard "file system" mechanisms; instead the data model has been designed to support out-of-band access to attachments, and accompanying tools have been developed.

Also, many teams integrate a "Developer on Support" (called a *reliability engineer* in Chapter 1) in their development life cycle where team members are also rotated into a support role (e.g., for two weeks at a time). During their rotation, developers work closely with the support team to investigate issues related to the particular software. A Developer on Support does reduce the resources available for feature development in the short term, but the intent is that in the longer term there will be less need for the rostered Developer on Support to be involved in troubleshooting and for developed software to be more easily supported by the operations team through better design and tooling.

Build and Deployment Pipeline

BlobStore code and configuration are kept in a Git repository (Atlassian Stash). The team uses a feature branching strategy; a feature branch is created for each new task or story and is short-lived, typically two or three days. One or two developers typically work on a branch at any one time. To merge into master, a pull-request for the feature branch is raised and must be approved by two developers who have not worked on the branch; a successful branch build is required as well.

A series of Bamboo build and deployment plans have been created to automatically build, test, and deploy changes on the master branch to the environments for both the server and client code. Figure 13.3 shows the key steps in the continuous delivery pipeline. Notice that the path for deployment of the client plug-in is different from the deployment of the BlobStore server.

Some key features of the deployment pipeline are:

- The pipeline has been streamlined so that code can be deployed to production within about one hour from the time of merging to master. During early stages of deployment, it was common for server code to be deployed to production two or three times a day. The BlobStore client pipeline is available to Atlassian developers after approximately three hours because of more extensive tests with applications. Rollouts to production can happen as a portion of weekly deployments if necessary.
- Code is "released" (i.e., built, tagged, and deployed into a central Nexus artifact repository) early in the pipeline. This is done to negate the possibility of changes in the build infrastructure at different points in the pipeline (e.g., a different Java SDK version). The downside of this is that it does not fit well into the way Bamboo operates. Bamboo works best with branches and releases being performed as part of deployment plans.
- BlobStore follows standard semantic versioning. This is required primarily to support the BlobStore client and possible changes to the server API; nonbreaking changes result in an increment of the minor version, and breaking API changes result in a major version increment. Changes to the server itself only result in a patch version increment.
- Our intent is to maintain one mainline, which is the master branch. The current build pipeline means that issues on the master branch prevent releases. This is mitigated by thorough testing prior to merging to master, and discipline to ensure the build pipeline for master is always green. One other option would be to have a separate "stable" branch where code

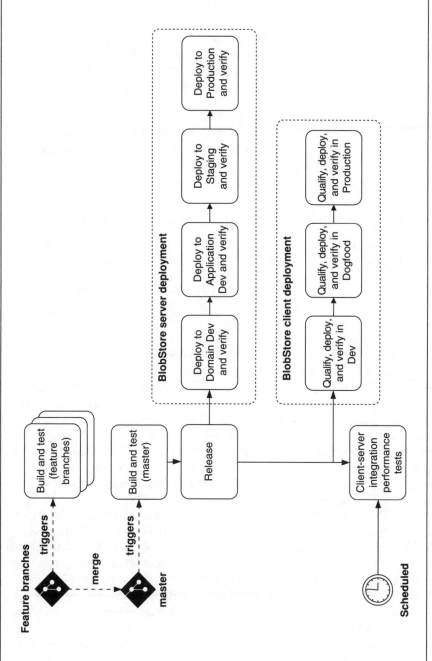

FIGURE 13.3 BlobStore deployment pipeline [Notation: BPMN]

is released, and only when the master builds have successfully passed would the master be merged onto stable. The BlobStore team decided this involved too much of an overhead considering the small size of the team.

- Automated unit testing, client-server integration testing, and integration testing with AWS resources must all pass before BlobStore client and server components are deployed to the "development" environment for others outside of the immediate team to use. Deployment of the server to subsequent environments automatically occurs after successful "smoke" tests, including end-to-end acceptance tests that test the full path from consumer applications through to the BlobStore server deployed in the appropriate environment. Performance tests are also regularly scheduled.

No-downtime Path to Production for Consumer Applications

In addition to production deployments of BlobStore server, the BlobStore team was also responsible for rolling out necessary changes in consumer applications to production with no additional downtime. This proceeded as two independent steps that were run in parallel: data migration and consumer application code migration/deployment. This meant that data migration could occur even while application code changes could still be made, and hence shortened the time required to reach production state.

Data migration was done as an out-of-band operation triggered through a new data migration plug-in deployed to application instances; this plug-in was independent of application code changes required for BlobStore. Data migration was an idempotent operation, meaning it could be rerun at any time without overwriting any previously migrated data. Since the content hash for a blob was stored as part of the key mapping, determining whether a blob had already been migrated was trivial and did not require comparing binary data. Migrations were continually run over a period of several weeks while application code changes were being rolled out, providing controlled and incremental migration of data without excessive network and other resource consumption.

Application code changes included three modes of operation—local only (i.e., no BlobStore), local primary (i.e., asynchronous operations to BlobStore), and remote primary (i.e., synchronous operations to BlobStore, fallback to local for read caching). These modes were enabled using feature flags that could be changed at runtime without restart. The interim "local primary" mode was used to ensure that the full code and network path to the BlobStore server was tested for reliability and also to gather performance metrics to determine real-world latency of operations and potential impacts on end-user experience. This staged approach gave us confidence in the overall solution prior to reaching full production state.

Both stages of rollout, namely, data migration and switching feature flags to enable code changes, started gradually with canary instances (approximately 10 with random distribution of attachment size and count). When successful, the rollout moved to a group of 100 instances, followed by a rack (~1,000 customers), then to racks in the two datacenters, before finally switching on all customers. This process took several weeks to ensure that the BlobStore development team could respond to issues without significant customer impact.

13.5 Evolving BlobStore

During the course of the project, the BlobStore microservice has evolved, including significant changes in the back-end implementation and the addition of new functionality such as per-customer encryption keys, copy/move blobs, and byte-range requests. So far, the changes have been smooth, with minimal, if any, impact on the consumer application code.

One good example was the addition of per-customer encryption keys. Initially, encryption was implemented using AWS server-side encryption on S3 buckets. During development, a requirement was generated to support per-customer encryption keys, which led to a change to perform the encryption within the BlobStore server itself. In the end, this required significant server-side changes, changes to the S3 key structure, and a relatively minor change to the HTTP API, but no noticeable change from the consumer application's point of view was needed. These changes were achieved as follows:

- Customer encryption keys were managed on an instance by the BlobStore in the interim, with the intent to delegate it to a separate microservice in the near future. This meant that consumer applications were not aware of the encryption process.
- In order to maintain data immutability, blobs in S3 became keyed on both plain-text content hash and a secure hash of the encryption key. This made it easy to ensure that data could only be decrypted with the correct key; if an incorrect key was provided, the blob in S3 simply would not exist. This also makes it possible to support multiple encryption keys for the same content concurrently, which is important when customer encryption keys are changed over time as it allows clients with the "old" key access to data during the re-encryption process, so this process can be run online without downtime.

Atlassian PaaS and BlobStore servers are currently serving customers in production. BlobStore functionality in one major application (JIRA) is enabled for all Atlassian Cloud instances. To date, there have been no significant defects or production incidents. The BlobStore team believes that this can be attributed to the "safety-first" approach taken for BlobStore, specifically:

1. Use of functional architecture and functional programming to ensure high code quality, and to prevent inadvertent destruction of data.
2. Care taken in developing rollout plans for both data and code migrations.
3. Focus on supportability of the solution, including developing necessary tools and metrics.
4. Automation of most testing and deployment, including performance tests to ensure that the system can handle predicted loads.

In general, even at this early stage of microservice transition, we have already observed a number of benefits:

- *Significantly shorter time to deployment for new functionality or bug fixes* compared to making changes in existing monolithic applications. This can be attributed to:

  - A smaller, more focused code base that can be modified quickly. For example, server-side changes in BlobStore to add or delete functionality were implemented and deployed to production within a couple of days, with most of the time spent waiting for reviews. The small code base meant the architecture could be kept clean, and the code has thorough test coverage.
  - With well-defined interfaces for microservices, the build pipeline includes only a small number of integration tests focused on specific functionality being provided by the microservice. This significantly reduces the cycle time of the build pipeline.
  - Changes to microservices can be made and deployed independently from the consumer applications. This means microservices are decoupled from application deployment cycles, which are longer due to running comprehensive integration tests across the entire monolithic application.

- *Significant consolidation of resources.* For example, we are able to service all existing customers with a handful of BlobStore server instances, instead of occupying resources (CPU, RAM, disk) in each customer's container, which is difficult to share between customer instances. A similar scenario has occurred with Atlassian ID single sign-on.
- *Ability to utilize non-JVM packages that are better suited to tasks.* By bundling up applications into a Docker image and deploying to the PaaS, we are no longer tied to what can be done within one JVM (e.g., we can integrate with native tools for better performance where necessary).
- *Ability to use more appropriate languages for specific microservices.* We are no longer tied to Java or even using a Java virtual machine (JVM) for implementation, which has led to new microservices to be developed quickly using a variety of languages (e.g., Node.js, Python, and Clojure).

As with all new technologies, though, many challenges have appeared and been addressed, but more challenges are on the horizon as we start building many more microservices that interact with each other. Some of these challenges include:

- *Microservice deployment is more "complex" than monolithic applications with more moving parts.* While microservice code bases are smaller, there are additional considerations and infrastructure required, such as new deployment pipelines, networks, logging, metrics collection, and so forth. This has added a lot of time to the development and deployment of early microservices. Atlassian PaaS simplifies these issues considerably, and much of the work on early microservices is being reused, which has greatly reduced development time for subsequent services.
- *New architectural concerns come into play that are quite different from traditional monolithic applications.* Many of these concerns are not difficult to implement; the challenge is ensuring that all engineers, including those working on consumer applications, are aware of them. These concerns include:

  - *Need for stateless business logic to support horizontal scalability.* Services need to be designed with no session state between requests and careful, if any, caching of data.
  - *Need for services to be designed to support multiple tenants.* For example, services need to be able to look up a specific tenant's data for a request, compartmentalize data between tenants, and ensure that a tenant can only access their own data.
  - *Increased network latency due to extra hops to microservices.* In the short term with early microservices, caching is relatively easy to implement with immutable HTTP APIs. However, as we develop networks of services where requests traverse multiple network hops, this may become problematic. Greater care needs to be taken to ensure that data remains cacheable as much as possible.
  - *Low-latency authentication and authorization between microservices.* Microservices need to authenticate and authorize requests between each other and may also need to impersonate end users as part of those requests. Handling this in a performant way, especially when a request traverses multiple microservices (each of which may need to perform authentication and authorization checks) is a challenge that is currently being worked through. However, existing mechanisms such as Kerberos have shown that it is possible.
  - *Deploying and rolling back microservices in new environments independently without an excessively long-running suite of integration tests.* Microservices should be deployed independently of each other, yet changes need to be compatible with other services in the same environment. Integration tests are currently being used to verify this,

but as the number of microservices grows this could become a bottleneck. Investigation into concepts such as consumer-driven contracts, maintenance of metadata around test runs, and reliability of specific microservice version combinations is being done, but this is still an outstanding problem.

- *Ensuring that microservices stay "small" and focused with well-defined APIs.* In a monolithic application, it becomes a habit to add functionality to the same deployment unit, and this behavior can be easily transferred to microservice development. To address this, Atlassian SaaS and application architects have developed a roadmap to define boundaries of microservices. Also, this may be less of an issue within Atlassian, as our monolithic applications are already architected to be highly modular through OSGi (and now HTTP) based plug-in systems. Finally, microservices may need to be refactored over time to further split out functionality as new services come online; the small code base with well-defined interfaces makes this relatively easy.

- *Dependencies on to-be-built microservices.* Being small in scope, microservices typically need to work with other microservices to become fully featured. However, in the early stages, not all dependent microservices are available for use, which leads to interim solutions and workarounds. For example, customer data encryption and key management is strictly not within the scope of BlobStore microservice, but an interim solution needed to be developed before such a service was available. Going forward, BlobStore will need to be refactored when a suitable microservice is developed. This requires a refactoring mindset and time scoped for refactoring of microservices. Having said that, it should be relatively easy to refactor the services because they are small.

- *Dependencies on other projects (applications or services).* This challenge exists with any architecture, but becomes more pronounced because microservices are "cross-application" and hence have more touch-points. Well-defined APIs and project scope are helping to clearly identify these dependencies so that they can be managed. Also, the experiences from early microservice work such as Atlassian PaaS and BlobStore have led to process improvements especially around inter-team communications and dependency tracking, and better utilization of the outputs of agile methodologies to identify delays and adapt accordingly.

- *Supporting microservices is different from supporting monolithic applications.* As discussed previously, tooling and process for dealing with microservices is quite different from supporting monolithic applications. Development of these needs to be factored into microservice work. The close interaction between microservice development teams, service operations, and support is extremely important to ensure smooth transition to support.

Operations team onboarding processes are being developed to standardize and streamline the process. In addition to general support, debugging a distributed network of microservices is significantly different and more difficult than a monolithic application stack. Further investigation is required into distributed tracing solutions such as Twitter Zipkin that track requests at relevant points via a unique ID generated upon ingress of requests.

So far, the benefits of microservices far outweigh the negatives, and Atlassian expects the challenges to become fewer as they gain experience, build templates and infrastructure to speed up development, and reduce the size of the monolithic applications. There are several factors that should allow Atlassian to build on the momentum of early microservices to complete a successful transition to fully tenantless architecture:

- There are pressing business problems of how to reduce cost per customer and increase scalability of applications to serve new customers while being able to rapidly deliver new functionality and applications. As can be seen from large web-based businesses such as Amazon, Netflix, and Google, shared microservices represent a good solution to these challenges if done correctly (i.e., ensuring issues are addressed with minimal technical debt accumulated along the way).
- Microservice development, agile methodologies, and DevOps concepts promote a similar outcome of rapid delivery of small high-quality pieces of functionality at a time. As discussed in this case study, agile and DevOps are well embedded within teams in Atlassian, so microservices, which by nature are small pieces of functionality that can be delivered quickly, are a natural evolution to support faster team velocities.
- Development of the PaaS was a turning point in the adoption of microservices within Atlassian. The PaaS introduced a convenient platform for developers to investigate and innovate on, similar to public PaaS offerings such as Heroku or Elastic Beanstalk, while also providing standardized common infrastructure to help with production support. As a result, within weeks of wider internal release, a plethora of microservices with different technology stacks were in development.

As this case study was being written, several more microservices were being deployed to Atlassian PaaS, and BlobStore functionality was being integrated with other Atlassian Cloud applications and microservices (e.g., a new document conversion microservice). Going forward, Atlassian PaaS will be incorporating additional useful infrastructure components, including better centralized metrics collection, secrets store, and AWS asset management. There are also a number of other core microservices in the pipeline, such as tenant management, authentication/authorization, and external task scheduling. In true agile style, Atlassian is picking the low-hanging fruit first, ramping up velocity, and adapting the plan as new challenges emerge.

13.6 Summary

Migrating to a microservice architecture can be done incrementally. It requires identifying commonality among services to migrate initially and adapting the application architecture to take advantage of these common services. For Atlassian, it also required developing a PaaS on which the microservices would rely. These two different development streams introduced a necessity for coordination, but the PaaS became relatively stable once several microservices had been deployed.

BlobStore is a microservice that affects persistent data, and, consequently, its implementation is perhaps more sensitive than other types of services. It was implemented in a fashion that made the blobs that it stored immutable. This immutability supported rollback as well as error tracking since all copies of the blobs remained until garbage-collected.

13.7 For Further Reading

Further details on the technologies mentioned in this chapter can be found at the following links:

- Amazon Direct Connect http://aws.amazon.com/directconnect/
- CloudWatch: http://aws.amazon.com/cloudwatch/
- DynamoDB: http://aws.amazon.com/dynamodb/
- ELB: http://aws.amazon.com/elasticloadbalancing/
- Elasticsearch: http://www.elasticsearch.org/
- Finagle RPC: https://twitter.github.io/finagle/
- Fluentd: http://www.fluentd.org/
- Kibana: http://www.elasticsearch.org/overview/kibana/
- OpenVZ: http://openvz.org/Main_Page
- Route 53: http://aws.amazon.com/route53/
- RDS: http://aws.amazon.com/rds/
- S3: http://aws.amazon.com/s3/
- Simple Queue System: http://aws.amazon.com/sqs/
- Squid: http://www.squid-cache.org/
- SNS: http://aws.amazon.com/sns/
- Stackdriver: http://www.stackdriver.com/

PART FIVE

MOVING INTO THE FUTURE

In this part, we discuss how DevOps might evolve over the next few years. First, we have been doing research into DevOps for several years, and we describe our research results and directions. Second, we speculate more broadly about how DevOps will evolve.

In Chapter 1, we defined DevOps as a collection of processes specific to the goal of reducing the time between a commit and the code being in normal production. The business process management community had been working on process mining and modelling for many years. Our research has revolved around creating a process model for individual DevOps processes from logs and using that model to drive error detection, diagnosis, and recovery for the processes. We describe this in Chapter 14.

DevOps has been evolving quickly and will continue to evolve. Its evolution will touch the three areas of DevOps activities: organizational structure, process definition, and technology. In Chapter 15, we provide our guesses as to how these activities will change in the next three to five years.

14

Operations as a Process

With Xiwei Xu and Min Fu

> *If you can't describe what you are doing as a process,*
> *you don't know what you're doing.*
> —W. Edwards Deming

14.1 Introduction

As we discussed in Chapter 9, the continuous deployment pipeline is not just another software *product* with system-of-systems characteristics, it also has strong characteristics of a *process*. This is also true for many other operations such as diagnosis, backup and recovery, upgrade, and maintenance. Even your favorite Cron jobs and scripts may be pipelining a set of small tools—a familiar concept in the administrator's world. We can view the operations world as a large number of such process-oriented systems operating on your applications and your systems. These processes are not just sequential, but have a lot of simultaneity and parallelism both at the process and task levels.

The purpose of this chapter is to discuss the implications of treating operations as processes. By treating, we mean you can discover a process model from existing operations software/scripts and their logs. You can:

- Analyze the discovered process models for improvement opportunities.
- Use the process models to monitor the progression of various operations, to detect errors and to recover from them as early as possible.
- Set monitoring thresholds at a level that reflects the active operations processes. You want to achieve this at the step level rather than the whole process level, since that leads to earlier error detection and recovery.
- Use the process models to help other activities such as root cause diagnosis.

Performing these activities is difficult as they often lack context information on what is happening. The process model and the monitoring of progression provide that context. The process models can also be a central place to correlate different events and monitoring metrics to improve your understanding of the runtime system. The opportunities are ample. The discovered process model can be used to orchestrate variations in the original process and could become a mechanism for executing future applications of the process.

Process-oriented systems can be seen as workflow systems or business process management systems. Relevant results from these areas include mining process models from logs and event traces, process analysis, runtime monitoring and prediction, process quality improvement, and human-intensive processes. You can see an example of this perspective in our discussion about rolling upgrade in Chapter 6. In this chapter, we focus on the workflow or (business) process perspective on operations processes.

One final introductory issue that you should consider is the level of abstraction of your process models. A process model is a specification of a set of activities which, when carried out, result in the completion of a desired result. This set of activities can be modeled at a fine-grained level (every step in carrying out the process) or at a coarse-grained level (the major activities performed during the process). The modeling level depends on the richness of the source of discovering the process model and the results you wish to obtain from the model. As with a software system, a process model can be understood from its runtime properties (performance, reliability, and security being three important qualities) as well as its development time properties (interoperability and modifiability being two). In this chapter, we focus on research that we have performed into the reliability of operations processes whose process model specification is correct. Other perspectives involve ensuring the correctness of the process (and its model), improving the performance of the execution of the process, or constructing the model efficiently at a desired level of granularity.

14.2 Motivation and Overview

As we discussed in Chapter 9, reliability refers to the capability of the overall deployment pipeline and its individual pieces to maintain service provision for defined periods of time. A typical pipeline has to deal with different types of error responses from different types of systems—ranging from the error code of a cloud application programming interface (API) call to the potentially silent failure of a configuration change. The uncertainty inherent within clouds that we discussed in Chapter 2 also introduces some random failures so that a script that was previously successful may produce an invalid outcome. What this means is that defensive programming strategies, while important, are not going to be sufficient. Instead, we advocate deriving an understanding of what should be the desired state of a process and comparing that with the actual state. In essence, that is the basis of the approach we discuss in this chapter. Operations processes have several characteristics that make this approach more tractable than for general business processes. In particular:

- Operations processes manipulate only a few types of entities. In the rolling upgrade example we use in this chapter, these are Elastic Load Balancers (ELBs), autoscaling groups (ASGs), launch configurations (LCs), and virtual machines (VMs). In general business processes, there can be a large number of different types of entities that are being manipulated.
- Operations processes have a time frame measured in tens of minutes if not in hours. This means that gathering logs, detecting errors, and recovering from errors in a few minutes is useful. In general business processes, the time frames can be much shorter.
- Operations tools typically generate high-quality logs that can be used to create the process model without a lot of noise.

In order to know what the desired state of a process should be, we first need to discover a suitable process model. Once we have done this, we can prepare for error detection, diagnosis, and recovery. We discover the process model by analyzing logs from successful executions of the process. This discovery is done offline after we have achieved successful execution and generated associated logs.

During an execution of the process, we compare the desired state of the process with the current state of the process. Any difference indicates a reliability problem and provides the seeds of a recovery strategy. These activities happen online (concurrently) with the process.

We use the process of rolling upgrade as our running example throughout the chapter. A rolling upgrade places a new version of an application into service, one or more servers at a time. It removes a server from service (possibly deleting the server), loads the new version of the application onto that server or a replacement server, and starts the newly loaded server. We discussed rolling upgrade in more detail in Chapter 6. Figure 14.1, repeated from that chapter, shows the rolling upgrade process used by Asgard on AWS.

14.3 Offline Activities

As we said, the process model is created offline. It can be created manually based on your understanding of the operation and the code/scripts. Alternatively, process mining techniques can be used to discover the process, especially from logs. In this section we describe the process mining activities that are carried out offline based on successful executions of the process. These activities provide the basis for the online error detection and recovery.

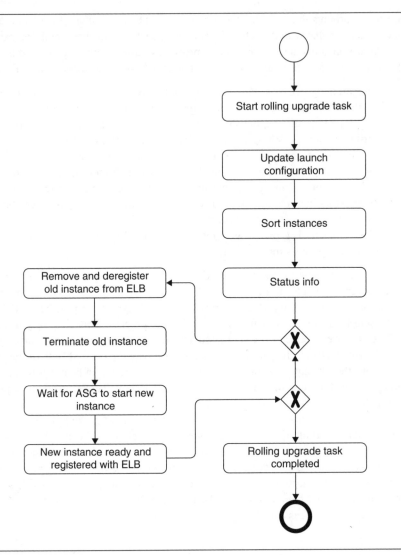

FIGURE 14.1   Rolling upgrade process from Asgard on AWS (Repeated from Figure 6.2) [Notation: BPMN]

There are a number of reasons for preferring process mining techniques over manual process model creation. First, automation is critical for technology adoption. It reduces the skill level required to create the process model. You will have a large number of constantly evolving operations. Manual model creation and later maintenance incur a high cost. Second, frequently we do not have access to the source code/scripts of the operation software, so understanding of it has to be derived from externally observable traces such as logs. Third, runtime logs can be used to trigger tests and diagnosis as the operations process progresses without modifying the original operation software.

Recall that in a rolling upgrade, a small number of k instances at a time currently running the old version are taken out of service and replaced with k instances running the new version. The time taken by each wave of replacement is usually in the order of minutes. Performing a rolling upgrade for hundreds or thousands of instances using a small k will take a long time.

The Asgard tool performs a rolling upgrade and produces logs such as the ones shown in Listing 14.1.

LISTING 14.1 Logs produced by Asgard rolling upgrade (shortened version)

```
"2014-05-26_13:17:36 Started on thread Task:Pushing
ami-4583197f into group testworkload-r01 for app
testworkload."
"2014-05-26_13:17:38 The group testworkload-r01 has 8
instances. 8 will be replaced, 2 at a time."
"2014-05-26_13:17:38 Remove instances [i-226fa51c] from
Load Balancer ELB-01"
"2014-05-26_13:17:39 Deregistered instances [i-226fa51c]
from load balancer ELB-01"
"2014-05-26_13:17:42 Terminating instance i-226fa51c"
...
"2014-05-26_13:17:43 Waiting up to 1h 10m for new
instance of testworkload-r01 to become Pending."
```

If you look at the log lines, you get a sense of what the operation is doing as a process without looking at the source code. For example, the software is pushing an Amazon virtual Machine Image (AMI) to an instance group that has eight instances. This AMI contains the new version of the software. The plan is to upgrade two instances at a time until all instances are upgraded. The old instances are removed/deregistered from the ELB and terminated while the system waits for an instance containing the new versions to be launched. Later this new instance will be added/registered to the ELB (not shown in the listing). And you would expect a loop for the replacement step until all instances are upgraded to the new version.

Process mining techniques allow the discovery of a process model as shown in Figure 14.1 from these logs without having access to the source code. There are two basic steps in creating a process model from logs: 1) group the logs based on the activity they represent and tag them with an activity name, and 2) use the tagged logs to create the process model using a tool such as ProM. Figure 14.2 shows the logs from Asgard being stored in Logstash—a log management tool—and then being used for generating the process model.

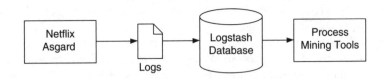

FIGURE 14.2   Using Asgard logs to produce a process model [Notation: Architecture]

Asgard logs are not the only source of log information for this operation. In Amazon Web Services (AWS), a feature called CloudTrail logs all the Cloud API calls. The Asgard rolling upgrade operation calls the Cloud APIs to complete certain steps, such as deregister/terminate/start instances. These Asgard operation steps leave a trace in the CloudTrail logs but at a lower level of abstraction—the API call level. Some other steps such as "Status info" do not involve any Cloud API call, thus they do not leave any traces in CloudTrail. It is possible to combine or correlate multiple sources of information for the same operations process. This correlation might not only provide a more useful process model, the correlation itself can be used to associate causes with effects and use that information for assertions, diagnosis, or even recovery. Listing 14.2 shows a sample log entry from CloudTrail. Notice that this log entry identifies the AWS resource being

LISTING 14.2   Sample CloudTrail log

```
{ "awsRegion": "us-west-2",
  "eventName": "TerminateInstances",
  "eventSource": "ec2.amazonaws.com<http://ec2.amazonaws.
com>",
  "eventTime": "2014-01-24T01:59:58Z",
  "eventVersion": "1.0",
  "requestParameters": {"instancesSet": {"items":
[{"instanceId": "i-5424a45c"}]}},
    "responseElements": {"instancesSet": {"items":
[{"currentState": {"code": 32,"name": "shutting-
down"},"instanceId": "i-5424a45c","previousState":
{"code": 32,"name": "shutting-down"}}]}},
"sourceIPAddress":"autoscaling.amazonaws.com<http://
autoscaling.amazonaws.com>",
    "userAgent": "autoscaling.amazonaws.com<http://
autoscaling.amazonaws.com>",
    "userIdentity": {"accountId": "066611989206","arn":
"arn:aws:iam::066611989206:root","invokedBy":
"autoscaling.amazonaws.com<http://autoscaling.amazonaws.
com>","principalId": "066611989206","type": "Root"}}
```

manipulated—VM instance—as well as identification information and parameters associated with the request.

Figure 14.3 shows how the process activities can be correlated with the CloudTrail logs based on time stamps. This correlation allows you to determine which AWS resources are being manipulated during which activities of the process model. Furthermore, knowing the state of these resources at the beginning of an activity and knowing the type of manipulations that should occur allows you to determine the expected state of the AWS resources at the end of each activity. We elaborate on this idea in Section 14.4.

There are two steps in the development of the process model that require human intervention.

1. A human must examine the groups of activities to determine whether they are at a desired level of granularity and to assign names to the groups. At the two ends of the spectrum, every log line could be a separate group, or there could be only one group including all of the log lines. Choosing the correct level of granularity takes some judgment.
2. A human must also examine the generated process model. It is possible that there are spurious activities or transitions within the process model. A human must determine that the model, in fact, represents the process being modeled.

Creating the process model is an activity that should take less than a day for a skilled analyst.

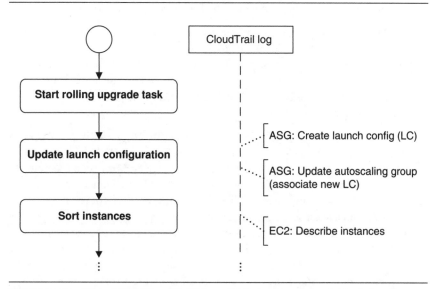

FIGURE 14.3 Correlating CloudTrail logs with the process model to determine the AWS resources manipulated by each activity of the process model [Notation (left): BPMN]; [Notation (right): UML Sequence Diagram]

14.4 Online Activities

Recall that our current focus is on the reliability of the rolling upgrade process. This means we want to detect, diagnose, and recover from errors that occur during the execution of a rolling upgrade. Error detection and recovery can be done online during the execution of the rolling upgrade. Diagnosis is an activity that occurs subsequent to the detection of an error, which can be online or offline; fast online diagnosis can lead to more informed recovery, but detailed analysis of underlying issues are better done offline, after recovery brought the system back to a stable state.

Some timing information is useful at this point. Asgard logs are created and can be processed quickly. CloudTrail logs, on the other hand, are not available, currently, for up to15 minutes after the API calls have been made. This means that the error detection and recovery proceed using just Asgard logs. The CloudTrail logs are useful for understanding the desired state of AWS resources at the end of each activity but they cannot be used directly in either error detection or recovery because of the time delay.

Error Detection

From the log lines being produced by Asgard, we can detect the start and end of each activity step. From the process model, we know the desired sequence of steps. One error detection mode is to look for steps out of the desired sequence. Such an occurrence is called a "conformance error."

Conformance checking can detect the following types of errors:

- Unknown: a log line that is completely unknown.
- Error: a log line that corresponds to a known error.
- Unfit: a log line that corresponds to a known activity, but that should not happen given the current execution state of the process instance. This can be due to skipped activities (going forward in the process) or undone activities (going backward).

For example, after seeing the log line `"2014-05-26_13:17:38 Remove instances [i-226fa51c] from Load Balancer ELB-01"`, we should expect a log line about terminating that instance `[i-226fa51c]` soon according to the discovered process model. If we do not see that log line within a time period or see a different known or unknown log line, it indicates some type of error.

A conformance error triggers a message to the operator and also triggers the error recovery mechanism. The message to the operator is produced within seconds of the production of the log line out of sequence. This enables the operator to know where in the thousands or millions of log lines being produced to start from when manually diagnosing and recovering from the error.

The second type of error detection relies on the AWS resources manipulated by activities. Recall that through correlating CloudTrail logs with the process model, we can determine the AWS resources manipulated by each activity. For example, the activity "Remove and deregister old instance from ELB" should result in one fewer instance being registered with the ELB at the completion of this activity than there was at the beginning of the activity.

The concrete instance that will be removed during the runtime execution of the process will be different from the instance that was removed during offline analysis, but we know that one instance fewer should exist. By recording the state of the ELB at the beginning of the activity and comparing that to the state of the ELB at the end of the activity, we can determine 1) in fact, a particular instance has been removed from the ELB, and 2) the instance ID is known so that in the next activity "Terminate old instance," we know exactly which instance should have been terminated.

The rolling upgrade process manipulates only four AWS resources: ELB, ASG, launch configuration, and VM instances. This means that saving the state of these resources at the beginning of an activity can be done quickly. Furthermore, at the end of an activity, we can determine the current state of these resources by querying AWS. The response time of these queries depends on AWS, but our experience is that the response time is on the order of several seconds. These two times mean that comparing the state of these resources at the end of the activity to the desired state can be done on the order of seconds. Furthermore, the saving and comparing is done by a process operating independently from Asgard, so there is no degradation to the normal rolling upgrade process unless an error is detected.

The kinds of errors that can be detected by these means include errors caused by failures in the cloud such as the long tail and also errors caused by interference between two teams simultaneously deploying different instances. Examples of the kinds of errors we have detected are

1. AMI changed during upgrade
2. Key pair management fault
3. Security group configuration fault
4. Instance type changed during upgrade
5. AMI unavailable during upgrade
6. Key pair unavailable during upgrade
7. Security group unavailable during upgrade
8. ELB unavailable during upgrade

Error Recovery

Now suppose an error has been detected. We have three sets of states of the AWS resources that are relevant.

1. The state at the beginning of the last activity
2. The current erroneous state
3. The desired state

We know that the current state is erroneous for some reason. There are at least two options to automatically recover from the error: roll back to the state at the beginning of the last activity or roll forward to the desired state.

The difficulty of performing either of these activities varies with circumstances. Suppose, for example, that an old instance was not deregistered from the ELB. Then recovery would involve retrying the deregistration operation. On the other hand, with more complicated processes, it may not be possible to return to the state at the beginning of the last activity. When a VM is paused or deleted, its IP address is lost. Recovering the VM with its original IP address is not possible.

14.5 Error Diagnosis

Repairing an error may not repair the root cause of an error. For example, some of the errors we mentioned in the previous section on error detection are caused by race conditions and release conflicts because of two different teams simultaneously deploying different versions of a system. If the conflict is not resolved, the system may be subject to the same error again. Consequently, we now turn our attention to diagnosing errors.

We are looking for error diagnoses due to typical causes in cloud operation rather than bugs in software. Diagnosing bugs in software is certainly important and useful but outside of the current scope of our research. For diagnosing operations errors, we use *fault trees* as a reference model. In such a fault tree, each node represents a failure or an error, which in turn could be caused by the errors in the child nodes. The children of these child nodes, in turn, could have caused that error. Figure 14.4 shows a part of the fault tree we use for detecting rolling upgrade errors. Although it involves some effort to build this tree, this is a once-off effort and the tree can be reused for many different cloud operations.

Our knowledge of the process progression helps us in diagnosis. Knowing during which step an error occurred restricts the possible causes to those involving the AWS resources involved in that step. We can then prune the trees to retain those elements that affect those resources but exclude the others. Furthermore, historical data for the types of errors that have occurred allows us to associate probabilities with each branch of the fault tree and use those probabilities to guide the diagnosis process.

14.6 Monitoring

As we mentioned in Chapter 7, one of the problems with using thresholds for alerts or alarms is the number of false positives if the thresholds are set low. Relaxing the thresholds raises the possibilities of false negatives—namely,

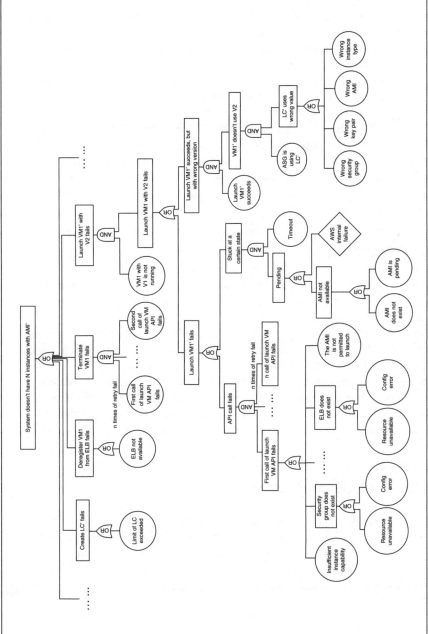

FIGURE 14.4 Part of a fault tree for automated error diagnosis [Notation: Fault Tree]

missing actual errors. Normal practice is to adjust the thresholds to achieve a tolerable number of false positives.

The number of alerts or alarms is increased during the execution of an operations process because VMs are being taken out of or added to service during these processes. Some organizations turn off alerts and alarms while such operations are ongoing, so that they are not flooded with alerts or alarms.

Knowing the fact that a process is under way and knowing the current activity of the process allows for dynamic adjustment to monitoring thresholds. For example, if you are performing a rolling upgrade, you know when an instance is going to be taken out of service. This has the effect of temporarily increasing the load on the other servers, assuming a relatively stable workload during this period. The CPU threshold, for example, can be increased temporarily when a server is taken out of service and lowered again when a new server becomes active and is sharing the load.

14.7 Summary

In this chapter we have summarized some of the research we have been performing over the past two years. Viewing operations as a process allows us to create a process model from log lines and to use that process model to detect and sometimes repair errors caused by operational reasons. The crucial element in our research is the use of the process context to provide information enabling the determination of the desired state of the AWS resources manipulated by the process being modelled. Knowing the desired state allows, in turn, the detection of errors and, potentially, recovery from these errors. Furthermore, knowing the process context can allow for dynamic adjustment of monitoring thresholds to reduce the false positives generated when an operations process is ongoing.

14.8 For Further Reading

You can find more about process mining in van der Aalst's book [van der Aalst 11].

To learn more about our line of research in error detection, diagnosis, and recovery, see the papers by Xu et al. [Xu 14] and Weber et al. [Weber 15]. You can go to our website for updates: http://ssrg.nicta.com.au/projects/cloud/

You can find more information about the technologies we mentioned at the following links:

- AWS: "Error Codes—Amazon Elastic Compute Cloud," http://docs.aws .amazon.com/AWSEC2/latest/APIReference/api-error-codes.html
- Logstash: http://logstash.net
- Asgard: https://github.com/Netflix/asgard

15

The Future of DevOps

The best thing about the future is that it comes one day at a time.
—Abraham Lincoln

15.1 Introduction

In this chapter, we speculate about the future—always a dangerous proposition. We begin with the assumption that DevOps is in the process of "crossing the chasm." This phrase is a creation of Geoffrey Moore, and it describes the process of the diffusion of technology. In this model, a technology is initially adopted by innovators. It is next adopted by the mainstream beginning with early adopters. In order to have mainstream adoption, a large amount of material describing how to use the technology, success stories, and business considerations are needed to convince the mainstream that the technology is worth the investment. The requirement for the material necessary for mainstream adoption is called the "chasm." Technologies that do not provide this material tend not to survive. From the early adopters, the technology enters the mainstream and is adopted by the majority, and finally by the late adopters and the laggards.

For DevOps, the innovators are the Googles, the Amazons, or the Netflixes. The material being created includes talks, meetups, books (including this one), new tools, LinkedIn groups, and blogs.

Now a variety of other organizations are investigating and adopting, in one way or another, DevOps practices. These include

- *Internet companies that are well established but have not needed the agility of the innovators.* Atlassian (see the case study in Chapter 13) fits into that category.
- *Enterprises.* Organizations large and small are investigating or adopting continuous delivery and deployment and better integration of Dev and Ops.

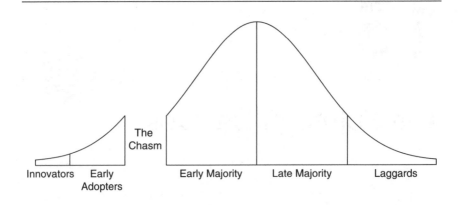

Innovators   Early   Early Majority   Late Majority   Laggards
          Adopters

FIGURE 15.1 Crossing the chasm

> See the case study in Chapter 12 for the kind of organizations that Sourced Group works with.
> - *Startups.* A startup's first goal is to gain a customer base. They are not particularly concerned with the processes they use. Their architecture is often monolithic to begin with and their operations processes are typically carried out by the developers. Once a startup grows, they find a need for a more flexible architecture and more organizational structure. This is the stage where they begin to adopt DevOps.

As we have discussed throughout this book, DevOps touches organizational, process, and technology issues. The speculation about the future in this chapter is structured according to these categories.

15.2 Organizational Issues

We discuss three different organizational issues: other groups that may be involved in DevOps-style activities, ownership and reorganizations, and empowerment versus control.

Other Groups That Might Be Involved in DevOps-Style Activities

DevOps began as a movement to break down barriers between Dev and Ops with the goal of reducing organizational inertia in putting systems into production. There are other groups that cause potential problems with both Dev and Ops.

- *Business initiatives*. Business initiatives impact most areas of an organization. New products, discounts, test marketing, and changes in the supply chain all have impacts on both Dev and Ops. Most established organizations have processes in place to plan for and manage these types of events. If the time between development and production is reduced, the coordination between the units responsible for the business initiatives and DevOps becomes a larger percentage of the total time. This will create pressure to smooth out coordination between those business units and both Dev and Ops. This "BizOps" is being accomplished by moving relevant information into a content management system and using the content management system to coordinate.
- *Data scientists*. Big data is used to get business insights that drive both strategic thinking and real-time customer acquisition. Operating complicated big data analytics clusters, maintaining data ingestion pipelines, and integrating data analytics (machine learning models and predictive results) into products introduces additional requirements for prompt response for DevOps, and a new type of business analyst— the data scientist.
- *Security*. The case study in Chapter 12 includes a discussion about the role of a security group while establishing a continuous delivery pipeline. We also discussed security audits in Chapter 8. Making the security process and security audits more agile is not only an organizational matter but also a matter for the regulators. There is work ongoing on automating compliance and compliance testing. This work can be applied not only to security matters but also to compliance with accounting regulations such as Sarbanes-Oxley.
- *Strategic planning*. Having a continuous deployment pipeline may open up other business opportunities. Netflix, for example, had an opportunity to develop a suite of operations tools but chose not to because it was not their core business. Other organizations may develop other business opportunities as a result of their DevOps activities.

Ownership and Reorganizations

Microservices are owned by small teams but also consumed by many other teams. Whenever a microservice is updated, not only does the team have to be sure that it works with all downstream services, but, more importantly, that it does not have negative impacts on upstream services. This is the traditional dependency problem, but the complexity, scale, and real-time performance requirements of microservices are exacerbating the problem. One emerging solution is to let the upstream consumers' development team have co-ownership of the testing suite of a downstream service and allow the change negotiation to happen through the testing suite. On the other hand, end-to-end testing in the microservice environment is expensive. The collective ownership of end-to-end tests by a large number of teams is impractical because people liberally add new tests to this test suite, causing each run of them to be expensive (due to time needed and flaky tests).

Organizations reorganize their structures frequently. When an organization has been developing microservices over a period they will own a variety of microservices, some undergoing development and some just in a maintenance phase. When a reorganization occurs, it is possible that a team may end up owning a microservice that is unfamiliar to them. This raises standard, long-lasting software engineering issues about documentation and knowledge transfer.

Furthermore, a microservice may be sufficiently old that it does not take advantage of newer tooling. Monitoring, for example, depends partially on the application providing appropriate information. An old microservice, inherited by a new team, may not conform to the team's standards for generating monitoring data and may not have an appropriate quality of automated tests.

Empowerment Versus Control

Empowerment versus control is another organizational issue that arises. On the one hand, some key decisions (such as releases and A/B testing) are delegated to small teams and individuals rather than enforced through a hierarchical, human-intensive approval process. This delegation increases the velocity but also introduces significant risks to your production system. One way of resolving this is to place automated quality controls in the pipeline process itself. Locking down the production environment unless automated tests and other gates have been passed is an example. Two potential problems can be foreseen:

1. *Processes have a tendency to be all-encompassing.* One reaction to a problem is to add new elements (such as flows, gates, and structures) to the process. Over time, processes lose their original motivation and no one recalls exactly why certain elements are in the process. Alternatively, the reason for a feature in the element may have changed and may no longer be relevant but the element remains.
2. *Ownership of the process.* Development teams can own the process to deployment, or the organization can own the process. In the case study in Chapter 12, there is an organization-wide base process that each development team can tailor. Amazon has a group responsible for creating build tools, and these tools provide the basic process, where parameters allow for some tailoring. Again, once reorganization occurs, the ownership of the process may pass to a team unfamiliar with the process or its rationale.

15.3 Process Issues

Some of the process issues that will arise in the future are old ones such as concern about vendor lock-in, some are due to the use of the cloud as a platform such as charging models, and some are due to the increased velocity of changes that are being deployed.

Vendor Lock-in and Standards

A continuous deployment pipeline utilizes many different tools and deploys onto a platform. All of the tools as well as the platform raise the possibility of vendor lock-in. This is not a new problem, but one that has existed in the computer industry for at least 50 years. That does not make it less of a concern.

One solution to the problem of vendor lock-in is the use of standards. Although the use of standard languages and interfaces does not guarantee portability, it does simplify the problem. As yet, there are no widely adopted standards for the tools in a continuous deployment pipeline, although one of our predictions is that as DevOps crosses the chasm, the pressure for standards will grow.

Lacking standards, the solutions for resisting vendor lock-in include the following:

- *Defensive programming.* In Chapter 9, we discussed techniques that can be used to support modifiability. Changing from one tool to another in a deployment pipeline is a modifiability scenario.
- *Migration programs.* It is possible to move programs from one tool to another through the construction of a specialized migration program. Such programs work best when the target concepts are a superset of the source concepts. Emulation of source concepts in the target environment is a technique that is used when there is no straightforward mapping. Such emulations typically involve making assumptions about particular choices of parameters on the target and are not an ideal solution, although such emulations are frequently cost-effective in terms of human effort versus machine efficiency.

Another technique to avoid vendor lock-in is to provide open application programming interfaces (APIs) and promote an active plug-in ecosystem for interoperation among tools. For example, Jenkins is a popular continuous integration product that interoperates with a large number of other tools through externally developed plug-ins. This enables people to choose their favorite version control, testing, and dependency management systems.

Charging Models

The models used to charge for resources in a cloud platform fall into four categories:

1. *Consumption-based.* Pay for the resources that you use based on a preannounced schedule.
2. *Subscription-based.* Pay for unlimited or capped usage during a particular time such as a month.
3. *Advertising-based.* Allow advertising to appear on your web pages or displays for price reductions.
4. *Market-based.* Pay based on supply and demand at a particular time. Auctions are used to allocate resources to consumers.

Combinations of these charging models also exist. Amazon Web Services (AWS), for example, will charge per hour (subscription) based on the characteristics of the virtual machine (VM) that has been allocated (consumption).

One strategy when facing a combination of subscription and consumption models is to use a pool of VMs and change the contents of the VMs through the use of containers. If this strategy is used then autoscaling rules, for example, have two levels. One level allocates and deallocates containers within VMs, and the other level allocates and deallocates VMs. The container model also aligns well with the microservice architecture where a single microservice is best deployed into containers.

Velocity of Changes

A successful continuous deployment pipeline should increase the frequency of deployments, and this will have a number of consequences.

- *The qualities of concern with a deployment will change.* When you deploy once a month, it is important to ensure that the new version is correct and that the deployment proceeds smoothly. The actual time of the deployment is not that great a concern as long as it happens within some, fairly lengthy, window. When you deploy 10 times a day, these considerations change. The major quality concern with deployments is avoiding outages. A failed deployment, for example, caught in time to avoid impact on the service to the user is not a major concern since another deployment will occur within a short time. The concern is with repeated failed deployments, not a sporadic failure of a particular deployment. Rolling back in the event of a failure is a reasonable strategy for stateless services, since changes will be picked up with the next deployment.
- *Automatic error detection/recovery is important.* When you deploy once a month, there is time to carefully examine each deployment for correctness and to manually troubleshoot errors. When you deploy 10 times a day, manually repairing an error is infeasible since the error may affect other deployments as well. Hence, tools to monitor and detect errors and to roll back automatically become important. Diagnostic tools also are important. Ideally, a diagnostic tool would be able to pinpoint the source of an error to the application system or to the deployment pipeline.
- *Workload and application behavior changes.* Through continuous delivery, an organization can rapidly introduce new services and features into their product. These will change user behavior and subsequently workload and traffic patterns. Even when such a change is not significant, a more performing or reliable version of your software also consumes internal services differently. Existing monitoring systems rely on carefully derived thresholds using historical data and benchmarking of a particular version of the system. This may work if a version of your software usually runs for

weeks or even months. If you deploy new versions 10 times a day, adjusting the threshold for new versions is a major challenge. Without proper adjustment, this may create many alarms that are false positives.

- *Environment changes.* Current monitoring tools also assume the environment in which the application is executing remains, essentially, unchanged. Frequent deployments can violate that assumption and introduce a different type of false alarms. Given a higher frequency of deployment, this would mean turning off the monitoring tools during the deployment, which is happening quite frequently. Monitoring tools need to become deployment-aware and aware of other process interferences.

In other words, high velocity of changes eventually becomes continuous change, which can fundamentally alter the way testing and monitoring is done. Organizations may rely more on production environment canary testing and intelligent monitoring rather than time-consuming end-to-end testing. All of these are blurring the boundary between end-to-end testing and monitoring and will require whole new solutions. On the other hand, intelligent monitoring can enable predictive analytics to pre-scale infrastructure and application, while adaptive monitoring can dynamically change the entities to be monitored and the thresholds using various context information.

15.4 Technology Issues

Our prediction with respect to technology is that the continuous delivery pipeline will begin to be viewed as a single entity rather than as a collection of individual tools. Currently, a continuous delivery pipeline is almost always a chain of individual tools, each with their own scripts and tied together with several integration scripts. The integration scripts will evolve, and the environment of the continuous deployment pipeline will also evolve, together forming a collection that can be viewed as a single entity with parts, rather than a collection of parts loosely tied together. Some major problems exist when you just integrate existing tools through scripts:

- There is little traceability throughout the full pipeline. For example, it is difficult to know which particular builds are deployed to what environment. Some major outages were caused by connecting a testing build to production environment components.
- The lack of traceability makes error diagnosis very difficult. A production environment error log usually contains no information relating to upstream build, test, or commit activities and artifacts. Establishing the trace not only takes significant time and manual effort but also makes more intelligent automated recovery actions less practical.

- Security credentials often need to be passed from one tool to another, which causes security risks. The security features provided by the cloud introduce extra complexity.
- Many existing popular tools were created before the era of continuous delivery and deployment. It is difficult to express the new concepts and practices naturally using these tools.

Some of the things we foresee in this evolution are: the introduction of continuous deployment pipeline concepts and the achievement of various qualities in the pipeline.

Continuous Deployment Pipeline Concepts

Throughout this book we have discussed a variety of concepts that are specific to the operation of a continuous deployment pipeline. These concepts should be given first-class status in the specification of a continuous deployment pipeline. That is, the integration scripts should have mechanisms to allow the specification and execution of these concepts. In the following, we list the most relevant of these concepts.

- *Environment*. Moving committed code through the pipeline is largely a matter of deploying the code to different environments. As we defined in Chapter 2, an environment typically contains a load balancer, the system operating in that environment, and necessary support entities such as a database and configuration parameters. In addition, the environment may also contain other services or mock versions thereof. A pipeline tool should have the ability to specify an environment, to create an environment, to move code or a deployable artifact built from the code into or out of environments, and to tear down an environment while maintaining mappings, traces, and correlations of activities. For the production environment, concepts such as traffic matching and warmup should also either be built in or their specification be allowed.
- *Deployment*. A variety of different considerations involved in deployment should be specifiable in the pipeline tool while the specific implementation details are hidden and provided by different platform/systems-specific "providers." These are:
  - *Blue/green (or red/black) deployment*. Specifying a blue/green deployment should just be a matter of specifying the image to be deployed and the target of the deployment (number of VMs, autoscaling rules, location of the VMs). The support infrastructure should take care of a) ensuring the new version is properly installed and b) shifting traffic to the new version when appropriate. The deletion of the old versions could be included in this concept, or it could be a separate concept included in teardown.

- *Rolling upgrade.* Specifying a rolling upgrade should be a matter of specifying the image to be deployed, the instances to be replaced, and the granularity of the rolling upgrade.
- *Rollback.* A rollback should be able to be specified just by giving the ID of the deployment. All other parameters should be retrievable by knowing the prior deployment and how it was specified.
- *Canary deployment.* Both of the deployment styles should have the ability to be done with canaries. Specifying the number of canaries and the criteria for their placement (random, customer-based, geographically based).
- *A/B testing.* While canary deployments run two versions in parallel to ensure the new version is working correctly, A/B deployments are used to test if the new version, say, "B," is performing better in terms of some metrics, for example user acceptance of a special offer.
- *Feature toggles.* Specification of the activation or deactivation of a feature toggle should include the feature ID, whether it is to be activated or deactivated, and the scope of the change to specify if all or only specified servers should be toggled.
- *Teardown.* An environment is torn down by deleting its VMs and other resources and removing it from any Domain Name System (DNS) entries in which it occurs. This could be specified as an activity distinct from deployment, or it could be included in the blue/green deployment.

- *Monitoring.* Monitoring during deployment includes both monitoring the performance of the pipeline as well as monitoring the behavior of the application being deployed in the staging and production environments. The pipeline should explicitly inform the various monitors of the changes of the application and the environment. This information is vital for monitoring tools to adjust thresholds and suppress false alarms about legitimate changes.
- *Replicating data or versions.* Although the number of organizations that maintain multiple datacenters will likely decrease with re-architecting to take advantage of cloud provider replication services, there will be some organizations that will maintain their own datacenters or hybrid private/public clouds. Synchronizing across datacenters should be specifiable in the pipeline tool. Furthermore, specifying the type of data replication and the frequency of that replication should also be possible.
- *Service level agreements (SLAs) for the pipeline.* Organizations need to be able to predict the time it takes to complete each stage of a deployment. A canary deployment, for example, might impact 5% of the users. How long will it take to roll out the canary, and then how long to roll out the remainder? A rolling upgrade might save $40, but take 30 minutes longer than a blue/green deployment. A declarative approach for deployment (often used by configuration management tools such as Chef/Puppet)

hides the procedural complexity of deployment but also introduces some uncertainty in achieving what you want both in terms of time (unpredictable convergence time) and in terms of error recovery (using dumb retry as the only mechanism). Communicating application SLAs and pipeline SLAs to the underlying systems can help achieve better predictability in the declarative approach. Another way is to introduce the process view at a higher level of abstraction, as we suggested in Chapter 14. All these will help both Ops and Dev to plan and schedule deployments.

- *SLAs for the applications.* While a new version of an application is being deployed, the SLAs for the current version may be maintained or modified. There should be the ability to specify these adjustments to the application SLAs.
- *Configuration management database (CMDB).* A CMDB is an essential portion of an integrated continuous deployment pipeline. As such, it will have special requirements in terms of replication, access control, and usage. At the moment, the data models in typical configuration management tools have a limited scope and do not satisfy cross-pipeline configuration requirements needs. Making the CMDB a first-class concept with a broader scope allows for these special requirements.

Achieving Quality in a Continuous Deployment Pipeline

There are three different aspects to achieving quality that can be performed with an integrated continuous development pipeline.

1. *Don't do anything stupid.* You should be able to specify a series of constraints that prevent certain configurations from happening. For example, do not allow any environment except the production environment to access the production database. For another example, ensure that deployments to a particular region have specific configuration settings. For a third example, ensure that any change in an environment has passed through particular quality gates.

2. *Automatically detect, diagnose, and recover from errors.* In Chapter 14, we discussed techniques that can be used to detect, diagnose, and recover from errors that occur during an operations process. These techniques can be automated and should be a routine portion of an integrated continuous deployment pipeline. Many of these techniques should also be integrated with a more intelligent monitoring system. The operational process context plays important roles in suppressing false alarms, detecting subtle problems, and diagnosing root causes.

3. *Predict completion time of operations.* Associated with the SLAs that we identified as an important concept is the monitoring and prediction of the performance of an operation. This will allow planning of deployments,

where necessary. It will also provide visibility into the progress of an operation beyond just knowing that a given step is currently being processed or has been completed.

Implementation

A variety of possibilities exist for implementing such an integrated continuous deployment pipeline. These possibilities range from defining a new tool-independent domain-specific language to creating a Ruby Gem that integrates the deployment possibilities already existing in Ruby Gems or creating a superstructure over other sets of tools.

Regardless of the implementation strategy, the concepts we identified should be first-class entities in the implementation and achieving quality of the pipeline should be built into the infrastructure for the pipeline.

15.5 What About Error Reporting and Repair?

We began this book by defining DevOps as a collection of processes intended to reduce the time between committing code and placing that code into normal production.

The best and most effective method to achieve normal production is to reduce the number of errors that escape the deployment process. So the line between ensuring high quality of the deployed code and detecting errors after deployment is not a clear one.

Live testing such as that done by the Simian Army, which we discussed in Chapter 5, is one technique for detecting and repairing errors without exposing those errors to the end users. When an error is detected by a member of the Simian Army, the cause of that error is known because essentially it was a test case run during production.

Formal methods may finally have achieved sufficient maturity to be used in conjunction with microservices. The state of the art of formal methods is the ability to prove correctness of code that is less than 10,000 lines. Microservices, as described in Chapter 13, are often less than 5,000 lines of code. Thus, formally verifying a microservice seems within the realm of possibility. Furthermore, a microservice communicates only through message passing. This simplification seems as if it would also serve to support the formal verification of microservices. Formal verification may not be possible for the whole stack because of the inherent complexity of some lower-level services or protocols.

Even if a microservice has not been formally verified, a combination of static analysis together with hooks usable during execution, such as with debuggers, seems likely to enable faster repair of application errors.

15.6 Final Words

DevOps is in the middle of the chasm of adoption, but its momentum and growing number of materials will carry it into the mainstream and into normal practice. The gained effectiveness and effectivity will then allow Dev and Ops to deliver software innovation at a higher pace to the world. For the moment, we are pleased to be able to contribute toward moving DevOps over the chasm.

15.7 For Further Reading

Crossing the chasm is described in a Wikipedia entry: http://en.wikipedia.org/wiki/Crossing_the_Chasm

Ethann Castell has written about cloud pricing models in an IBM blog [Castell 13].

References

[3Scale 12] J. M. Pujol. "Having Fun with Redis Replication Between Amazon and Rackspace," July 25, 2012, http://tech.3scale.net/2012/07/25/fun-with-redis-replication/

[Agrasala 11] V. Agrasala. "What is IT Service?" December 6, 2011, http://vagrasala.wordpress.com/2011/12/06/what-is-it-service/

[Allen 70] T. J. Allen. "Communication Networks in R&D Laboratories," *R&D Management*, 1(1), 1970.

[Ambler 12] S. W. Ambler and M. Lines. *Disciplined Agile Delivery: A Practitioner's Guide to Agile Software Delivery in the Enterprise*. IBM Press, 2012.

[Ambler 15] S. Ambler. "Large Agile Teams," January 9, 2015, https://www.ibm.com/developerworks/community/blogs/ambler/?lang=en

[Barros 12] A. Barros and D. Oberle (Eds.). *Handbook of Service Description: USDL and Its Methods*. Springer, 2012.

[Bass 13] L. Bass, P. Clements, and R. Kazman. *Software Architecture in Practice, 3rd Edition*. Addison-Wesley, 2013.

[BostInno 11] J. Evanish. "Continuous Deployment: Possibility or Pipe Dream?" November 21, 2011, http://bostinno.streetwise.co/2011/11/21/continuous-deployment-possibility-or-pipe-dream/

[Brutlag 09] J. Brutlag. "Speed Matters," Google Research, June 23, 2009, http://googleresearch.blogspot.com.au/2009/06/speed-matters.html

[Cannon 11] D. Cannon. *ITIL Service Strategy*. The Stationery Office, 2011.

[Castell 13] E. Castell. "The Present and Future of Cloud Pricing Models," IBM Cloud Products and Services, June 12, 2013, http://thoughtsoncloud.com/2013/06/present-future-cloud-pricing-models/

[Clements 10] P. Clements, F. Bachmann, L. Bass, et al. *Documenting Software Architectures, 2nd Edition*. Addison-Wesley Professional, 2010.

[Confluence 12] M. Serafini. "Zab vs. Paxos," March 28, 2012, https://cwiki.apache.org/confluence/display/ZOOKEEPER/Zab+vs.+Paxos

[Dean] J. Dean. "Designs, Lessons and Advice from Building Large Distributed Systems," http://www.cs.cornell.edu/projects/ladis2009/talks/dean-keynote-ladis2009.pdf

[Dean 13] J. Dean and L. André Barroso. "The Tail at Scale," *Communications of the ACM*, 56(2), pp. 74–80, 2013.

[Dumitras 09] T. Dumitraş and P. Narasimhan. "Why Do Upgrades Fail and What Can We Do About It?" Middleware '09 Proceedings of the 10th ACM/IFIP/USENIX International Conference on Middleware, Springer, 2009, http://dl.acm.org/citation.cfm?id=1657005

[DZone 13] P. Hammant. "Google's Scaled Trunk Based Development," May 9, 2013, http://architects.dzone.com/articles/googles-scaled-trunk-based

[Edwards 14] D. Edwards. "DevOps is an Enterprise Concern," InfoQ QCon interview with Damon Edwards by Manuel Pais, May 31, 2014, http://www.infoq.com/interviews/interview-damon-edwards-qcon-2014

[Erl 07] T. Erl. *Service-Oriented Architecture: Principles of Service Design*. Prentice Hall, 2007.

[FireScope 13] "What is an IT Service?" November 12, 2013, http://www.firescope.com/blog/index.php/service/

[Fitz 09] T. Fitz. "Continuous Deployment at IMVU: Doing the Impossible Fifty Times a Day," February 10, 2009, http://timothyfitz.com/2009/02/10/continuous-deployment-at-imvu-doing-the-impossible-fifty-times-a-day/

[Fowler 06] I. Robinson. "Consumer-Driven Contracts: A Service Evolution Pattern," June 12, 2006, http://martinfowler.com/articles/consumerDrivenContracts.html

[Gilbert 02] S. Gilbert and N. Lynch. "Brewer's Conjecture and the Feasibility of Consistent, Available, Partition-tolerant Web Services," *ACM SIGACT News*, *33*(2), pp. 51–59, 2002.

[Gillard-Moss 13] P. Gillard-Moss. "Machine Images as Build Artefacts," December 20, 2013, http://peter.gillardmoss.me.uk/blog/2013/12/20/machine-images-as-build-artefacts/

[Hamilton 12] J. Hamilton. "Failures at Scale & How to Ride Through Them," November 30, 2012, Amazon Web Services.

[Humble 10] J. Humble and D. Farley. *Continuous Delivery: Reliable Software Releases through Build, Test, and Deployment Automation*, Addison-Wesley Professional, 2010.

[Hunnebeck 11] L. Hunnebeck. *ITIL Service Design*. The Stationery Office, 2011.

[InfoQ 13] A. Rehn, T. Palmborg, and P. Boström. "The Continuous Delivery Maturity Model," February 6, 2013, http://www.infoq.com/articles/Continuous-Delivery-Maturity-Model

[InfoQ 13] E. Minick. "A Continuous Delivery Maturity Model," July 17, 2013, http://www.infoq.com/presentations/continuous-delivery-model

[InfoQ 14] D. Edwards. "Introducing DevOps to the Traditional Enterprise," June 18, 2014 http://www.infoq.com/minibooks/emag-devops

[InformationWeek 13] J. Masters Emison. "Cloud Deployment Debate: Bake Or Bootstrap?" October 30, 2013, http://www.informationweek.com/cloud/infrastructure-as-a-service/cloud-deployment-debate-bake-or-bootstrap/d/d-id/1112121

[ITSecurity 14] D. Raywood. "Shellshock hit our old unpatched server, admit BrowserStack," November 13, 2014, http://itsecurityguru.org/shellshock-hit-old-unpatched-server-admit-browserstack/#.VGVvZskhMuI

[Kandula] S. Kandula, G. Ananthanarayanan, A. Greenberg, I. Stoica, Y. Lu, B. Saha, E. Harris. "Combating Outliers in Map-Reduce," Microsoft Research, http://research.microsoft.com/en-us/um/people/srikanth/data/combating%20outliers%20in%20map-reduce.web.pptx

[Kreps 13] J. Kreps. "The Log: What Every Software Engineer Should Know About Real-time Data's Unifying Abstraction," December 16, 2013, http://engineering.linkedin.com/distributed-systems/log-what-every-software-engineer-should-know-about-real-time-datas-unifying

[Lamport 14] L. Lamport. "Paxos Made Simple," ACM SIGACT News 32, 4, December 2001, http://research.microsoft.com/en-us/um/people/lamport/pubs/pubs.html#paxos-simple

[Ligus 13] S. Ligus. *Effective Monitoring and Alerting*. O'Reilly Media, 2013.

[Lloyd 11] V. Lloyd. *ITIL Continual Service Improvement*. The Stationery Office, 2011.

[Lu 15] Q. Lu, L. Zhu, X. Xu, L. Bass, S. Li, W. Zhang, and N. Wang. "Mechanisms and Architectures for Tail-Tolerant System Operations in Cloud," *IEEE Software*, Jan-Feb 2015, pp. 76–82.

[Massie 12] M. Massie, B. Li et al. *Monitoring with Ganglia*, O'Reilly Media, 2012, http://ganglia.sourceforge.net/

[Mozilla] C. AtLee, L. Blakk, J. O'Duinn, and A. Zambrano Gasparian. "Firefox Release Engineering," http://www.aosabook.org/en/ffreleng.html

[Nelson-Smith 13] S. Nelson-Smith. *Test-Driven Infrastructure with Chef, 2nd Edition*. O'Reilly Media, 2013.

[Netflix 13] "Preparing the Netflix API for Deployment," November 18, 2013, http://techblog.netflix.com/2013/11/preparing-netflix-api-for-deployment.html

[Netflix 15] J. Kojo, V. Asokan, G. Campbell, and A. Tull. "Nicobar: Dynamic Scripting Library for Java," February 10, 2015, http://techblog.netflix.com

[Newman 15] S. Newman. *Building Microservices: Designing Fine-Grained Systems*, O'Reilly Media, 2015.

[NIST 11] P. Mell and T. Grance. "The NIST Definition of Cloud Computing," National Institute of Standards and Technology, NIST Special Publication 800-145, http://csrc.nist.gov/publications/nistpubs/800-145/SP800-145.pdf

[NIST 13] "Security and Privacy Controls for Federal Information Systems and Organizations," NIST 800-53, Rev. 4, April, 2013 http://csrc.nist.gov/publications/PubsDrafts.html

[OMG 11] "Business Process Model and Notation," Version 2.0, OMG, January 2011, http://www.bpmn.org]

[Puppet Labs 13] C. Caum. "Continuous Delivery Vs. Continuous Deployment: What's the Diff?" August 30, 2013, http://puppetlabs.com/blog/continuous-delivery-vs-continuous-deployment-whats-diff

[Rance 11] S. Rance. *ITIL Service Transition*. The Stationery Office, 2011

[Schad 10] J. Schad, J. Dittrich, and J.-A. Quiané-Ruiz. "Runtime Measurements in the Cloud: Observing, Analyzing, and Reducing Variance," Proceedings of the VLDB Endowment, 3(*1*), 2010.

[SEI 12] G. Silowash, D. Cappelli, A. P. Moore, R. F. Trzeciak, T. J. Shimeall, and L. Flynn. "Common Sense Guide to Mitigating Insider Threats, 4th Edition," December, 2012, http://resources.sei.cmu.edu/library/asset-view.cfm?assetid=34017

[Seo 14] H. Seo, C. Sadowski, S. Elbaum, E. Aftandilian, and R. Bowdidge. "Programmers' Build Errors: A Case Study (at Google)," *Proceedings of the 36th International Conference on Software Engineering* (ICSE 2014).

[Sockut 09] G. H. Sockut and B. R. Iyer. "Online Reorganization of Databases," *ACM Computing Surveys*, 41(*3*), Article 14, July 2009.

[Spencer 14] R. Spencer. "DevOps and ITIL: Continuous Delivery Doesn't Stop at Software," Change & Release Management blog, April 5, 2014, http://changeandrelease.com/2014/04/05/devops-and-itil-continuous-delivery-doesnt-stop-at-software/

[Steinberg 11] R. A. Steinberg. *ITIL Service Operation*. The Stationery Office, 2011.

[Tonse 14] S. Tonse. "MicroServices at Netflix," August 8, 2014, http://www.slideshare.net/stonse/microservices-at-netflix

[van der Aalst 11] W. van der Aalst. *Process Mining: Discovery, Conformance and Enhancement of Business Processes*. Springer, 2011.

[Weber 15] I. Weber, C. Li, L. Bass, S. Xu and L. Zhu. "Discovering and visualizing operations processes with POD-Discovery and POD-Viz," International Conference on Dependable Systems and Networks (DSN), Rio de Janeiro, Brazil, June, 2015.

[Xu 14] S. Xu, L. Zhu, I. Weber, L. Bass, and D. Sun. "POD-Diagnosis: Error diagnosis of sporadic operations on cloud applications," International Conference on Dependable Systems and Networks (DSN), Atlanta, GA, USA, June, 2014. http://ssrg.nicta.com.au/projects/cloud/

About the Authors

Len Bass is a senior principal researcher at National ICT Australia Ltd. (NICTA). He joined NICTA in 2011 after 25 years at the Software Engineering Institute (SEI) at Carnegie Mellon University. He is the coauthor of two award-winning books in software architecture—*Software Architecture in Practice, Third Edition* (Addison-Wesley 2013) and *Documenting Software Architectures: Views and Beyond, Second Edition* (Addison-Wesley 2011)—as well as several other books and numerous papers in computer science and software engineering on a wide range of topics. Len has more than 50 years' experience in software development and research, which has resulted in papers on operating systems, database management systems, user interface software, software architecture, product line systems, and computer operations. He has worked or consulted in multiple domains, including scientific analysis, embedded systems, and information and financial systems.

Ingo Weber is a senior researcher in the Software Systems Research Group at NICTA in Sydney, Australia, as well as an adjunct senior lecturer at CSE at the University of New South Wales (UNSW). Prior to NICTA, Ingo held positions at UNSW and at SAP Research Karlsruhe, Germany. His research interests include cloud computing, DevOps, business process management, and artificial intelligence (AI). He has published over 60 peer-reviewed papers, and served as a reviewer or program committee member for many prestigious scientific journals and conferences. Ingo holds a Ph.D. and a Diploma from the University of Karlsruhe, and an MSc from the University of Massachusetts at Amherst.

Liming Zhu is a research group leader and principal researcher at NICTA. He holds conjoint positions at the University of New South Wales (UNSW) and the University of Sydney. Liming has published over 80 peer-reviewed papers. He formerly worked in several technology lead positions in the software industry before obtaining a Ph.D. in software engineering from UNSW. He is a committee member of the Standards Australia IT-015 (system and software engineering), contributing to ISO/SC7. Liming's research interests include software architecture and dependable systems.

Index

Big Data: Architectures and Technologies

About the Course

Scalable "big data" systems are significant long-term investments that must scale to handle ever-increasing data volumes, and therefore represent high-risk applications in which the software and data architecture are fundamental components of ensuring success. This course is designed for architects and technical stakeholders such as product managers, development managers, and systems engineers who are involved in the development of big-data applications. It focuses on the relationships among application software, data models, and deployment architectures, and how specific technology selection relates to all of these. While the course touches briefly on data analytics, it focuses on distributed data storage and access infrastructure, and the architecture tradeoffs needed to achieve scalability, consistency, availability, and performance. We illustrate these architecture principles with examples from selected NoSQL product implementations.

Who Should Attend?

- Architects
- Technical stakeholders involved in the development of big data applications
- Product managers, development managers, and systems engineers

Topics

- The major elements of big data software architectures
- The different types and major features of NoSQL databases
- Patterns for designing data models that support high performance and scalability
- Distributed data processing frameworks

Three Ways to Attend

- Public instructor-led offering at an SEI office
- Private, instructor-led training at customer sites
- eLearning

For More Information

To learn more and to register for the course, visit www.sei.cmu.edu/go/big-data

 Software Engineering Institute | **Carnegie Mellon University**